Insights

Violence
and its causes

Jean-Marie Domenach
Henri Laborit
Alain Joxe
Johan Galtung
Dieter Senghaas
Otto Klineberg
James D. Halloran
V. P. Shupilov
Krzysztof Poklewski-Koziell
Rasheeduddin Khan
Pierre Spitz
Pierre Mertens
Elise Boulding

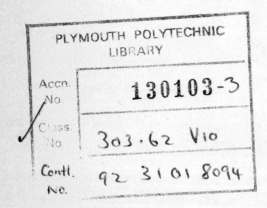
Published in 1981 by the United Nations
Educational, Scientific and Cultural Organization
7 place de Fontenoy, 75700 Paris
Printed by Imprimerie des Presses Universitaires
de France, Vendôme

ISBN 92–3–101809–4
French edition: 92–3–201809–8

Contents

history. 9. - are we more or less violent today
257
34

Preface

Since its creation, Unesco has undertaken a number of projects bearing on violence and in particular on the tensions that endanger international understanding, on human aggression, on the impact of violence on the mass media and on the Gandhian message of non-violence. It is obvious that violence in its different forms and expressions affects education, science, culture and communication. The Organization's efforts have sometimes been concerned with the consequences of violence in Unesco's spheres of competence and sometimes with its underlying causes.

Until the very recent past, however, the activities of Unesco were limited to several of the dimensions of the abundant research that had been done on the causes of violence, especially the analysis of individual behaviour and the contributions of ethology, psychology and physiology to the understanding of human aggression. Examination of the social and economic factors that determine violence at the different levels of contemporary society had not yet been the subject of systematic research. The same was true of examination of the relations between violence and those problems to which Unesco gives priority, i.e., respect for human rights, the strengthening of peace, and development.

On the occasion of the Interdisciplinary Expert Meeting on the Study of the Causes of Violence, convened at Unesco in November 1975, a research programme was elaborated with a view to investigating thoroughly those dimensions of violence that had been insufficiently studied previously.

This publication is one result of the recommendations of the 1975 meeting. It contains a series of chapters grouped in three sections, of which the majority were written by the specialists of various disciplines who participated in the meeting. Alain Joxe, rapporteur of the meeting, agreed to

serve as general editor of this book and has written the
general introduction as well as introductions to the three
sections. The opinions he expresses, like those of the other
authors, do not necessarily represent the views of Unesco,
for a plurality of viewpoints, Unesco believes, is necessary for
the reader to understand a problem such as violence in all
its complexity. The Organization would like to extend its
warmest thanks to all the authors and to the general editor
for their valuable collaboration. It is the hope of Unesco,
in making available this fourth volume in the 'Insights'
series, that the fruits of their knowledge and their reflection
will promote thinking about and understanding of violence,
so that solutions may be found in a spirit of justice, fairness
and respect for the rights of individuals and peoples.

General introduction

Maître-Assistant, Groupe
de Sociologie de la Défense,
École des Hautes Études
en Sciences Sociales, Paris

Alain Joxe

The theme of violence as something new is one of the topics
that has been most bandied about by the mass media. However,
included in the understanding this word—the totality of human
actions involving the use of force and in particular armed
force—there is, in fact, little that is new. The means and the
victims of kidnappings, machismo and hooliganism, of gang
warfare, of prison and university riots, of hold-ups and wars of
repression, of conquest or the destruction of military weapons,
are not altogether the same today as under the *ancien régime*,
during the Middle Ages or in antiquity. Yet we cannot conclude from this that our century is more violent than any other.
Depending on what one chooses to include when measuring
this violence, one might even show eventually that it is less so.
It is fashionable to use 'violence' as an all-embracing category.

However, Unesco is not simply following fashion in turning
its attention to the causes of violence after having already devoted considerable effort to the study of aggressivity. It should
also be said that the concept of violence, to which the Organization is here referring, is not the same as that widely used
in the media. Unesco's interest in the question of violence stems
fundamentally from its Constitution and also from a resolution adopted by its General Conference during its 1974 session
on the Organization's contribution to peace and its tasks
with respect to the promotion of human rights and the elimination of colonialism and racialism (Resolution 18 C/11.1).

In this text the Member States of Unesco considered
that 'peace cannot consist solely in the absence of armed
conflict but implies principally a process of progress, justice
and mutual respect among the peoples. . . .' They also
affirmed that 'a peace founded on injustice and violation of
human rights cannot last and leads inevitably to violence'.

The text adopted by Unesco may be seen as providing

the following implicit definition of violence and its causes. The inevitable cause of violence is the conclusion of a type of precarious peace that corresponds merely to the absence of armed conflict, without progress in justice, or worse, a peace based on injustice and the violation of human rights.

This implicit definition (the analysis of which is solely the responsibility of the author of this introduction and of not Unesco itself) can be seen to encompass the approach of the Unesco meeting of experts on the study of the causes of violence, held in 1975, which was authorized by the resolution and was the point of departure for the studies leading to this book. The definition raises more questions than it answers. It constitutes a normative definition of peace and of justice: peace and justice should make for the absence of violence. But it is also a definition of violence through its causes that seems to take no account of the violation of human rights as violence; the word 'violence' appears to be used exclusively for forms of revolts and conflicts that are the consequence of these violations. Of course, as the violation of human rights is universally considered a form of violence, Unesco's definition is interesting in that it attributed to the violation of human rights the quality of primary violence in a chain of causality that allows for retroactive effects. Therefore one can say that the point of view of the Organization is very open, very normative, very idealistic, and generally not subject to state influence and, finally, not at all hostile to violence in itself. It is almost a militant declaration; it fully endorses the right of resistance to oppression, what Thomas Aquinas called the legitimate revolt against the tyrant.

From a sociological point of view the study of violence called for by the Member States of the Organization (which are usually members of the United Nations) is more in line with the spirit of the many international juridical texts than with the totality of the concrete practices of the human race. But one must not underestimate the effect of such texts on actual practice. In the scientific study of violence we always find that it is never suppressed without some essential political mediation that one can call the 'recognition of the illegitimacy of the use of force'. But the definition of the causes of violence suggested by the adopted texts is coloured by a legal point of view and a system of interpretation with which the authors represented in this collection were certainly not obliged to agree.

However, because of its openness, the Unesco definition serves to orient peace research. Violence in such a widely humanistic sense is a concept that does not necessarily have the same elements when considered from the point of view of the North, the East, the West or the South, as one says in the language of world-wide diplomacy.

In asking, as does this collection, what point research into the causes of violence has reached, the prior question of a definition of violence for non-normative purposes arises all the time. This writer is inevitably thrown back on the definition bandied about by the media and therefore to a sort of naive anthropological question: 'What is it that twentieth-century men want to express by this word?' or 'How can they use only one word to express such very different things?'

The articles in this collection represent a response to this question. Each specialist in his own discipline states at least why and how he writes about violence. Moreover, a certain number of the articles, those in the first section, try to formulate a cross-disciplinary definition of violence, while others, in the third section, turn their attention to the definition of different kinds of violence. This plan doesn't fully take into account the discussions of the experts (included in the appendix), which consist of an epistemological consideration of the concept of causality, as well as a particular preoccupation with the historical background necessary for the study of the causes of violence, including the necessity of taking into account a wide variety of cultural differences. The meeting became aware of the essential need for trans-disciplinarity in research into violence; this is necessary because of the significant disparities in the definitions of violence put forward by the respective disciplines. It is these points that we should like to emphasize in this introduction, by suggesting several definitions and questions.

In order to contribute to a definition of violence let us adopt a certain Socratic irony. Is not violence a professional quality in certain occupations? Undoubtedly it is the principal weapon of the armed forces, the police, criminals and revolutionaries. Good sense should prevent us from using the same word for all the 'tools' of such different professionals. Indeed, if one term has now emerged, it is because something has changed. The specific nature of these tools—or the differences among these 'occupations'—particularly as they were understood during the eighteenth and nineteenth centuries, is

very blurred now. The animal cunning of the juvenile delinquent from the 'dangerous classes', the 'astuteness' of the
police inspector in disguise, the 'discipline' and 'courage'
of the military man, the 'heroism' of the revolutionary—these
distinctions are becoming invalid because the social contexts
in which they played their roles are no longer as distinct as
they once were. These different attributes now appear to be
present as essential factors of the entire range of social
relations in the production process, where they are influential
and efficacious as well as 'violent'. The purely animal juvenile
delinquent, the purely astute police inspector, the purely
brave and disciplined military man and the purely heroic
revolutionary are today considered either marginal or manipulated. Even if these stereotypes persist at a certain level, the
divisions between occupations and types of violence common
in the nineteenth century are beginning to appear more and
more archaic, a sort of secularized vestige of the medieval
structure of 'orders'—the military deriving from the order
of the nobility, the police inspector from the order of the
clergy and the juvenile delinquent and revolutionary from the
order of the Third Estate—in the structure of power relationships that has determined the class struggle since the beginning of capitalism. In this hypothesis, the unification of the
field of coercion, typical of the merging process that is
perhaps the essence of capitalism, necessarily leads to the
unification of the concept of violence as the prime mover of
the system of domination and the anti-systems of revolt. A
transdisciplinary approach legitimately corresponds to this
transprofessional knowledge.

Cross-discipline and hierarchy in violent systems

It is because of its cross-disciplinary nature that this meeting
of experts was important, but the necessary transdisciplinarity
has not yet evolved, and the theory of violence that would
emerge from it is still unclear. This collection is based on this
paradox, and it is this that gives us food for thought.

Violence is necessarily 'violence by' and 'violence against'.
Individual violence, group violence, institutional violence,
class violence, state violence, violence of the international
system, these generic terms categorized from microcosm to

macrocosm are already assumptions about types of causality. Indeed, if there is violence by the individual, its origin or form must, to some extent, be determined by the individual himself. On the other hand, violence by the individual concerns his environment only to the extent that it acts against a higher level of organization; research into its causes is naturally accompanied by a curative preoccupation that expresses the determination of the group to suppress the causes. If we remain at this micro-sociological level, we see that the study of the causes of individual violence at the biological and genetic level necessarily stems from a medical need (eugenic, therapeutic, euthanasic). The same kind of observation can be made about each of the types of violence listed hierarchically above. If there is violence by the group—ultimately to control the violence of the individual—the study of this violence must be established on the assumption that this violence, too, either has its origin or takes its form in the group itself; similarly, research into the causes of group violence stems from a police need (prevention, surveillance, punishment) and generally an institutional one. If there is institutional violence, particularly by repressive institutions, against the entire social structure, the social control of this violence must stem from the assumption of the existence of police violence at the level of the institution itself; research into the causes of police violence necessarily proceeds from a political need (political struggle, political control, legislation). In the same way, we find that the inquiry into the cause of state violence calls for a diplomatic approach and the inquiry into the causes of the violence of cross-national forces

System (units)	Causality (discipline)	Control practice	Methods of intervention		
			1	2	3
Individual	Biology, genetics	Medical	Eugenic	Therapeutic	Euthanasic
Group	Psycho-sociology	Police	Prevention	Surveillance	Repression
Institution, organization	Sociology	Political	Political struggle	Political control	Legislation
Nation-states, politico-economic structures	Sociology of international relations	Diplomatic	Consultation	Negotiation	Agreements, alliances
		Military	Recruitment, armament	Manœuvre, threat	Operations
Transnational system	Peace research, strategic studies, macro-economics	Generalized military	Consultation	Control of flow	Economic, military intervention

an economic and military approach at the international level.

At each of the foregoing levels there is a corresponding educational step: the education of children with respect of the acquired aspects of violent behaviour, the education of the police, diplomats, politicians, the military. There is also the education of the exploited and oppressed.

Research into the causes of different levels of violence undertaken by the theorists of different disciplines—which gives hope to teachers of either non-violence or violence—throws us back on to the need for a praxeology more than for a theory. So far we have schematized the psychologist and the biologist acting 'for' the doctor, the sociologist 'for' the politician, the macro-sociologist of international relations 'for' the diplomat and/or the military, the macro-sociologist of transnational relations 'for' the transnational economist and/or military, in a generalized response to the demands of transnational institutions.

In establishing this double structure of competence around each of the interlocking fields involved in studying violence, we are still offering only one model—not for violence itself but for the current social reasons for the use of one word that brings together such varied research, so many levels of causality and such different practical applications.

Divide *ut impera*

It must be noted—as is manifest in most of the essays of this collection—that no specialist today adheres to a single system of explanation. The biologist studying the causes of violent behaviour at the level of the structure of the brain does not pretend that his discipline alone can account for all the causes and forms of violence; he refers to a multiple causality, particularly social apprenticeship. He admits that the field of this research is legitimately cross-disciplinary. The boundaries between disciplines are thus understood as inevitable divisions of labour. But if it were still humanly possible, there is no scientist who would not wish to be a *homo transdisciplinarius*, one of the sacred monsters of the Renaissance capable of embracing everything. Today this dream has been replaced by the concept of multiple causality and by the practice of holding multidisciplinary congresses.

Despite all this the research, practices in the different

disciplines are far from uniform or concerted. Transdisciplinarity remains only a wish. Indeed, the fields of research are partitioned even more finely. Now, what poses an extremely serious problem is that, confronted with this partitioning, we are witnessing an accelerated transdisciplinarity by those who practice socio-political control; police medicine (in fact, the medicine of torture), police politics, military politics and the militarization of the economy are perfectly articulated praxeological units that drain important resources and systematically orient or exploit the discoveries of basic science. What is termed 'economic warfare' seems to bring together into a 'package' that is very militarized, very police-oriented and very biologically geared, a global domination that extends from torture of the individual to the organization of mass murder through hunger.

Certainly, as academics, scientists or moralists, we can avenge our current impotence by terming this domination 'structural violence' or 'imperialism', but its practitioners could not care less and are already moving towards a higher level of logic, genuinely transdisciplinary, by bringing together for practical purposes the diverse specialists whom they use. Those who practice social control exploit the discoveries of research into the causality of violence for the sake of violence. They bear out the terrible statement that must be attributed to Thomas Schelling: 'It is easier to destroy than to produce.'* They thereby contradict the deontology of the scientist. For some twenty years this contradiction has produced a moral revolt by scientists of all disciplines. The best known example is the appearance of the Pugwash movement, which has brought together scientists (largely from the exact sciences) protesting against the consequences of their own discoveries, particularly in nuclear physics. But we would like to put forward a 'non-moral' definition of this revolt in the human sciences, to show how the struggle of scientists against their domination by those who exercise power can take the form of an epistemological struggle for transdisciplinarity.

Peace as a verification of war

* Thomas Schelling, *Arms and Influence*, p. 15, New Haven, Yale University Press, 1966.

At all levels of research into the causes of violence, scientific discussion generally holds that violence is explicable and that, because it is explicable, it is avoidable. Experimental scientific method demands—without any moral connotation—that one prove a hypothesis about a phenomenon by demonstrating that, by eliminating certain causes, one can eliminate certain effects. With respect to violence, the scientist will seek proof by experimenting with a system free of violent factors. For every theoretical assertion on the existence of any given cause of violence, we should be able to identify a concrete social experience from which that cause is absent and which would therefore prove the hypothesis being tested. Scientists investigating violence are therefore necessarily pushed towards wanting non-violent experiments. All peace researchers could perfectly well be violent people who favour war, which obviously isn't the case; but, in fact, that would change nothing because their scientific approach would inevitably push them towards the creation of non-violent systems, without which their theories could not be scientifically based. The non-violence of social scientists therefore has a basically epistemological aim.

But the social scientist himself is incapable of creating social situations alone. He depends for that on those who hold power. His dependence is very different from that of the physicist, the biologist or the mathematician, but very similar to that of the astrophysicist who depends on God to see novae under certain conditions. His dependence is therefore fundamental. When a social scientist becomes so powerful that he can influence the politico-social process, he is more often asked to show his knowledge by the violent rather than non-violent manipulation of situations—certainly wherever macro-sociological problems are involved. Consequently, in general, theory about the causes of violence makes little headway because it relies almost exclusively on practices and experiments that are themselves violent.

Nevertheless, this dependence is temporary. The expectations of the social scientist, his dependence, are not identical to those of the astrophysicist because the object of his study is also a stake in social struggles and depends on human practice itself. The dream of transdisciplinarity in the social sciences capable of guiding social practices is a conceivable aim; it will therefore one day be conceived. Moreover, the day when transdisciplinary practices based on a scientific knowledge of the multiple causality of violence yield several solid discoveries, that is tangible proposals for social experiments from which the multicausality of violence would be excluded, all traditional discussion of the necessity of using violence to control violence will be re-examined at a level of logic higher than that of the practices of domination. Transdisciplinary study of violence is for this reason—in the long term—a struggle against all the types of political power that have been organized since neolithic times on the basis of *si vis pacem, para bellum*. This old Roman adage is in fact always evident in a field fragmented into causalities, corresponding to a field fragmented by struggles between human groups. It is obviously inseparable from that other adage, *divide ut impera*, and until the present time, in political history whether of empires, states or classes, we can find no non-violent society that isn't in fact an island or cell of non-violence surrounded by violent fortifications. Those who wield power enjoy refuting utopians with 'common sense'. But as the struggle to revise these two adages has already begun, it is clear—or it should be clear—that the struggle against maintaining or deepening the divisions between disciplines, which permits the domination of scientific praxeologies by political ones, is in fact an integral part of the struggle itself.

Violence and data processing: centralism against self-management

It is only an optical illusion that allows certain schools to maintain that knowledge is the source of all power. Everyone knows, however, that power is the application of the knowledge of violence. This struggle for transdisciplinarity is not simply a scientific task or a cultural struggle; it is the current form of an attempt to change the nature of power, to replace 'violence in the last resort' by 'knowledge in the last resort' as the source of political power. This struggle is therefore closely linked to the old Platonic dream of the philosopher-king, but with greater force than during the fourth century B.C., since our knowledge is more scientific today than it was then. Moreover, the logic of this debate centres on the material achievements that can support the absorption of collectively accumulated knowledge. We are not involved in a phenomenology of the mind in the Hegelian sense but in a phenomenology of software and hardware. Violence and knowledge always depend on the international division of labour, on the appearance of new social relations of production and new

productive forces, and the struggle for information about
these new productive forces is, in effect, the political struggle
of the classes. The problem of the subordination of knowledge
to violence is, in the end, very concrete.

The unification of certain economic fields by electronic
storage procedures and the extension of the range of options
for large corporations or nation-states has already 'regionally'
modified the relationship between knowledge and power
and between violence and power—even in the military field
—because greater knowledge allows a less frequent use of
physical violence. Prevention and dissuasion have become the
key concepts of military thinking, equal to the concept of
operation, which recently predominated alone and the sole
implication of which was the recourse to force. However, one
can understand the contemporary situation only by studying
the relationship that brings together in time the unifying
concept of violence and the unifying hardware and software of
control and decision-making in data processing. One can try
to describe this phenomenon as follows: the co-ordination of
the decision, whether violent or economic, along with the information that supports it, belongs now to overwhelmingly
powerful centres of control that in the West do not necessarily
exercise state power in the traditional sense. These centres
create violence at the same time as they control it, for they preserve and guard, violently if necessary, a central restricted fund
of knowledge, as well as the means of shaping, violently if
necessary, the reality to be integrated into this knowledge.

To a system of centralized information and decision-
making, based on a costly infrastructure, which integrates
advanced techniques, 'violence' is everything opposed to this
centralization. Conversely, for all social forces opposed to
this centralization, 'violence' is the sum of all those procedures
that reduce human action (if need be, by force) to inter-
changeable elements, that can be easily integrated into and
manipulated by this central knowledge pool.

In addition, it should be noted that this discussion is being
conducted simultaneously within the organization of the
dominant classes and those that are dominated and exploited;
centralization and state control versus neoliberal 'anarcho-
capitalism' among the bourgeoisie, democratic centralism
versus the concept of self-management among the working
classes, or in countries suffering from imperialism. These are
two parallel discussions the general aim of which is the articu-

lation of old and new practices of coercion through old and new practices of consensus in the deployment of class power.

This discussion is taking place at the heart of the developed capitalist system and so it is, in its birthplace, induced from the development of certain productive forces and in particular advanced electronics. It is clear that the terms are not exactly the same everywhere. They derive from the degree of development and distribution of these techniques within a concrete social framework and, therefore, can assume the character of a purely ideological discussion or a formal recapitulation of traditional arguments about basic democracy and despotism with a background of the social relations of precapitalist production.

We therefore feel that only an abuse of formalism could permit one to transform everywhere the struggle between centralization and decentralization into the 'main contradiction' of the contemporary world, and consequently to declare the end of class struggle and the end of Marxism as a theoretical tool of analysis. Instead of becoming involved in such a debate, let us look at how it might eventually affect a cross-disciplinary approach to violence.

Hegemonic violence and coercive non-violence

What Gramsci called the 'hegemony' of class referred to a non-violent class power that was diffused throughout the whole of civil society and based on an acceptance by the dominated classes of their own domination. It was therefore the objective manifestation of certain common interests of the exploiters and exploited within a framework determined by the dominant. This Gramscian hegemony covered an ensemble of decentralized practices that were institutionalized to some extent in certain central state mechanisms but in essence were manifest in social relations, companies, corporations, the church, schools and political parties; their power was effective only to the extent that they were locally and autonomously perpetuated.

By contrast, the concept of 'coercion' or of 'class dictatorship' which, according to Gramsci, is the other side of class domination, refers to practices carried out by centralized organizations of coercive class power, which resort to violence, generally in state military form, particularly when hegemonic relations break down. Today the development of new productive forces, particularly the electronic ones, allows for the simultaneous existence of centralized hegemonic ruling practices (essentially television) and decentralized coercive practices (proxy wars, repression delegated by the state to more or less private and centrally informed militia). Violence becomes a fragmenting instrument of power and therefore plays a hegemonic role; and non-violent political action, because of its massive nature, appears to be 'coercive'. In this confusion violence appears to be general.

It is no accident that television and violence maintain a particular relationship in which some people even see a more or less complex causality. Television is a non-violent instrument; in contrast to universal military service it keeps separated without violence the audience it unites in depersonalized form. It implements the proverb *divide ut impera* through the attraction of information alone, albeit information that is hardly distinguishable from fantasy and its attractions, and it appeals to the highest associative zones in the cerebral structure (not to the zones where the most primitive reflex actions coalesce in the process of learning violence for the defence of 'the desired object'). That it why one can say that television is superior to the institution of universal military service, which organizes the simultaneous depersonalization and uniting of individuals under the banner of war, while leaving aside half the human race, that is to say women. It is also superior to the institution of universal suffrage because it does not involve a phase of human interaction, even the verbal combat which, under the military term of 'electoral campaign', precedes the vote. It leads the individual directly to the placid polling booth of the evening at home.

At least in the capitalist world, television creates the unified representation of violence that becomes the instrument of political hegemony. Violence is the risk that begins 'from the other side of the screen', that is to say, right in the street. From their own hearths, the citizens of the developed world penetrate a special space that can encompass even the most remote theatres of war. Because its representation of practices brings together the whole of the non-domestic area, televised violence has as its opposite not non-violence but tourism. The corollary of this double character—both violent and touristic—in the non-domestic space of the TV-citizen is the absolute need to repress political violence, even brutally, in certain countries, so as to permit the organization of large-scale tourism and sports. It is no longer a question of taking risks to reach a touristic area (as was the case with the 'conquering tourism' of the English in the nineteenth century).

Violence must be suppressed, if necessary by violence, in order to create tourist areas and lines of communication; hence the security fences and the fortifications that protect airports and resorts in developing countries—and also, increasingly, in the developed ones themselves. Hence also the migration towards huge fortified housing complexes or residences in outlying suburbs, which reproduce, up to the edge of the real countryside, a sort of touristic security.

This system of representation is obviously Eurocentric, like the idea of the TV-citizen; the violent area and the unified touristic area are not universal phenomena. In Third World countries the masses without television, tourism or houses, subjected to famine and permanent insecurity, would necessarily put forward a totally different definition of violence. The Eurocentric concept of violence is not the one most widespread, but it is the dominant one and imposes itself on the entire world because of the fact that the privileged groups of underdeveloped countries themselves tend to adopt as a way of life and criteria of status the same symbols as the élite of the rich countries, and so to adopt through television, air travel and tourism, domestic enclosures all the more fortified because social inequalities are more flagrant.

Violence is imposed as the world-wide currency of struggles, revolts and revolution. In the long term, it is a far more effective myth than nuclear war, because nuclear warfare is not taking place, whereas violence exists—and it exists everywhere.

Research into the causes and perceptions of violence outside the European ambit could not be fully explored during the meeting at which several of the papers of this collection were presented. But the idea is put forward in the extracts from the Final Report, which appears in the appendix of this volume.

Transdisciplinarity and totalitarianism

We are therefore in a confused transitional phase: a great
number of hegemonic practices in the Gramscian sense can
be termed violent; they are, in effect, totalitarian and muti-
lating. Conversely, a great number of coercive practices can
be termed non-violent; they are in fact based fundamentally
on the meticulous preparation of threats—which can transform a citizen into a prisoner or a country into a proxy
battlefield—and not on the actual use of force.

The appearance of the unified concept of violence can be
explained by a double metamorphosis of the two sources of
power when the stick becomes the carrot and the carrot
the stick. The pressure of political power in the organization
of knowledge entails the slowing down of transdisciplinarization and the development of praxeologies.

One may well wonder if greater transdisciplinarity may
not be a cure worse than the illness. If we end by explaining
violence better through a set of causes stemming from
different levels of the organization of society, might not we
soon see the emergence of totalitarian powers—indeed, a
worldwide totalitarian power based on the transdisciplinary
use of violence?

This development has even begun before our very eyes.
But we have good reason to believe that, as a plan, it is a sort
of Frankenstein monster peculiar to certain praxeologies of
power in a technocratic utopia. The failure of this plan, if it
is indeed envisaged somewhere, perhaps in certain armies,
is written into the inevitable structural contradiction that
exists between the centralization of a complex system and
its local effectiveness. Grassroots struggles already under
way will deliberately contribute to the erosion of this
effectiveness.

Obviously, we cannot pretend that, in articulating these
prospects, we can forecast the development of revolutions.
We can only clarify the way in which transdisciplinarization
in the study of the causes of violence, as begun here, can
seriously affect the future of mankind.

Part one

Transdisciplinarity and multiple causality

We are beginning this collection with certain essays that treat the general question of transdisciplinarity by an approach to the theory of violence.

Violence remains subject to philosophical inquiry, like all questions concerning the human condition that have not yet been definitively answered. This is demonstrated by Jean-Marie Domenach in his discussion of a number of major thinkers, from Anaximander to Heidegger and from Diderot to Sartre; he has no doubt that the definition of violence in Lalande's dictionary of philosophy—'the illegitimate or, at all events, illegal exertion of force'—is a function of the evolution of the democratic spirit. For violence is a phenomenon opposed to freedom and happiness; it must be fought. But it remains an aspect of human, non-animal behaviour and is sometimes the last resort against violence itself. To abolish it, even as its control by sacrosanct institutions such as religion is tending to disappear, seems to be difficult because its excess has been transmitted into the development of the ultimate instruments of destruction—which, however, have led violence to deadlock. This is Domenach's moderately optimistic conclusion for our age of nuclear violence: 'Idealism becomes essential when it converges with the imperative of survival.'

Rapid progress in the functional research on the higher nerve centres, linked with the development of cellular biochemistry and the emergence of both information theory and systems theory, already permit us, as Henri Laborit's article demonstrates, to elaborate and prove hypotheses on the systematic causality of violent behaviour at the biological level.

Like other Laborit writings, this article manifests a constant search for the junction points of interdisciplinarity; whatever the reader's level of scientific knowledge, no one today can be unaware of the implications of debate on cerebral chemistry and the effects of the debate on all the human sciences.

Laborit contends that man's innate behaviour—centred in the hypothalamus, the primitive part of the brain also known as the 'reptilian brain'—is very limited in extent and, moreover, not particularly violent (it includes predatory behaviour caused by hunger, thirst or sexual drive; defensive aggression, flight). Innate behaviour is, in fact, subject to the 'limbic' part of the primitive brain possessed by all mammals; it is capable of long-term conditioning and, consequently, of selection, reinforcement or suppression through learning. Furthermore, in man's case, the more or less fortunate experience of violent behaviour comes to nourish the highly developed associative zone of the brain where new behaviour is created and verbalized. The clarification of predatory instincts and the affective investment in reinforced violent behaviour, conveyed to the human being by learning and by verbalization, is one of the structural—although not inevitable—causes of violent behaviour in mankind today. Man's characteristic is not the 'territorial instinct' nor the 'property instinct'—these are acquired behaviours that cannot be found in certain societies—but, rather, the capacity to verbalize and create new structures, including non-violent behaviour. As the paucity of gratifying goods can, technically, be eliminated, man can deliberately stop rewarding the aggressive.

The next article, by Alain Joxe, criticizes the theoretical impasses created by the misapplication of quantitative methodology to the macro-sociological and cross-cultural study of the causes of violent behaviour. The issue, in a certain type of statistical manipulation of data on violence, is essentially the disappearance of history itself; and this disappearance is itself a form of violation of the heritage of exploited classes or peoples in so far as this knowledge is a collective memory or learning experience; the movement towards generalized aggregates sweeps away a specific determinant. The 'scientific'—or 'economistic'—taste of today's political technocrats for quantification not only fosters the creation of theoretical monstrosities (several are illustrated in the Joxe article) but channels the sociological mind into explaining phenomenon by 'statistical causality' alone—a method that cannot take into account different levels of political awareness and often proves to be nothing but 'quantified tautology'.

In agreeing to play the game of producing a typology of violence as a tool for the definition of the concept itself, Johan Galtung emphasizes the concomitant need for a theory of violence that extends the concept and that, therefore, must be transdisciplinary. Starting by defining violence as 'anything avoidable that impedes human self-realization' and is linked to a more general idea of 'destruction' as it affects man, Galtung dismantles and dismisses one by one a number of typologies that are often implicitly accepted in ordinary political discourse or in the strict vocabulary of the behavioural sciences. He demonstrates that these do not respond to three absolute requirements for the establishment of a typology: the formulation of subsets that are exhaustive, exclusive and fit for use in developing a theory. He concludes by proposing a typology that meets these needs.

In the last article of this first section, Dieter Senghaas describes the necessary contribution of peace research to the definition of a transdisciplinary field and, therefore, to the emergence of complex causality in a sociology of violence. In his effort to take stock of the research conducted over the last decade within this new framework, as well as his recommendations for approaches to future research, Senghaas goes well beyond a 'progress report'. A transdiscipline adequate to a concrete praxeological end raises problems of definition that are far more acute and far more dynamic in their evolution than those that arise in relation to a narrowly defined discipline that is well established in the traditional social sciences. This transdiscipline immediately entails the constant correlation of research carried out in many fields, as well as the consequent creation of different types of 'configurative causality' that allow for a complex feedback process and a basic re-examination of the concepts of 'independent variable' and 'dependent variable'.

Violence and philosophy

Jean-Marie Domenach, writer
and journalist, edited the
French periodical *Esprit*
from 1957 to 1976. He has
taught at several European
and North American
universities and now works
for a publisher in Paris. He
is the author of a number of
books, among them *Le
christianisme éclaté* (1975)
and *Le sauvage et l'ordinateur*
(1976). Address: Éditions
du Seuil, 27 rue Jacob,
75261 Paris, Cedex 06.

Jean-Marie Domenach

Violence is as old as the world; in cosmogonies, mythologies
and legends it is presented as something linked to the
beginning of history, always attendant upon the deeds of
heroes and innovators. Why, then, is it looked upon as a
contemporary issue—almost as a new problem—as if it had
emerged yesterday or at most during the last century?

It is noteworthy that violence had never been taken as a
theme in itself for the great thinkers of the Western philo-
sophic tradition before the nineteenth century. It had to wait
for a Georges Sorel to make it the centre of his studies. If
we succeed in distinguishing the reasons for what was
virtually a blackout of the subject of violence, we shall
perhaps arrive at a better understanding of the reasons for
its emergence into daylight and its present prominence, and
thus gain insight into its true nature. A further advantage
of this method is that it should enable us to take an objective
view of the violence that surrounds us on all sides, so
as to assess the threat it represents and seek appropriate
remedies.

Admittedly, we find a reference to violence in the well-
known fragment of Anaximander which Heidegger called
the oldest utterance of Western thought: 'The infinite mass
of matter out of which all things arise, and into which they
return by their destruction, in order to render to each other
atonement and punishment for their offence against the order
of time'. And Greek cosmogony proclaimed, with Hera-
clitus, that 'strife is the father and king of all things'. But
this is a datum, a self-evident fact that does not present the
philosopher with a problem, even if it is the cause of his
death. What irritates Socrates is the misuse of power and
the misuse of language, for they are impediments to reason,
beauty and harmony: violence is reprehensible because of

its effects and not in itself. However, the question from which philosophy turned aside was taken up and represented by tragedy. Violence is shown here in the forms of revenge, anger and the many excesses of passion. But it is not isolated and considered for its own sake; it is the result of arrogance (*hubris*) or reckless behaviour (*ate*), which are concerns of the gods. Human violence expresses and, at the same time, transgresses divine law, demonstrating the 'impossibility of distinguishing between the divine and the demoniac' (Paul Ricœur) that constitutes the horrifying content of Greek tragedy and that still lies, as we shall see, at the root of the ambiguity of violence.

We find no difference in the way the subject was approached by the Latin philosophers, whose language did not even draw a distinction between force and violence (*vis*). Until the end of the eighteenth century, Western culture continued to evade a question that the thinkers of our time regard as vitally important. Evade? It would be more correct to say that the concept of violence did not yet exist, or at least was slow in forming. What we today call 'violence' gradually came to be understood from three main points of view: (a) the psychological aspect, an explosion of force assuming an irrational and often murderous form; (b) the ethical aspect, an attack on the property and liberty of others; and (c) the political aspect, the use of force to seize power or to misappropriate it for illicit ends.

It is the third aspect that commands the most attention in the twentieth century, as is shown by this definition from the Lalande dictionary of philosophy: 'Violence: the illegitimate or, at all events, illegal exertion of force.'

It is undeniable that the progress of the spirit of democracy has generated the modern concept of violence and has also given the word a pejorative overtone. From the moment that every individual is entitled to the status of citizen, with the recognition of his right to freedom and happiness, violence can no longer be confused with force; it no longer pertains to inevitable physical processes (natural calamities) or to political necessities (hierarchies established by divine right) but becomes a phenomenon that has to do with freedom and can—and must—be fought and overcome. Sensitivity to the violence inflicted on men develops simultaneously with the belief that political power must be used to pursue reasonable and constructive aims, transcending the need to maintain the social order and ensure the efficient administration of municipal affairs. 'To have slaves is of no consequence', said Diderot, 'what is intolerable is to have slaves while calling them citizens'. To have slaves is part of the natural pattern of relations based on force in a world where freedom is a privilege of the aristocracy, but as soon as freedom emerges as a value to be promoted by political systems, the divorce between principle and practice is clear and the real state of affairs is regarded as a form of intolerable violence.

The study of the origins of the concept clarifies the definition; violence is, historically, a human phenomenon. I do not think we can follow the example of the *Encyclopedia Universalis* and speak of the 'violence of nature' except in anthropomorphic terms. We can of course talk about the 'violence of an earth tremor' but this is an extrapolation and, in my view, an improper use of the word, for there is no violence in the depths of volcanoes unless we believe that a deity hides in their recesses. Storms, waves and collisions can be described as violent only as a figure of speech.

If nature is not violent, are animals violent? It is precisely because of the growing sensitivity to the issue of violence that scientists have turned their attention to this point and, as is generally known, many recent studies, particularly those of Konrad Lorenz and his disciples, have dealt with aggressiveness in animals. These studies seem to point to the conclusion that the species observed avoids violence, or at least keeps it within strict limits, by two methods in particular: separation (delimitation of a 'territory') and hiearchization (domination of the weakest by the strongest). It could be said, then, that the species both stops short of violence and transcends the need for violence: it stops short of violence because it does not wish to run the risk of revolt and internecine strife; it transcends the need for violence because it establishes a peaceful *modus vivendi*. In any event, by these two methods the animal group succeeds in avoiding self-destruction. Can we speak, at least, of violence in relations between different species? In our eyes, the lion devouring its prey is violent. But we have learned, to our cost, that this 'violence' is a basic factor in the equilibrium of ecosystems. Here again, we ought to be consistent and ban the use of the word 'violence'. Man alone is capable of turning his strength against himself. Only the human race is capable of destroying itself, precisely because it has lost its capacity for self-regulation.

If we wish to use the word to denote an observable reality, violence must be recognized as a specifically human phenomenon inasmuch as it consists of the freedom (real or presumed) of one person to encroach upon the freedom of another. I shall apply the term violence to the use of force, whether overt or covert, in order to wrest from individuals or groups something that they do not want to give of their own free will. Theft is not always violence. Rape always is. And if rape is a conspicuous and, so to speak, pure form of violence, it is because it obtains by force what is normally won through loving consent. Violence is horrifying and yet fascinating in that it enables the strong to establish profitable relations with those who are weaker without expending any energy on hard work and discussion. In this sense it is not murder that is the apogee of violence (it annihilates the very object of this violence), but torture, because it associates the victim in spite of himself with his torturer. This brings us to consider that enigma of violence that Jean-Paul Sartre presented so well on the stage: violence creates its own society—a society that is the repulsive caricature of a society based on reason and love. However, the caricature has a special appeal because it achieves, easily and rapidly, what individuals or groups despair of accomplishing through the channels of persuasion, debate and negotiation.

But we must clarify this point: if recourse to violence were dictated only by the principle of economy, men would not have found it so powerful nor so attractive throughout their history and in their hearts. This supposedly economic instrument ultimately proves, in fact, to be a costly one, and the benefits it secures are short-lived and fragile. It should therefore be possible, through persuasion, critical analysis of results and extrapolation, to deter individuals and peoples from resorting to violence. It is significant that, both in the case of a delinquent and in the case of a group setting out to battle, violence is decided upon almost invariably on the spur of the moment, without regard for the foreseeable consequences: punishment, physical injury and material damage. But, as Greek tragedy or the great novelists, from Dostoyevsky to Faulkner, have shown, and as modern philosophers, from Hegel to Sartre, including Nietzsche, help us to understand, violence concerns not only a person's property or physical security, but the very essence of his being.

From the earliest months of life, the child's desire for the Other is directed towards the external world, in order to take possession of it. But this possession is not immediate: it passes through other persons, the first stage being, as Freud has shown, the desire for the Other that lies nearest to the child, namely, the father. But the father is also regarded as an adversary, for the very person who becomes the focal point of desire and who initiates and teaches, is the one who must be eliminated. The Oedipus complex leads to the slaying of the father. Violence is thus included, at the very beginning of life, among the factors contributing to the growth of self-awareness and the assertion of personal autonomy.

Animals seek their prey. Man's prey is freedom. Violence also seeks freedom. Love and sadism, democracy and tyranny, honest reasoning and sophistry—there are always two rival courses of action, one gentle, the other violent. They are mutually antagonistic but, in a way, share a common objective: both strive to obtain that most precious of indispensable possessions—the innermost being of the Other, so as to win him over or force him into submission. But here, too, we are oversimplifying: violence is rooted in the depths of human nature, a condition, as we have seen, of birth itself, and it is sometimes reflected in the expression of man's noblest aspirations: mysticism, art, revolt, love. It is, indeed, too easy, too ineffective, to condemn violence as if the phenomenon were extraneous and even alien to man, whereas it is constantly with him and may even be present, as Nietzsche sensed and as our epoch more readily understands, in the structure of discourse, not excluding the presentation of rational evidence. To be sure, we can protest against 'all forms of violence, whatever the source may be', but we will not thereby rid ourselves of violence.

Hegel was the first philosopher to show that violence was an integral part, not only of the rationality of the history of societies, but of the very genesis of consciousness. Consciousness only emerges from life and becomes 'for itself' in negating the Other. But this produces only subjective certainty. If I am to be sure that I exist, the Other must also exist and must recognize me as existing. The struggle for life thus becomes a struggle for recognition. It is by engaging in the struggle that I shall free myself from the natural, animal life of man, and doubly so: by showing that I am prepared to risk my life—by inducing the Other, compelling him if necessary, to give me proof that he recognizes my existence. 'It is only by risking one's life that one preserves one's freedom.'¹ This risk implies violence, whether confronted or exercised. Hegel does not reject violence. Through the master-slave dialectic he incorporates it into the process of human development. Similarly, he holds that war is a normal form of relations between states. It is true that violence is not glorified; work and culture offer more satisfactory forms of self-expression and relationship. But violence is justified inasmuch as it is seen, paradoxically, to be a prerequisite to the humanization of interpersonal and international relations.

The Hegelian analysis continues to dominate a whole line of thought in contemporary conceptions of violence. It obliges us, particularly if we conduct it in terms of the Marxist categories, to pose the problem of the duality of violence: positive or negative, good or bad, according to the ends it pursues or, rather, the historical forces that support it. We know the reply given by Marx and Engels: class struggle is the driving force of history. Therefore, we cannot escape violence, unless we take refuge in the illusions of utopias or religion. But we have to distinguish the violence of the dominant class, which is at present the bourgeoisie, from the violence of the oppressed class, the proletariat, for the former impedes the advance of historical forces, whereas the latter's violence is used only in the interests of the emancipation of all men. Georges Sorel expressed this idea in its most extreme form: according to him, force is bourgeois, violence is proletarian. By reversing the connotations of the usual vocabulary and extolling violence, he sought to reverse the prevailing situation; his aim was to unmask the 'natural' use of the means of domination that had ceased to scandalize because they were cloaked in legality, habit and morality, and to rehabilitate the use of force when it was employed openly and collectively in order to overthrow an unjust social order.

This dialectic, which was directed at that time to justifying general strikes, has been the theme of countless proclamations, discussions, plays and novels. It was the problem that was raised at the turn of the century by the violent actions of anarchists and nihilists. We find it in Dostoyevsky,

Malraux, Sartre and Camus. We also find it in contemporary events; we recognize it in the problem of terrorism, the problem of hostages. It is not a simple issue and I cannot claim to solve it, nor even to go into it here. What is more, I am convinced that it is useless to seek a categorical answer, in philosophy or ethics, to the problem raised by violence. Because of its ontological aspect, violence is inseparable from the human condition. It is futile to condemn it in moral pronouncements or political resolutions. However respectable 'non-violence' may be, I do not think that it can represent a coherent, tenable position in a world where violence is widespread and bound up with almost every aspect of human relationships. Violence has a multitude of concrete aspects that call for precise definitions and specific replies. The violence of a strike is not of the same nature as the violence of the atomic bomb. Again, 'institutional' or 'structural' violence, which is concealed behind a screen of legality and is exercised peacefully, is very different from revolutionary or military violence. It is sufficient here to note that openly avowed violence tends to attract more attention than insidious forms of violence, and hence to be denounced more vehemently.

An inquiry into the nature of violence cannot be conducted separately from a study of means, circumstances and ends. To condemn all forms of violence is absurd or hypocritical. To extol violence is criminal. Judgement on the moral value of violence should depend, first, on the relationship between the doctrine proclaimed and the means employed; secondly, on the relationship between the means and the end; thirdly, as Malraux and, subsequently, Camus understood very well, on the relationship between an individual and his violence: up to what point does he assume the responsibility and take the risk that it implies? The worst example is 'blind' violence—blind as regards its victims but also as regards its perpetrator. We must not forget that violence possesses its own power of reproduction; it begets itself. Accordingly, it must always be analysed sequentially, as a network. The forms of violence that outwardly are the most frightening and at times the most reprehensible usually conceal other situations of violence that seem less scandalous, because they have lasted a long time and are protected by seemingly respectable institutions or ideologies. The violence of individuals and small groups must be measured against the violence of the states; the violence of conflicts against that of the established social order. This is what Dostoyevsky seems to have had in mind when he asserted, in a provocative phrase, that the real cause of war is peace itself.

To refuse to subscribe to abstract declarations of disapproval and to accept the ambiguity of violence is the first step in the right direction. But we have to go farther. Precisely because we have to confront, not violence in itself, but one particular form of violence or another, we must examine the way in which violence besets us, and proceed from our findings to seek such means as will put an end to it.

Wondering whether there is more, or less, violence today than formerly will lead us nowhere, for several reasons, and first of all because, as we have just seen, sensitivity to violence and intolerance of violence are recent phenomena or, at least, have recently assumed very significant dimensions. It is true that, in the past, violence was flagrantly displayed in ways that are disappearing in industrialized societies. Duels, executions, other punishments inflicted in public, and street fights are becoming rare. Violent forms of delinquency are not ceasing to increase, for all that. There is a paradox here to which we should give some thought. As a 'civilized' conscience develops that cannot tolerate the spectacle of violence, the violence is driven to disguise itself and to do so moves in two directions. On the one hand, it turns inward and finds an unexpected and indirect form of expression, as, for example, in philosophical and critical discourse, which is becoming increasingly peevish and self-opinionated (there is much that could be said about the way ideology is used in the accusation and condemnation of an opponent who refutes an argument) and, also, in everyday life, through the brawls and riots that break out during demonstrations and celebrations, at dance-halls, and so on. The pent-up violence of the common man is 'let out' in many different ways, expressed through vague feelings of aggressiveness, which all too often become focused on a chance antagonist.

But on the other hand—and the two phenomena are linked—violence turns outward and becomes embodied in collective, anonymous forms designed for it by technology and political systems. There is a technical, impersonal, abstract violence that has been the subject of many studies. But there is, at a much deeper level, a violence of technology. Ernst Jünger and Martin Heidegger have seen in technology the combined expression of universal rationality and the will to power. Technology, which enables men to communicate with each other and is creating a common universe for all nations, is at the same time tearing the earth apart and taking advantage of nature and man. Thanks to technology, we are becoming used to moulding the world to suit our ends. But to reduce nature to slavery, the very process that is the great adventure of the Western mind, imperils not only nature but also the human reason that is attempting to subjugate nature. This is where we should heed the warning of the Frankfurt school of philosophers: Theodore Adorno and Max Horkheimer tell us that mathematical and technological reason, now that it has destroyed the mythologies, is crushing the Self under its imperialism. Behind the collective forms of violence that man has experienced in our epoch, do we not find a kind of technocratic hysteria—the desire to subject men as well as things to a single will, to an all-embracing and transparently authoritarian state? Technology does not confine itself to providing the political system with unprecedented instruments of supervision and control; it offers a model, an incitement to secure total domination over men. When one has reached the ultimate stage in winning power over matter, it is difficult to concede that the spirit may resist.

So we see that violence, although intrinsically unreasonable, is bound up with the very process of reasoning. To quantify, to organize is already an act of violence. Discourse itself and the structure of ideas within the framework of an established vocabulary and syntax can be regarded as violence.

We find the same implication and the same intrinsic ambiguity in political history. What, in fact, is the *polis* if it is not the organization of a community against external and internal violence? What is the state, if it is not the means of taking violence out of the hands of individuals and groups and bringing it under a single authority, as Max Weber showed when he defined the state as holding 'the monopoly of the legitimate use of violence'? The state is indeed the authority that exercises total power over the lives of citizens, not only through the right to mete out punishment but also through the right to organize national defence. And the state, to the existence of which we owe the retreat of savagery, banditry and summary justice, is precisely the authority that makes of violence an institution having no obligation to conform to any moral or legal norm, for it is always prepared to use the maximum of force if it considers its survival threatened. War is that 'extremity-situation' described by Paul Ricœur, in which the citizen finds himself placed by his state in the 'kill or be killed' dilemma (kill or be enslaved is only a variant), which conscientious objectors refuse but do not resolve.

Whether we see the state absorbing violence or unleashing it, it is always tied to violence. As a matter of fact, every political institution is immersed in violence to a greater or lesser degree, for violence is the driving force of history, which brings to the fore governing classes, nations, civilizations. 'The history of man seems to be identified with the history of violent power; in the end, we no longer find that the institution legitimizes violence, but that violence generates the institution by redistributing power among states and among classes.'[2] There is no question of justifying violence; history has been steeped in too much blood and suffering. But violence can be a constructive factor. It sometimes goes hand in hand with social and cultural changes that were historically necessary and have proved beneficial.

Such is our difficulty, our perplexity. We cannot easily evade it. We must, of course, always prefer persuasion to violence. But what if our rulers turn a deaf ear? It is, of course better to be kind—but naive kindness, on certain occasions, can be more disastrous than hard-heartedness, as Bertolt Brecht has shown. We should, no doubt, hold on to the modest conviction that violence is the ultimate recourse, but a dangerous one because it is contagious, because it soon destroys those who employ it and the end it is intended to serve; this is illustrated, for example, by the logical sequence of events in operations of terrorism.

But we have a final step to take. If violence is becoming both more menacing and more intolerable, is there any hope, are there any means, of holding it in check? There are some who dream of eradicating it by attacking it at what they suppose to be its source. For instance, many thinkers are convinced, as was Sartre, that conflict originates in scarcity. But can we not equally well say that scarcity originates in the exploitation, monopolization and unequal distribution of sources of wealth? If this is so, where does the origin of exploitation lie if not in the violence of an individual or a group? And here we come back to the enigma of primitive violence, which was a stumbling-block to Engels and Marx. In fact, it is the aporia of all humanism and, perhaps, of all religion, for although original sin, as presented by the Bible, explains everything, it cannot itself be explained. We shall therefore abandon the attempt—in itself a source of some of the worst violence—to extirpate the root of the evil. It is probably better to take our stand on other grounds, and to seek to wear down forms of domination and exploitation through active practice of language, democracy and justice.

However, on the horizon there is a glimmer of hope, born of the very magnitude of the threat.

Human cultures have long sought to control violence by measures taken under sacred auspices, in two ways: first, by legitimizing certain forms of violence (holy wars, justice rendered in the name of God, and so on); secondly, by religious rites whereby violence is purified through the selection and sacrifice of a victim. But as men's belief in the supernatural weakens, the violence of institutions is laid bare; justice becomes confused with revenge, order with repression. Desacralized institutions are seriously challenged on all sides, and as fast as these institutions lose their legitimacy, the violence of individuals and groups becomes legitimized by the cause that it claims to serve.

Furthermore, sacrifice, as René Girard[3] has so clearly shown, once gave ritual expression to the expulsion of violence. The victim was designated as the symbol of evil influences, and his execution was intended to reconcile enemies and pacify the city. But the decline of religion has made it more difficult to designate a scapegoat and drive out evil in this way. Recent holocausts in Europe have shown that the reflex is still there; but sacrifice, despite the growing number of victims, has lost all its religious value: now it is the appointed enemy that is destroyed and no longer his symbolic substitute. In other words, violence continues to respond to violence, but since religion has been far less active in attempting to circumscribe its domain, violence is rapidly gaining ground in the minds of men, in the entertainment industry and in everyday life. It is indiscriminate and polymorphous violence, which refuses to keep within the traditional and almost honourable framework accorded to it and prefers to seek an outlet in delinquency. The feeling of being the prisoner of a highly organized system, which nothing legitimizes save its own functioning, aggravates this spread of violence and creates a dangerous situation that could become explosive.

Yet this very peril gives us the inkling of a remedy. In the past, violence was limited by other violence, under the control of the political and religious system. The development of the spirit of democracy has removed, as we have seen, the deep-rooted reasons that justified violence. But at the same time, as we have also seen, it has removed the reasons that justify the counter-violence organized by religious ritual and the state apparatus. The complete anarchy that is liable to result from such a situation cannot be tolerated, and makes it essential to resort to recognized processes other than those of ritualized and institutionalized violence. This is all the more urgent because the extreme limit of state-legitimized violence is the atomic weapon, the use of which would be contrary to the reasonable objective that counter-violence has set itself. We see, then, that the progress of philosophy and the progress of technology have brought them together at the point at which they can take a radically new approach to the problem of violence and the solutions it calls for. Since we can no longer count on violence to check violence, each society, and mankind as a whole, must realize that, if they are to survive, they will have to give precedence to ecumenical aims over particular interests. They have to be made to see that a readiness to engage in dialogue, and an ethical system based on love, or simply on understanding, will change institutions and customs.

For the first time in history, violence, that typically human way of behaving, fails to justify itself. It no longer seems feasible to contain the effects of its own logic. When the maximum possibilities of violence mean the destruction of mankind, it is not enough to demand limitations and controls. We should turn our attention to a different set of problems, different practices and different policies in the expectation that we shall eventually be compelled, as it were, to accept them, for idealism becomes a necessity when it coincides with the demands of survival.

Notes

1. Hegel, *Phénoménologie I.*
2. P. Ricœur, *Histoire et vérité*, Paris, Le Seuil.
3. René Girard, *La violence et le sacré*, Paris, Grasset.

The biological and sociological mechanisms of aggressiveness

Director of the Entomology
Laboratory, Boucicaut
Hospital, Paris

Henri Laborit

We have repeatedly proposed that aggression be defined as the quantity of kinetic energy capable of accelerating a given system's tendency towards entropy or thermodynamic equalization: that is, towards more or less total destructuralization. If structure is defined as the sum total of relationships existing between elements comprising a whole, then aggressiveness is the quality that characterizes those agents capable of bringing this energy to bear on an organized whole, thus creating increasing disorder within it and diminishing its information content, or structuralization.

Using these definitions as a point of departure, it becomes apparent that aggression can assume various forms, because the mechanisms that cause the release of destructuralizing energy are themselves varied. It is this variety that has led many writers in the field to draw up lists tabulating the most frequently observed types of aggression. Unfortunately, these lists have often been based on descriptions of different aggression-provoking situations with, however, no account taken of the concurrent central nervous system processes involved. What we now need to examine is the relationship between the ecological situation and the nervous system's response to it.

When we are dealing with hypercomplex systems, we can today no longer look for a simple 'cause' for a given action; this is because causality can no longer be thought of in linear terms ('cause-effect') as it was by the determinists of the late nineteenth century. We now think in terms of whole 'systems' whose organization must be understood before we can proceed to an analysis of how they work.

All living organisms conform to the second law of thermodynamics in that they are open systems relative to the energy they degrade. We can say that the energy flowing in

them, through the intermediary of photosynthesis, is solar
energy. On the informational level the problem is a more
complex one, however, because in living organisms we find
different 'levels of organization'. Using 'information' in the
etymological sense of the term, we will refer to 'structure-
information' as that controlling organization in either a living
being or a social complex; and 'system-information' as that
comprising the totality of messages circulating between
subcellular, cellular, organic and social individuals. System-
information ensures the continuity of structure-information
in time and space.

   In the organizational schema, each level includes within
it the one just below it and is itself included within the one
just above it; the complexity of the system as a whole will
reflect the number of organizational levels it contains. We
thus proceed from molecule to enzyme, from the intra-
cellular level of the organoids (mitochondria, nucleus,
cytosol, membranes, etc.) to the cell, from cell to organ,
from organ to systems of organs and then on to the total
organism itself. Structurally, each of these levels of organization constitutes a closed system, and as a rule it will be
regulated functionally by feedback. This is why it is possible
to study it experimentally in isolation. But the information
received at each level comes from other levels of organization, and this is what transforms the original 'regulator'
into a 'servomechanism' that opens the closed system to the
outside. The ultimate opening occurs between the total
organism and the environment. If information flow were
only one way, from environment to organism, then the
organism would be entirely dependent on the environment.
As it is, however, continuity of the structure-information,
expressed in terms of satisfaction of the cell group constituting the organism, requires that the nervous system
receiving this information be able, in return, to act upon the
environment: to inform, transform and reform it in terms of
its own structure. We can already see, from even this rather
cursory systemic schematization, that each level of organization inside a system is finite only at the level of the
organization as a whole and that the limits of this whole
condition those of each organizational level beneath. We
can also see that there is no structural analogy to be drawn
between the various levels of organization. The important
thing is, rather, the relationship of their separate structures

to the whole and how it works. Looked at from this point of view, a being's only purpose is to be; to preserve the continuity of its structure-information at whatever level of behavioural complexity. This is its 'teleonomy', or purpose as a structure, the goal without which there would be no living creatures.

There is no hierarchy or system of dominance within individual organisms, and this is because each separate cell, organ and system fulfils a 'function' whose ultimate purpose is participation in the continuity of the structure as a whole, without which none of these organizational levels, from the simplest to the most complex, could survive. Thus, from the system-information point of view, the system is an open one throughout, becoming closed only when the boundaries limiting the total individual have been reached. For, although the individual as a whole constitutes a system that is open to the environment, and registers and acts upon the variations presented by the environment to it, creating system-information between them, it nonetheless also constitutes a system that is virtually a closed one in terms of structure-information. Any change in the structure-information resulting from the action of memory or imagination will occur within the context of its own specific environmental biotope. When a structure's limits are reached and it becomes closed, we can say that its continued existence will depend on whether or not it assumes as its ultimate purpose, or *raison d'être*, the maintenance of its own organization.

In the course of the millions of years it has taken for unicellular organisms to evolve into pluricellular ones, evolutionary determinism has allowed for the constitution within each individual element of structures that are open-ended. In man, however, inclusion of the total organism within the species as an open-ended structure has so far not been possible. Furthermore, the absence of homogenous structure on the species level has precluded the flow between various groups of humans of information that would be valid for the entire species. Current information flow is valid only relative to specific dominant or dominating subgroups. We will be discussing below the ways in which patterns of dominance are established; in any case, once they have been established, the only information circulating within an individual group will be that favourable to continuation of its dominance structure.

This is why, in the last analysis, we cannot take etho-
logical observations of animal behaviour that are based on
the functional anatomy of the organizational levels found in
their central nervous systems and that result in certain
behaviour patterns, and transpose them whole into human
behavioural terms. Because only man possesses sufficiently
well-developed associative zones to enable him, on the basis
of his own imagining, to create information and to employ
a symbolic language.

The first appearance of intraspecific aggression in man
seems to have occurred in neolithic times, at the end of the Ice
Age. It was then that the ethnic groups located in the
northern hemisphere at about the 45th parallel began to
develop agriculture and to domesticate animals. The prevalence in these areas of what today we call a temperate
climate—that is, one characterized by the seasonal alteration
of hot and cold weather, making survival easy in the summer
but difficult during the winter months—resulted in the stock-
piling of gratifying objects to ensure survival through the
winter. It seems probable that certain less favoured groups
desired a share in these reserves and so attempted to impose
their domination on the early neolithic peoples. Studies into
prehistory have shown that, in ancient Europe in any case,
these early neolithic peoples were matrilinear and egalitarian,
and that they did not bear arms.[1] The notions of property and
intraspecific aggressiveness both appear to have developed
in this area at this time, although amongst other, ecologically
more favoured groups, such as those in the South Pacific,
they were until recently quite unknown. Certain other groups,
such as the Eskimos—hardly a favoured one, ecologically
speaking—have also avoided the phenomenon of aggressiveness, owing to the fact that mutual co-operation is essential
for individual survival in their climate. In the temperate zone,
the creation of technological information, in its early stages,
protected the ethnic group and facilitated its growth in a
hostile environment. Later, however, it was increasingly
made use of to form dominance hierarchies between individuals, between groups and, finally, between nations.

The functional significance
of the higher nerve centres

The essential functions of the nervous system can be said to be the following. First, interception of energy variations coming from the environment and capted by the senses; the degree of sensitivity in this area will depend on sensory structure, differing from species to species. Second, conduction of intercepted information to the higher centres, where there is also a confluence of the third function. Third, conduction to the higher centres of internal signals that reflect the relative equilibrium or disequilibrium of the organism as a whole.

For example, when several hours have elapsed since ingestion of the last meal, the resulting biological disequilibrium will trigger internal signals that stimulate certain lateral regions of the hypothalamus and set in motion the behaviour patterns associated with a search for food; if the sense organs record the presence nearby of appropriate prey, the behaviour pattern will be predatory. If, further, this act on the environment is successful (prey attacked, slain and eaten), then internal equilibrium will be re-established and other cellular groups in the hypothalamic region will be stimulated, setting in motion the behaviour pattern associated with satiation. Biochemically and neurologically, these behaviour patterns are extremely complex, and yet they are among the simplest we know and are indispensable for immediate survival. The mechanisms governing the satisfaction of thirst or the urge to reproduce are similar and result in patterns such as mating dances, nesting activity and the instruction of offspring. This category of behaviour pattern, in so far as it fulfils a programme built into the nervous system itself, and as it is necessary for the survival both of the individual and of the species, is the only one that can be qualified as truly instinctive. These patterns are activated by the hypothalamus and the brainstem, a primitive region of the brain common to all species that possess a higher nervous system. When the environmental stimulus coincides with the internal signal, these behaviour patterns are stereotypical, invariable and immune to memorized experience. This is due to the fact that, in this simplified nervous system, memory is short-term, with a span of only a few hours. These behaviour patterns correspond to what we can call basic needs.

We must keep in mind that originally it is only through a motor activity exercised upon the environment that the individual can satisfy his search for biological equilibrium, for 'well-being', for 'pleasure'. In reality, this motor activity results in the conservation of the complex structure of the organism in a less 'organized' environment, thanks to energy exchanges between the organism and this environment that are kept within certain limits. On the other hand, the absence of a nervous system makes vegetables entirely dependent on the biotope in which they exist.

When the brains of the earliest mammals evolved to include additional formations, the latter 'derived' from the preceding system and became known as the limbic system.[2] Usually thought to control affectivity, it seems to us more accurate to say that this system plays an essential role in the establishment of long-term memory,[3] without which affectivity, in turn, would of course be impossible. This is because long-term memory, now commonly agreed to be related to protein synthesis occurring when synapses are activated by experience,[4] is necessary if a given previously experienced situation is to be identified as agreeable or disagreeable, so that the appropriate 'affect', so-called, can be triggered by it. In the case of a situation that because of an 'information deficit' is not immediately classifiable, memory again plays a crucial role. Agreeable experience may be defined primarily as that enabling maintenance of, or return to, a state of biological equilibrium; disagreeable experience as that posing a threat to this equilibrium and hence to the survival and continuation of the organic structure in the environment. Long-term memory thus facilitates repetition of agreeable experience and avoidance of, or escape from, disagreeable experience. To be more precise, long-term memory makes possible temporal and spatial association within the synaptic circuits of memory traces identified with experience-related, information-bearing signals; this in turn facilitates development of conditioned reflexes, either the Pavlovian affective or vegetative type, or the Skinnerian[5] active, neuro-motor variety.

However, when memory facilitates the development of automatisms, or involuntary acquired responses, it creates new needs that can no longer be qualified as instinctive. In man, these acquired needs will more often than not be socio-cultural in origin. Nevertheless, they will, in their turn, become necessary to the individual's well-being and biological equilibrium. They will transform human impact on the environment so that a lesser energy output will be sufficient to maintain homoeostasis. Reaction range will narrow down and a progressive decrease in what we might call potential satisfaction scope will occur. By this we mean that the margin of environmental physico-chemical and energy variation tolerable to the increasingly demanding organism for maintenance of its biological equilibrium will be reduced. These acquired needs will produce satisfaction-seeking drives that will act on the environment in an attempt to be gratified. They will also run the risk of coming into conflict with other socio-culturally induced reflexes, or automatisms, that will prevent their fulfilment. We can thus define need as the quantity of energy or of information necessary for maintenance of a particular nervous structure, whether innate or acquired. When the structure is an acquired one, it results from interneuronal relationships that are established through learning. Thus, the basic underlying motivation is need. However, as we will see below, in social situations, needs can only be satisfied through domination by one individual or group of other individuals or groups. Basic motivation in all species is thus expressed in attempts to achieve dominance. This fact explains the development of hierarchic social structures, and also the existence of the majority of unconscious conflicts underlying what is sometimes called 'cortico-visceral' or 'psychosomatic' pathology. An apter term might be 'inhibition-behaviour' pathology, but we will return to this later. In man, socio-culturally conditioned needs and taboos are expressed, institutionalized and transmitted through language, and here again we find the cortex playing a role, this time providing, in the genesis of linguistic structures, a means or logical schematization for the conflict mechanisms occurring in other cerebral areas.

The higher forms of life possess a cerebral cortex, particularly well developed in man in the orbito-frontal regions, that furnishes a means for relating the various elements of memorized material to one another. We can assume, for example, that elements incorporated into the nervous system through sense-perception channels will subsequently be related to one another in long-term memory, just as, through experience, they were found to be related to one another in the environment: i. e. according to the natural relationships of perceptible objective structure. However, if we can also assume that the highly developed associative system characteristic of the orbito-frontal lobes in man is capable of recombining memorized material in new ways—ways that differ from those originally imposed by the environment—it then follows that the human brain is capable of creating new, imaginary structures. A newborn infant will be incapable of imagining anything, because it has not yet memorized anything. Imaginative scope will be proportionate to the quantity of memorized material, as long as this material has not been locked inaccessibly within the automatic response system. Through language, man is able to conceptualize, to gain detachment in relation to objects, to manipulate abstractions by means of associative systems and, in short, to command an almost infinite potential for creativity.

The biochemical and neurophysiological bases for primary behaviour patterns

In both animals and man we find instinctive behaviour patterns designed to satisfy endogenous biological needs arising from instinctive cravings triggered by hypothalamic stimulation caused when the internal biological equilibrium is disturbed: (a) If the action taken is rewarded and the need met, then a memory trace will subsist, reinforcing and facilitating repetition of the behavioural strategy employed. This system is catecholaminergic, i.e. a system in which the chemical mediators of nervous influx are catecholamines (CA). (b) If, on the other hand, the action taken is not rewarded, or is punished, this will trigger a behaviour pattern of flight or, if this too is ineffective, of confrontation or defensive aggressiveness. This behaviour pattern also activates various cerebral levels, but it does so through the periventricular system (PVS), which is cholinergic, in other words, a system in which the chemical mediator of nervous influx is acetylcholine (ACh). (c) Nevertheless, if flight or if confrontation is rewarded, leading either to satisfaction of the endogenous craving or to avoidance of an aggressive encounter, they too may be reinforced, as above, by memorization of the successful behavioural strategy employed. (d) However, if the behaviour is either punished or left unrewarded, or if both escape and confrontation prove ineffective, then an inhibition behaviour pattern, suppressing an acquired behaviour pattern, will intervene. This system of action inhibition (SAI) activates the median septal area, the dorsal hippocampus, the caudate nucleus, the lateral amygdala and the ventro-median hypothalamus; it is cholinergic and, possibly, also serotonergic, in other words, the chemical mediator of the nervous influx is serotonin (5 HT).[6]

Associated with the activation of these various areas and circuits of the central nervous system are certain endocrine actions, among which we shall single out those involved in the alarm system.[7] Called the Corticotropin Releasing Factor (CRF), they involve the hypophyso-cortico-adrenal pair, controlled by a hypothalamic factor triggering release of corticotrophin (ACTH) by the pituitary. The hypothalamus itself, of course, is controlled by the central nervous system in its functional relationship to the environment.

The role of behaviour inhibition

The system of rewards and punishments results in action reinforcement. It is catecholaminergic.[8]

The system identified by Molina and Hunsperger,[9] the PVS, controls flight and confrontation behaviour and is cholinergic. When it is activated, it triggers the release of the CRF and the secretion of ACTH. But if the behavioural strategy employed is effective and leads to gratification, then the secretion of ACTH and subsequent release of glucocorticoids will both be arrested. The ACTH released immediately following aggression stimulates the system of action activation of (SAA).[10]

However, behaviour that is unrewarded will be inhibited by the cholinergic SAI and secretion of these various endocrine factors will continue unchecked. In addition, we now know that the glucocorticoids themselves stimulate repression of inhibitory behaviour. The result is a kind of vicious circle that can be broken only by either effective action, or disappearance of the punishment.[11]

The essential function of the nervous system is to facilitate action by the organism on the environment. It is also responsible for motor inhibition, when action becomes impossible or dangerous. This inhibitory aspect of the nervous function seems to us to constitute the basis for such enduring biological disorders as psychosomatic illness, neurogenic hypertension

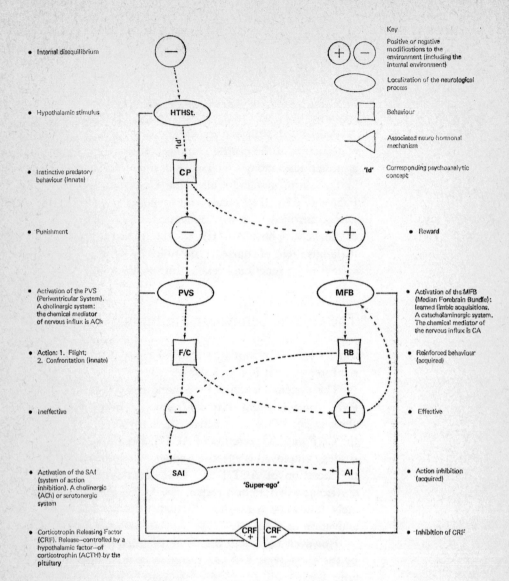

Diagram of the neurological and neuro-hormonal causality of innate or acquired behaviour*

* Diagram produced by the editor with the agreement of the author to help situate the various acronyms.

NB. The negative modifications to the environment and innate behaviour patterns have been arranged on the left-hand side of the diagram and positive modifications and acquired behaviour patterns on the right-hand side.

and gastric ulcers. We have demonstrated that when rats are able to avoid a plantar electric shock administered during a seven-minute period and repeated for seven consecutive days, they do not acquire chronic high blood pressure. But when the same experiment is performed with animals who have no way to escape, they are forced into a state of motor inhibition, causing high blood pressure to occur and to persist for as long as one month after the conclusion of the experiment. If the same experiment is conducted with animals which cannot escape but are placed in cages in pairs, they adopt an attitude of confrontation and there is no rise in blood pressure.

Motor inhibition and anxiety[12]

When dealing with the various functions of the nervous system we have traditionally placed too much emphasis, perhaps, on what is usually referred to as 'thought' and its source, 'feelings', and not enough on the physical interactions without which neither would be possible. Individuals have no existence outside of their material and physiological environment, and it would be absurd to consider either of these separately without taking into account the functional mechanisms of the system making interaction between them possible, i.e. of the nervous system. Despite its great complexity, which is the result of a long evolutionary process, its ultimate purpose still remains the facilitation of action that will ensure homoeostasis (Cannon), maintain the internal conditions necessary for life (Claude Bernard) and those necessary for pleasure (Freud). When circumstances render appropriate action impossible, then anxiety will develop. Our purpose here is to isolate the principal circumstances during which anxiety will occur. They are:

First, when learning has established in the neuronal network, through the long-term memory process, (a) experience of a noxious event, (b) experience of either a direct or an indirect punishment imposed by the socio-cultural milieu, or (c) experience of a punishment to come because of taboo transgression. If the taboo in question conflicts with a hypothalamic impulse seeking satisfaction of a basic need, the preclusion of effective action will activate the system of action inhibition. Alternatively, the impulse may proceed from another kind of socio-culturally conditioned learning, and be an acquired need, reinforced by gratification. When this type of gratification is forbidden or punished, it will also lead to action inhibition. I believe there is an obvious parallel to be drawn here between the hypothalamic impulse and the Freudian concept of the id and, on the other hand, between learned limbic acquisitions and the super-ego.

Second, anxiety will occur when there is an information deficit. This happens when the individual has already learned that certain events can constitute a threat to survival, biological equilibrium or pleasure, but is faced with a previously unrecorded event for which effective action is impossible because its potential for good or harm is not yet known. Paradoxically, 'future shock' (as described by Alvin Tofler), which results from an information surplus, also comes under this heading. When the individual is faced with an excess of stimuli and is incapable of ordering it in terms of preceding cultural schemas and behaviour patterns, the possibility of effective, and hence gratifying, action is denied him. Information deficit and information surplus thus both result in action inhibition followed by anxiety. By the same token, the contents of the space in which audio-visual media stimulate contemporary man's nervous system exceed the restricted range on which it is possible for him to have an impact.

Lastly, anxiety can be caused by the existence in man of the faculty of imagination, making it possible for him to use memorized experience, conscious or otherwise, as a basis for the elaboration of noxious scenarios. Whether or not they ever actually occur in reality, they constitute a source of anxiety because the taking of immediate appropriate action and a decision as to future effectiveness of a potential action are both precluded.

In order to avoid submitting to taboos, against which neither flight nor confrontation is effective, and to escape the psychosomatic consequences of submission, the only course of action left open is escape into the imagination. This can be achieved in various ways: through religion, drug addiction, creative work or psychosis. An explanation for the frequency of psychosis in man, although we can find no experimental model for it in animals, is probably to be found in this phenomenon of anxiety resolution through imagination. Another way in which the anxiety resulting from action inhibition can be resolved is through aggressiveness.

The progression from biological to sociological, from the individual to the collectivity[13]

Action takes place in space, or in spaces, occupied by objects and by beings. What we learn about reward and punishment is based on our experiences relating to them. A gratifying object must be preserved so that reinforcement can occur. Here we can see the origins of the so-called possessive instinct. The first object of gratification is the mother, and her importance is enhanced by the fact that gratification memory trace fixation precedes corporeal schema fixation. The spatial area containing the totality of gratifying objects for a given individual is what we will call the territory. It thus would seem that there is no more an innate instinct for defence of territory than that for the possession of property. There is simply a nervous system acting within a spatial area that is gratifying because it contains objects and beings appropriate for the facilitation of gratification. This nervous system is capable of preserving memory trace of actions, whether or not gratification followed them. This preservation, or learning process, is for the most part socio-culturally conditioned; it has yet to be shown that so-called 'altruistic' behaviour patterns, in either animals or man, are innate.

Now, if a given spatial area is occupied by two or more individuals, and if all of them are seeking gratification from the same objects and the same beings, then the inevitable confrontations will quickly establish hierarchic order among them. At the top of the hierarchy will be found the dominant individual, the one whose position allows him gratification without resort to aggressive behaviour. Once the hierarchy is definitively established, the biological equilibrium he thus enjoys will make him tolerant—that is, as long as his dominance remains uncontested. The dominated individuals beneath him, on the other hand, will experience continual activation of their systems of action inhibition, as the only means of avoiding punishment. They will feel anxiety and suffer its consequences according to the lines we have set

out above. In man, language has made it possible to institutionalize the rules that govern dominance. In human society,
we find that dominance has been successively instituted
through the production of consumer goods, the ownership
of means of production and capital and, in all contemporary
industrial civilizations, the degree of abstraction attained by
professional information. The latter has made possible the
invention of machines and the rapid mass production of
goods. These factors form the socio-cultural basis of industrialized society; all of its social structures, from the simplicity
of the family unit to the complexities of institutionalized
hierarchies, law, religion, moral codes and even ethics, are
derived from them.

The ability to create information that can be employed for
the purpose of manipulating matter and energy is the distinguishing characteristic of the human brain and its associative systems. This is as true for the palaeolithic man shaping
his flint while he carves it, as it is for the use of atomic energy
in modern times. Those human collectivities that have used
this ability in order to develop a high degree of technical and
professional information have, throughout the course of
history, been able to impose their domination on those that
have not. Information has made possible the construction
of more powerful weapons and the acquisition of raw
materials and energy sources lying beyond the ecological
biotope and belonging to groups unable to make use of them.
A high degree of information development also confers on the
groups that possess it a command of logical patterns of
discourse with which they can elaborate linguistic alibis for
their unconscious drive to domination. We are used to
thinking of technological progress as the only real progress,
as a highly desirable end in itself. At the same time, however,
the biological laws governing human behaviour have not
until recently evolved beyond the mechanisms acquired in
palaeolithic times. With the advent of civilization, the primitive responses have traditionally been presented with a verbal
garnish masquerading as truth; but it has been a truth valid
only for the predatory dominant group, never for the human
race as a whole.

Types of aggressiveness

The mechanisms for the appearance of animal aggressiveness also occur in man: predatory aggressiveness—an innate behaviour pattern motivated by hunger—is certainly an exception today and readily distinguishable from larcenous behaviour; competition aggression, which may take on the appearances of defence of territory or inter-male aggressiveness, is always a learned behaviour pattern linked to the acquisition of 'gratifying objects' and hierarchy establishment. This behaviour will be manifested through an aggressive attitude or by actual combat and will have the effect of reinforcing both the predatory drive as well as the aggressive behaviour of the dominant member. Defensive aggressiveness, an innate behaviour pattern (activating PVS), is activated by a painful stimulus when there is no possibility for escape. Defensive aggressiveness will not become an acquired behaviour pattern unless it is rewarded. It is inhibited by learned punishment expectation or by confrontation with unidentifiable circumstances.

However, man's highly developed associative cortex and his faculty for language have made it possible for him to institutionalize the notion of property ownership and the means for achieving dominance in competition aggressiveness.[14] The fact that man belongs to the only species capable of creating information, and of using it in the production of goods, has enabled him to base dominance rank on the degree of abstraction attained in his professional information. This has been especially true since technological information reached the point where the construction of machines for the rapid mass production of goods became possible. The industrialization of society has put the means for domination into the hands of technicians and bureaucrats.

We must also recognize the fact that what we call 'education' really consists simply of teaching children and adolescents how to acquire the technological information necessary for successful integration into the mass-production system. This education is motivated by a quest for dominance through acquisition of the technological information that today forms the basis of all social advancement. Competition between males, and nowadays between females as well, no longer manifests itself in combat behaviour patterns, as it does in animals and once did in man. The battle has become an abstract one, but is just as ritual and institutionalized as it formerly was. The conclusion to be drawn from this is that problems such as growth, production and pollution are actually rooted in competition aggressiveness, the true nature of which is camouflaged with a pseudo-humanitarian verbal logic designed to eliminate guilt, behind which structures of dominance are maintained within and between social strata, ethnic groups and nations. Mass (in the form of raw materials) and energy have always been available to the human race, but the only ethnic groups able to take full advantage of them have been those that acquired highly developed forms of technological information. Because of their more sophisticated weapons, they have also been able to impose their domination over other, technologically less advanced, groups. Competition aggressiveness today, more than ever before, is based on the efficiency of weapons and the number of patents.

The impetus behind the seizure and retention of power has always been this fundamental aggressiveness, ritualized and institutionalized until finally invisible, indeed assuming the appearance of legitimate rights, justice and the veritable absence of aggression; it enables those in power to profess humanitarian and charitable principles while they pursue aggression themselves and at the same time penalize those under their domination for any outward eruptions of violence. We must bear in mind, however, that every profound change in human social institutions has always been accomplished through revolutions bringing to power those previously under the domination of others. Once they achieve the dominant position for themselves, it is only a short time before they establish and institutionalize their own rules of dominance. The legislative process is never more than a logical alibi justifying the unconscious dominance drive and responsible for creation of the rules governing hierarchic structure in a given society.

Competition aggressiveness will then condition the dominated member to a pattern of behavioural inhibition aggressiveness or anxiety (sometimes referred to as irritability aggressiveness) as a result of failure of his defensive aggressiveness.

There also might seem to be a similarity between defensive aggressiveness and aggressiveness resulting from isolation. Certain authors[15] note that when animals are made aggressive through isolation, and are then replaced in a social situation, they are more likely to achieve dominance. The concurrent appearance of a CA surplus in the brain is observable and seems to be the cerebral biochemical characteristic of dominant animals, those who are the most aggressive and whose aggression is the most highly rewarded.[16]

In man, it would seem that defensive aggressiveness triggered by pain stimulus is relatively rare. On the other hand, language, the 'secondary system of signalization' (to use the Pavlovian term), perhaps constitutes a stimulus capable of activating the innate defence system. But to be effective, its semantics, i.e. its terms of insult, must first be learned. A whole set of values of a purely sociological utility must be culturally acquired as well; the values so learned include displays of courage and virility, adherence to codes of honour and personal subgroup identification, for example, as an outlaw or a pillar of society. Finally, the notions of merit and discipline must also be learned. The former will be rewarded by the social structure of dominance. The latter, if not respected, will result in punishment.

We have seen that when gratification is not obtained and when flight and confrontation both prove ineffective against aggression, a behaviour pattern of motor inhibition results. Defeat is preferable to combat that might end in death. But we have also seen that this pattern creates a vicious circle with, on the vegetative level, considerable increase in norehinephrin (NE) circulation and, on the endocrine level, the release of glucocorticoids that stimulate the system of action inhibition. This leads to a state of tension that can be resolved only by gratification, and that will sometimes lead either to explosions of aggressiveness or to a state of depression. In our opinion, this state of tension is responsible for the conditions generally known as psychosomatic diseases, although in this context we would prefer the term 'diseases of behavioural inhibition'. If a new stimulus is brought to bear in these situations, one that normally would not have led to aggressiveness, the new information will transform the overall behaviour pattern. PVS involvement can be assumed. It occurs as a reflex motor response to the anxiety and not to the factors that caused it; it makes possible the replacement of action inhibition by some kind of motor activity, even if ineffective.

Action inhibition is an acquired behaviour pattern. The ineffectiveness of certain modes of action must be learned. Rats unable to escape plantar electric shocks, isolated so they cannot fight, will develop chronic high blood pressure, as we have noted, when the experiment is conducted for seven minutes per day during seven consecutive days. If, however, immediately following each session, they are exposed to convulsive electric shock and coma, forestalling passage of the experience from short- to long-term memory, then high blood pressure will not develop. This is because the ineffectiveness of the action is forgotten from one day to the next. Aggressiveness based on inhibition or irritation, therefore, is a learned rather than an innate behaviour pattern.[17]

We come, finally, to suicidal behaviour, an anxiety, or gratifying action inhibition pattern, in which aggressiveness is directed towards the only object unprotected by the socio-cultural milieu: the subject himself. Drug addiction, for example, can be seen as an intermediary behaviour pattern allowing the individual to escape from socio-culturally imposed inhibitions in the environment by turning his aggression towards himself.

We should note that, according to Roslund and Larson,[18] in individuals who have committed crimes, dependence is a common character trait, and also that Glueck and Glueck[19] point out that delinquency prediction can be based on the extent to which a subject's personality is dominated, insecure or fearful of dependence.

To this may be added two additional defence factors: the first is addiction (particularly to alcohol), in the vast majority of cases the underlying cause for violence and in itself an attempt to block out anxiety. Both alcoholism and the violent behaviour to which it gives rise are complementary aspects of an attempt to escape painful feelings caused by gratifying action inhibition. The second dependence conditioning factor, again according to Roslund and Larson[20] results from an absence of anyone in whom the subject can confide his anxiety. The use of language would in itself constitute a course of action.

Everything we have said about individuals is also applicable at the level of organized social groups. War, for example, is simply confrontation between two closed structural systems, each attempting to establish dominance over the other in order to ensure the steady supply of energy and raw materials necessary for maintaining its own individual structure. Because the structure of all social groups up to the present time has always been based on hierarchic domination, we can thus deduce that war, regardless of the political or economic pretexts advanced to justify it, is always waged in order to maintain the specific dominance structures of the participants.[21] In man, language can be used as propaganda to convince each sector of the group that its own gratification territory and the objects and beings it contains are being defended. Actually, of course, very often the only thing being protected and defended is the prevailing structure of hierarchic dominance. In such cases, this structure is too frequently referred to as culture.

Conclusions

It seems obvious that, with the exception of predatory aggressiveness—and we may question whether this category should even be retained when considering aggressive behaviour in man—aggressiveness behaviour types result either from a learning process, making them amenable to socio-cultural transformation, or else from an elementary response to a painful stimulus.

Competition aggression seems to be the type most frequently encountered. We have seen that it rests on remembered gratification, hence on learning, and that this is the controlling factor in defence of territory occupied by gratifying objects and beings, as well as in notions of property, quests for dominance and the establishment of hierarchies. There seems little doubt, moreover, that until the disciplines we know as social sciences begin to devote serious attention to that fundamental property of the human brain through which it creates and uses information in order to dominate individuals, groups and nations, we are not likely to see any evolution in this area. A society calling itself a 'society of plenty' and claiming to have abolished 'scarcity' should be capable of an equitable global distribution of goods and people. It should stop camouflaging the principle of 'might makes right' in the discourse of humanism. A start must be made into investigating the dynamics of these most archaic of motivations, an attempt made to go beyond them, without distributing society's rewards to its most aggressive and least aware members.

There is no other way, in our opinion, to avoid an endless repetition, for millenniums to come, of the violence, exploitation, warfare and genocide that so far even the greatest of humanists have been helpless to abolish. Up to present times, humanism itself has always been at the service of predatory groups that dominated others and were convinced of their right to do so; it has never served the human race as a whole.

The peoples living in the temperate regions of the earth were the first, over the course of the centuries, to discover the laws of the physical world, including physics and its language, mathematics. They made technological progress possible, and for a long time technological progress was thought to be the only kind. The organic world and its point of culmination, the functional organization of man's own nervous system, were neglected. Let us hope that today's increasing knowledge in this area will furnish an effective instrument for the future exercise of a healthy scepticism in regard to conscious language, the value judgements it conveys and the historical structuring of man's unconscious automatisms.

Notes

1. M. Gimbutas, 'La fin de l'Europe ancienne', *La recherche*, No. 87, 1978, pp. 228–35.
2. P. D. McLean, 'Psychomatic Disease and the Visceral Brain. Recent Developments Bearing on the Papez Theory of Emotion', *Psych. Med.*, No. II, 1949, pp. 338–53.
3. B. Milner, S. Gorkin and H. I. Teuber. 'Further Analysis of the Hippo-campal Amnesic Syndrome: 14-Year Follow-up Study of H. M.', *Neuropsychol.*, No. 6, 1968, pp. 215–34.
4. H. Hyden and P. Lange, 'Protein Synthesis in the Hippocampal Pyr-amidal Cells of Rats During a Behavioural Test', *Science*, No. 159, 1968, pp. 1370–3.
5. B. F. Skinner, *Behaviour of Organisms*, New York, Appleton-Century Crofts, 1938.
6. H. Laborit, 'Action et réaction; mécanismes bio- et neurophysiolo-giques', *Agressologie*, Vol. XV, No. 5, 1974, pp. 303–22; 'Bases neuro-physiologiques et biologiques des comportements d'évitements actifs et passifs. Conséquences somatiques', *Ann. Med. Psychol.*, No. 133, 1975, pp. 573–603.
7. M. Selye, 'A Syndrome Produced by Diverse Noxious Agents', *Nature* (London), Vol. 138, No. 32, 1936.
8. L. C. Lorenzen, B. L. Wise and W. P. Ganong, 'ACTH-Inhibiting Activity of Drugs Related to -éthyltryptamine Relation to Pressor Activity', *Fed. Proc.*, No. 24, 1965, p. 128.
9. A. F. de Molina and R. W. Hunsperger, 'Organization of Subcortical System Governing Defence and Flight Reactions in the Cat', *J. Physiol.* (London), No. 160, 1962, pp. 200–13.
10. H. Bohus and Lissak, 'Hormones and Avoidance Behaviour of Rats', *Neuroendocrinology*, Vol. 3, No. 6, 1968, pp. 355–65. We have recently demonstrated that when ACTH is injected into a normal animal, a considerable quantity of epinephrin is released from the adrenal medulla. Cf. H. Laborit, E. Hunz and N. Valette, 'Rôle de l'apprentissage dans le mécanisme d'inhibition comportemental et de l'hypertension artérielle consécutives à l'application de stimuli aversifs sans possibi-lité de fuite ou de lutte', *Agressologie*, Vol. XV, No. 6, 1974, pp. 381–5. The ACTH facilitates flight and confrontation behaviour, and also

defensive aggression because epinephrin is a vasodilator in the organs crucial for the individual's motor autonomy in the environment. Cf. de Wied, 'Antagonistic Effect of ACTH and Glucocorticoids on Avoidance Behaviour of Rats' (2nd Congress on hormonal steroïds), *Excerpta Medica Inter. Congr.*, Series III, No. 89, 1966.

11. We have also recently been able to show that the injection of hydrocortisone into adrenalectomized animals causes the release of considerable amounts of noradrenalin into the plasma through the nerve ends of the peripheral sympathetic system. Cf. H. Laborit, E. Hunz, F. Thuret and C. Baron, 'Action de l'hydrocortisone sur le taux de norépinéphrine plasmatique chez le lapin surrénalectomisé', *Agressologie*, Vol. XVI, No. 6, 1975, pp. 351–4. Certain observations have led us to the conclusion that stimulation of the SAI is responsible for this. The PVS stimulates medullo-adrenal secretion of adrenalin with a vasodilator effect on the organs of motor activity in the environment. Noradrenalin, which is vasoconstrictive relative to all smooth vascular fibers, appears, on the other hand, to be the neuro-hormone of tense expectancy and adrenalin that of crisis reaction, when mobility of the individual in the environment is crucial.

12. H. Laborit, 'Des bêtes et des hommes', *Agressologie*, Vol. XV, No. 2, 1974, pp. 93–109.

13. H. Laborit, *La nouvelle grille*, Paris, Robert Laffont, 1974. ('Libertés 2000' series.)

14. H. Laborit, 'A propos de l'automobiliste du Néanderthal', *Presse Méd.*, Vol. 73, No. 16, 1965, pp. 927–9; H. Laborit, *L'agressivité détournée*, Paris, Union Générale d'Éditions, 1970. ('10/18' paperbacks.)

15. A. S. Welch and B. L. Welch, 'Isolation, Reactivity and Aggression: Evidence for an Involvement of Brain Catecholamines and Serotonin', in B. E. Eleftheriou and J. P. Scoot (eds.), *The Physiology of Aggression and Defeat*, London, Plenum Press, 1971.

16. The role of serotonin (5 HT) is still disputable, and results are contradictory. The pCPA, which lowers 5 HT levels in the brain, also lowers the pain stimulation threshold thought to control defensive aggression behaviour incidence. In the hippocampus, whose inhibitory role in aggressive behaviour patterns seems obvious, 5 HT is abundant. But it appears to us more likely that 5 HT intervenes either directly or indirectly (through release of cerebral polypeptides) in protein synthesis and the establishment of memory traces (unpublished findings).

17. H. Laborit, E. Kunz and N. Valette, 'Rôle antagoniste de l'activité motrice d'évitement ou de lutte à l'égard de l'hypertension artérielle chronique provoquée chez le rat par application journalière d'un choc électrique plantaire', *Agressologie*, Vol. XV, No. 5, 1974, pp. 33–5.

18. B. Roslund and C. A. Larson, 'Mentally Disturbed Violent Offenders in Sweden', *Neuropsychobiol.*, Vol. 2, 1976, p. 221–32.

19. S. Glueck and E. Glueck, *Predicting Delinquency and Crime*, Cambridge, Mass., Harvard University Press, 1959.

20. Cf. Roslund and Larson, op. cit.

21. H. Laborit, 'La communication sociale et la guerre', in *La communication sociale et la guerre (Colloque du 20–22 mai 1974)*, Institut de Sociologie, Centre de Sociologie de la Guerre, Bruylant, Brussels, 1974, pp. 173–83.

A critical examination of quantitative studies applied to research in the causes of violence[1]

Alain Joxe

The aim of studying the causes of violence is generally to make it possible to forecast the risk of antagonistic conflicts in order to be able to control, prevent or settle them. This links up with the practical concern of existing political systems seeking 'stability' and with the missions of international organizations responsible for maintaining peace.

The area thus defined embraces a disorderly conglomeration of peace research, strategic studies and works on international relations, as well as criminal studies ordered by government departments of justice or of the interior. Overlying all this, there also exists a considerable body of work devoted to an empirical examination of the relations between 'external violence' (between states) and 'domestic' violence.

In order to account for their decisions, whether made by democratic procedures or transmitted between different centres of power, and to provide an objective, 'politically neutral' basis for what are fundamentally political measures, public authorities now usually demand that research workers use as scientific a language as possible, i.e. that they base their conclusions on numerical data.

Translation into quantified terms represents not simply a form of expression of greater or lesser convenience but a limitation that may fundamentally modify, at its very roots, the process of creating concepts. Doubts are therefore expressed periodically (even in the social science field, which is most closely related to policy development in various countries) about the relevance of a certain number of heuristic approaches and about the theoretical presuppositions underlying these quantitative methods. To take an extreme case, it has on occasion been shown that the conclusions derived from a particular study on violence were completely contained in its premises.

The problem eventually arises of discovering whether it really is the conclusions of these studies that are used by the political authorities or whether these authorities, being little inclined to philosophize about primary causes, simply use sophisticated research as a mere source of data on which they can base a 'praxeology' completely independent of the concepts proposed to them.[2]

There is thus a whole area of applied social science research that has to be called into question.

In discussing such a crucial subject, we can naturally do no more than just open the debate. So as not to become overwhelmed by textual criticism, we shall first enumerate a certain number of principles that explain or motivate the critical approach to be followed. We shall then take a quick look at the origins of quantitative methods in the social sciences and at a definition of the types of impasse, illustrated by a number of examples.

Some principles

Analysis of two quantitativisms

It is not the quantitative method in itself so much as quantitativism that is under discussion. Viewed from this angle, the convergence between certain 'critical' branches of empirical sociology and critical Marxism that has appeared in recent years, especially in Western Europe, Latin America and the Middle East, reflects the relative impasse of both quantitativist methods and theories.

On the one hand, a behaviourist and empirical sociology that aims at being relevant at the macro- or mega-sociological level is incapable of accounting scientifically for class conflicts and national liberation struggles. The functionalist or structuralist systematic approach cannot compensate for the fact that it denies the specific nature of political polarization at the very level where the aggregates that govern the formation of concepts are established.

On the other hand, a certain form of Marxist economism, appropriate at the macro-economic level and at the industrialized centre, clearly finds itself in an impasse when it analyses the actual local socio-economic and political conditions of the periphery and accounts for the specific nature of the social formations in terms of the social relationships of production associated with the persistence of precapitalist modes of production. We believe that the specific nature of non-European social formations can be understood perfectly well by the Marxist approach, but this requires an extension of the Marxist theory of precapitalist modes of production.

As a theory of the capitalist mode of production, Marxism is still poorly equipped to analyze whatever does not form a part of that mode of production or that exists inside formations where the capitalist mode of production predominates but where the historical blocs are profoundly different from those found in Europe.

The Eurocentrism of Marxism is related to an economism that reflects the ideology dominant in the capitalist mode of production as it emerged in the 'centre' formations. Economism is a quantitativism, and one that probably acts as the model, historically speaking, for all other types.

'Cause', 'behaviour' and 'violence'

In the form we have suggested, the scope of the subject is considerable, especially since we have to include an examination of its very formulation. Everything that can be said about quantitative studies that seek to define the causes of violence could doubtless also be said about studies dealing with the cause of 'social peace' or fertility. At the epistemological level, it is essentially a question of studying the application of quantitative methods to an investigation of the causes of social behaviour.

In addition to examining the relevance of the methods and analyzing the concept of violence (which we do below) we would have to embark on a theoretical analysis of the concept of cause. Causality has recently been the subject of some interesting epistemological analyses. Causation is now almost always considered simply as one of the categories of determination. It is the 'determination of an effect by an effective external cause' (a bullet fired at a window pane causes the glass to break). Interaction (or reciprocal causality), structural determination (of the parts by the whole), teleological determination (of the means by the ends) and statistical determination (of a final result by the joint action of quasi-independent entities) are the principal categories in a group of categories of determination that can form combinations, and it will have to be demonstrated from the Marxist point of view that they are all encompassed by dialectical determination.[3]

The main point of the following remarks, in any case, is to acknowledge that the question raised by the determination of violence, and quantification as an approach to this determination, poses a fundamental problem because here we touch directly upon the Marxist conceptual field revealed by the concept of class struggle and contradiction, and upon the essence of dialectical and historical materialism.

The situation would be different if our subject were the determination of aesthetic feeling, for example.

Methodological or meta-theoretical analyses

Quantitative mathematics in the social sciences cannot be analyzed simply as a method. The social sciences make use of certain branches of particular mathematical theories. It should therefore be asked why, for what purpose, how and when a particular restricted branch of mathematics is considered to be capable of providing a causal or deterministic explanation of certain social phenomena. We have to draw up an inventory of the more or less explicit meta-theories or, in default of this, the dominant ideologies that serve as a basis.

We all know what the quantified mathematics of the social sciences owe to the spirit of physics, including endorsement of the most currently accepted causality or determination. The possibilities of a more 'biological' mathematics are barely being investigated. To deal with this question in all its subtlety, we would have to ask mathematicians and statisticians to replace the relatively poor mathematical tools used by the empirical sociologist, both in the mathematical sciences as at present constituted and in the historical process by which the mathematical concepts in question were formed. They would explain to us the significance of this poor invasion in comparison with the richness of their language.

This type of study would have to be accompanied by a more systematic historical anthropology of interdisciplinarity (the role of military requirements in the development of operational research groups, and so on).

It would, moreover, imply the development of a new discipline that is scarcely in its infancy, namely a study of the development of mathematics in terms of historical materialism, and the relation between mathematics and dialectical materialism.

The problem involved is not the purely practical one of matching the mathematical models to the subject of research but of the coupling of two heterogeneous processes for developing concepts and theories. It would, in fact, be necessary here to propose and criticize the theory of this coupling in order to raise the question of how this meta-theory matches the frame of reference of the research. We can, of course, do no more than just mention this problem.

Refining the equipment or returning to history

Since there is no question of attacking quantitativism in order to bring about some equally delusive return to the absolute supremacy of the qualitative, or of historical or anthropological reasoning, we must identify the profile of present theoretical trends by proposing certain lines of thought. There are two main natural tendencies.

One is to improve the existing situation by refining the mathematical tools and by exploring present mathematics to find other fragments, which might be used or which might prove stimulating to the sociologist's imagination. In addition and at the same time, the tendency is to refine the concepts, improve the theory and produce one capable of modelling situations of class and imperialist violence, while still maintaining the empirical approach.

The other tendency is to try and bring about a break with the existing position by means of a fundamental reappraisal and to try and show through practical work that, before a new quantification can be attempted, it is essential to return to the study of the most complex specific historical processes, whether contemporary or not.

We believe that a return to factual history and to current anthropology as the basic material for a socio-political survey supplementing the description of the economic interconnections of conflicts is now indispensable if we want, without repudiating the accomplishments of empirical social science, to advance the study of the determinations of violence through the history of dissatisfaction.

**From a mathematics of supervision
to a mathematics of violence**

It is only through new research practices (and in our opinion
after a period of complete break) that we shall be in a position
to reapply quantification, using mathematics probably completely different from the rigid mathematics of aggregates
and correlations, Gaussian curves and pay-off matrices.
Each period gets the social mathematics it deserves. We are
expressing a hope when we say that, through an examination
of quantitative methods of research into the determinations
of violence, we shall perhaps emerge from the mathematics
of supervision and oppression into the mathematics of self-
management and liberation.

Anthropology of the violent origins
of quantification

Quantification and atomization of the individual

'Violent behaviour' or 'state concept'

Opposed to political violence in general, but in favour of the
'regulatory functions of society' (which often stem from
police violence), the psychosociological behavioural sciences
developed in the United States (within the framework of a
very precise social structure where violence was by no means
the legitimate monopoly of the central state) have often
relegated the concepts of state and war to the level of the
'violent behaviour' of the groups involved. The research
hypotheses and methods likened human violence to animal
aggressiveness in a large number of instances.

The opposite approach raises the same theoretical problems. Opposed to military and police violence in general,
but in favour of machinery for the self-regulation of conflicts
inside groups and of the Fourierist exaltation of a free
democracy of pleasure, certain trends in critical psychosociology and certain recent anthropological studies equate
non-violence (and animal non-aggressiveness) with a faculty
lost through politicization and more exactly through the
formation of the state.

Whether it is a question of condemning violence so that

it can be eradicated, or of condemning the state so that it
can be eliminated, we are concerned perhaps in both cases
with moral progress, but in either case with an initial standpoint that represents a scientific regression when compared
to Machiavelli, Clausewitz and Marx, not to mention Sun-
Tzu, Aristotle and Thomas Aquinas.

It is thus the concept of violence that is uncertain in its
current state, inasmuch as it remains incompletely separated
from the category of 'behaviour', with its connotations of
the individual.

'Structural violence' and 'imperialism'

The concept of violence has nevertheless become gradually
separated from its behaviourist matrix. It has had its functionalist and finally its structuralist periods. The current
definition of 'structural violence' first appeared at the end
of the 1960s. However, as Senghaas[4] reminds us, it must be
noted that the definition is to some extent based on the
concept of 'institutional violence' that is used in the official
document of the conference of Latin-American bishops held
at Medellín in 1969. This concept arose out of the realization
that, in certain circumstances, 'people are not simply killed
by direct violence but also by the social order'. It must be
said that the language of the Medellín document is in one
sense more political than the idea of 'structural violence'
preferred by 'critical peace research'. Based on the Thomist
idea of the legitimate refusal to obey a tyrant, it connotes
and denounces not a structure but an authority. The Latin-
American bishops were thus raising fairly clearly the issue
of the class violence exercised by the state and of the
hegemony (in the Gramscian sense) over civil society. However, it is still a matter of violence towards people. Moreover,
the use of the word 'institutions' hardly enables it to mask the
violence which comes from a non-institutionalized source
and which Marxism calls the imperialist system.

The expression 'structural violence' thus endeavours to
mask completely that of 'imperialist system' in so far as
imperialism is linked to a whole set of latent or operational
repressive practices and leads to injustice and death. However, the same concept can be used to study violent and
unjust political relations which might arise in socialist
countries in the transitional stage. It therefore remains a very

theological concept, inseparable from a Thomist definition of justice.

The epistemological question is not whether the power of the state in socialist countries is just or injust, but whether the monopoly of political violence inherent in all state power can be analyzed in those countries with the same concepts as are used for capitalist states. The question is which theory of the state, not which theology of justice, must be applied.

Destruction of history and conquest of the periphery

The transformation of war into 'international violence', civil war and the class struggle into 'domestic violence', and criminality in the reserve proletarian army into 'individual violence' is usually inseparably bound up with designating 'spoil-sport nations', 'marginal groups' and 'neurotics and deviants' (respectively) as the source, i.e. the cause, of the violence.

In constructing the concept of 'structural violence', we reverse the order and attribute the origin of violence to the structure (meaning the structure of domination), thus establishing its asymmetric nature. However, there is no need to be any more precise than before about what this system is and whence and when it comes. A structure is by definition ahistoric. Despite the good intentions involved, the translation into non-Marxist language of a certain part of Marxist theory is extremely difficult. It is only possible through the destruction of everything that in Marxist language depends on the historical approach. It is true that this operation makes it possible to reconvert in an anti-imperialist direction a whole professional capacity to quantify, but history is lost in the process. Now, the loss of history seems to be precisely the fundamental operation of quantification. In addition, the destruction of history is related to the conquest of the periphery by the imperialist centre.

We can easily understand what this means when we see that the destruction of history plays a very definite role in the weakening of the precapitalist structures that still exist in the periphery, both as reactionary economic forces and as popular anti-capitalist ideologies. A poor knowledge of history is the rule amongst a large number of quantitativists. The dominant position of psychosociology with regard to other disciplines in the majority of dependent countries has the well-known result that the newly formed technical middle classes are incapable of understanding the societies which they come from and the traditional values of which they reject. It is the revolt of the Latin American sociologists at this amputation that lies at the root of the revival of studies of contemporary Latin American history. Much, however, remains to be done.

We now discuss what this destruction of history has in common with the atomization of the individual and quantification.

The reified individual

We see nowadays the rejection of history going hand in hand with the destruction of ideological superstructures that precedes the transformation of men into a working force, freely available on the market. This contemporary operation reproduces (with certain changes and certain special features that can be explained by a knowledge of the stage-by-stage transformations of the capitalist system) the procedure that marks the genesis of the capitalist mode of production. The rise of empirical sociology is inseparable, in its objectives and methods, from the provision of a framework for atomized man and from the appearance and management of free labour as a factor in capital.

Another point that it is important to note is that the breakdown of the precapitalist communal or feudal structures, the isolation of the individual on the labour market, his reattachment in the enterprise as a proletarian, the final production of goods—this whole process is paralleled by the isolation of the person surveyed and the reassembly of his behavioural elements inside the data-compiling machine that an empirical survey represents. This parallel between capitalist production and empirical research production provides a basic legitimacy and makes analysis more difficult, even, of course, in those social formations that are in transition towards socialism and where the social relations of capitalist production are not completely abolished.

Empiricist quantification in the human sciences, related in this way to the subject of its study, to which it moulds itself without any doubt, possesses a heuristic value. Marx himself, in studying the capitalist system, extolled the virtues of surveys based on the individual questionnaire. It is not claimed, either, that quantitative methods are necessarily related to the 'pacifying' aim of bourgeois society. A knowledge of 'free' individuals and of their links, via a given aggregate, with the system of social relationships of production can seek to release counter-aggregates: proletarian class consciousness. Research on the determinations of individual violence can facilitate the reorganization of this violence into a collective form directed towards liberation.

Class violence and quantitative sociology

However, the whole history of empirical sociology and of the sociology of violence, quantified on the basis of individual behaviour, can be properly justified only because of the level at which the bourgeoisie, from the earliest days of its hegemony, chose, as a class strategy, to deal with social conflicts: the 'micro' and 'intra' sociological levels, delineations that are opposed respectively to the appearance of class consciousness and proletarian internationalism.

This choice is itself a form of violence and is reproduced, when necessary, by armed violence, even in the 'centre' countries. In other places, it has been the deliberate product of the colonial wars of conquest. The majority of political struggles or even of cases of individual or intercommunity violence today cannot be explained outside the historical framework of the development of capitalism, in the sense that capitalism can only develop by destroying the communal structures that still exist in the world.

In this sense, we can say that all sociology in research into the determination of violence and also that all quantified sociology is a violence that reproduces the object of its own research: the individual who is first isolated and then agglomerated into the process of capitalist production.

It is not surprising therefore that the quantitativist school meets with insurmountable difficulties in carrying through its analysis to the end. Seeking to escape from the extraordinary limitations of the 'micro-intra' level, it has launched into the 'macro-trans', making a fetish of its methods in order to be equal to dealing with the world problems of the power system, and it has thus produced branches of research that are definitely sterile.

'Equality of nation-states'
and the current impasse of quantification

The formal equality of individuals that is indispensable for the appearance of the proletariat also has certain well-known corollaries in the development of the rules of bourgeois democracy: the ritualization of conflicts by voting and universal suffrage. It is no coincidence that quantitative methods in political sociology first appeared in 1928 with the studies by Stuart Rice[5] and that, for a long time, they were applied mainly to the analysis of electoral behaviour. Without this formal and legal equality, the idea of taking the individual as a legitimate basis of statistical aggregates to enable the entire complexity of a system to be understood only appears in surveys and medical experiments. In societies that are completely dominated by social relationships and a pre-capitalist ideology, a person who is questioned often replies in special stereotyped forms that depend not on the fact that he belongs to a 'group' but directly on his belonging to a social relationship of production that is not based on free labour.[6]

It is from this formal equality of individuals, in so far as it actually corresponds to a reality at the level of the economic infrastructure, that the human sciences develop, using methods that are comparable to those of the physical sciences. Behaviourism, positivism, functionalism and structuralism develop in layers, successive but not contradictory, in order to perfect this approach as the capitalist system moves from the competitive period to the monopolistic and imperialistic periods and eventually to the current stage of transnationalization.

If we now ask ourselves about the exact significance of the new phenomenon that first appeared in the 1960s with the proliferation of studies based on states rather than individuals, we shall find no immediate answer. That was the time when the transnational field of action, dominated by the American multinational corporations, was being organized and decolonization was quite rapidly achieving its aims. The number of independent Member States in the United Nations reached and passed the one hundred mark at that time. The temptation arose to consider this group as a 'population'. The legal framework, the 'formal equality between states', was comparable to that which established equality between all citizens in the early days of European capitalism. The play on words between the Third World and the Third Estate was very striking. However, it should be clear to everyone that compared to 'equality between states' (which only corresponds to a legal reality and a principle of sovereignty), equality amongst individuals seems to be a definite reality. We have clearly passed from a subtle myth to a legal principle that does not reflect any sociological reality but rather an ideal.

In order to arrive at this new quantitativist production, we therefore require a first fetishization that transforms the partition desired by the dominant section of the bourgeoisie (here the nation-states) into a natural datum allowing of enumeration. But a second fetishization is also required to transform into an absolute scientific method the technique that had been developed for the handling of quantified data based on a survey of individuals.

Once we have passed beyond the sociology of voting by states in international organizations, we arrive at misguided studies that attempt to get this sample population of nation-states to say something about interaction and aggression inside a group.

It is this double fetishization that explains the total impasse in which certain studies of the determination of violence find themselves. It is possible to make progress with one level of ideologization but not with two levels mechanically combined.

Types of impasse

We believe that it is very necessary to prepare as clear a statistical series as possible concerning military expenditure, the arms traffic, and the intensity of conflicts measured by the number of dead and the duration of the fighting, because we have to put the data supplied by states into an ordered form in which they can be compared. From a judicious use of indices such as the percentage of the GNP devoted to military expenditure we can get a precise, synthetized account of that area of state policy known as the defence effort. The only question that needs to be raised explicitly is whether in accepting that the basic unit of the study should be the nation-state, we can do anything more than describe and arrange these data in various ways, and not touch at all upon the quite different problem of the determination of violence.

If this determination is not to be found at the inter-state level, we shall surely be quite unable to comprehend it.

It is because this question cannot even be given explicit expression while we still rely on an approach based on a collection of states that the majority of quantitativist studies in this field can do no more than skin over the analysis of the determinants.

We can discuss some types of approach here only by way of example, e.g. the quantification of cycles of violence and of the causes determining their frequency; the quantification of national interests and the causes of the escalation of conflicts; the quantification of military effort and the causes of war. We conclude with a few points concerning the ideology of the approach.

Quantification of cycles of violence and the cause determining their frequency

In seeking regular patterns in human behaviour throughout history, one typically takes:[7] (a) a fairly long period (1400–1900); (b) a fairly large number of states; or (c) a set of facts sufficiently varied to constitute, by aggregate, some kind of 'violence index' (number of battles, number of belligerents, number of dead, etc.). It might be noted that the extended period exactly covers the history of the appearance of nation-states and that this is, in fact, the whole point of choosing it.

The problem thus vanishes in a statistical category. We next note that it is as a result of the proliferation of recorded data that attempts are made to construct a set that can be subjected to statistical treatment resulting in curves and indices. Not only does the methodology hide the theoretical emptiness of the undertaking, but it also forces the undertaking to remain theoretically empty, i.e. empty of the problem of the nation-state. On the other hand, the desire to form an aggregate connoting violence removes the possibility of mentioning (even at the most elementary level of collecting facts) the nature of the conflict, the victor and vanquished, the quality of what is at stake, etc.

It is true that this is not the object of the research, which leads to the simple conclusion that there could be a twenty-five-year cycle. Let us not forget that we are dealing with a law of global violence, considered between 1400 and 1900.

The cause of this amazing regularity (which exists only statistically) is then examined. The causes put forward are simply the 'succession of generations' and, more especially, the succession of 'political leaders, who from one generation to another forget the horrors of war'. It is as if the author had never heard of economic cycles, which would at least have enabled him to divide up his sample and his periods; as if, also, he was unaware of the fact that, in the fifteenth century, wars were not recorded by a world élite and, moreover, that the élite groups in very many cases considered war as being almost their *raison d'être*.

Quantification of national interests and causes of the escalation of conflict

In an attempt to get closer to the analysis of the true issues at stake, other quantified studies deal with interaction between states, the existence of conflicting interests, the problems of communication and 'perception' of the enemy, and finally the determinants of the escalation process. It is possible to achieve a certain degree of refinement, but one never gets away from the descriptive in so far as the agents are strictly identified with the institutionalized decision-making centres. As an example of all these studies we may quote the following dreadfully sterile sentence:

The relations of states may be studied from the viewpoint of the world as a whole by locating states in an analytic field of which the co-ordinates indicate their values and their capabilities. . . . Relations of conflict, competition, coexistence, or co-operation may exist in varying degrees between the members of a pair of states *because* (our italics) of their changing objective and subjective distances from each other in the field.[8]

We would like to draw special attention to the type of research and the definition of causality implied in this passage. The construction (even if imaginary and rhetorical) of a system of co-ordinate axes and a quantification scheme is enough for the cause to be placed effortlessly in that twilight zone where 'variables act and interact'. By giving the name of cause to the variations of variables, we no longer need to define 'what makes them vary'. The cause of escalation has become the relative movement of 'states' in this field rather than the increase of contradictions. The subtle pedagogical instruments of Schelling,[9] the deformations and the neighbour system of the analytic utility functions of his 2×2 matrices, did not at least claim to be useful for research on empirical causality.

Quantification of military effort and causes of war

A third type of study combines those that consider quantified data on the acquisition of armaments or on military budgets as being of primary importance. The search for the most varied types of correlation can lead to papers that attempt to establish empirically whether and how the arms race is the cause of conflicts.

In this context, the work of Newcombe is particularly significant. It establishes that war is a phenomenon that is statistically predictable from a study of the relative variations of military budgets as a percentage of the GNP of various states over a period of sixteen years. (With 4.63 per cent of the GNP devoted to military expenditure, a state has 6.61 per-cent greater chance of having a war within five years than it does with less than 4.63 per-cent expenditure).[10]

The cause of this phenomenon is not clearly expressed, and the author says he 'does not know why it is so'. The problem that arises is to understand whether the proof of this statistical determination represents a real contribution or whether it is only a numerical tautology.

The conclusion of the study resides in the proposition 'If you prepare for war, you get war', and this adage might be supposed to show the emptiness of the Roman saying, *si vis pacem para bellum*. In this epigrammatical form, Newcombe's conclusion places the origin of war clearly at the moment of budgetary decision-making. Even though it involves no desire to define a cause, the approach is centred on the idea of antecedence. In the circumstances, it is indeed a matter of antecedence, not of one fact over another, but of a co-ordinated set of concerted decisions aimed at the preparation of a complex activity in relation to the activity itself (war). In the guise of a 'statistical determination', there is in fact only the sum of a series of teleological determinations. The determination of war is by hypothesis situated in the decision to prepare for war by arming. The authors are certain, in advance, of the fact that, from a statistical standpoint, the processes of arming and of waging war must to some extent be correlated. They do their sums and come up with the figures of 4.63 and 6.61 per cent and state the hypothesis in a conclusion disguised as an adage.

This is not enough, however. It would quite clearly be necessary to explain why, at the level of the states, there is a desire to prepare for war. Newcombe is therefore obliged to present (explicitly, this time) another conclusion under the guise of a hypothesis, derived this time from a mechanistic determination: 'A nation's foreign policy changes when it becomes too heavily armed', in the same way that 'the personality of a man changes after he acquires a gun'.[11]

What are the relationships between these two determinations and what contradiction lies hidden behind the author's hesitation? The teleological explanation is of course bound to take the state as the source of the sovereign decision and the phrase 'if *you* prepare for war' certainly applies to it; but this says nothing at all about the decision of the arms suppliers, though in some sense, of course, it is all-important. The mechanistic explanation is bound to consider the state as a person behaving like an irresponsible young delinquent. In this case, the sovereign decision vanishes in the 'input-black-box-output' system and the fragile personality of your young delinquent is dominated and therefore determined by that of the man who can supply him with a gun.

The considerable amount of statistical work carried out thus only leads to a double question mark, and it cannot even help us to formulate correctly any hypotheses on the determination of wars by armament processes. This impotence is precisely a result of the fact that there is no theory of the state and no theory of war behind the entire approach. Any theory at all would be better than none. For example, it would be almost sufficient to say that 'the state is a political organization divided into two branches, the civil and the military'. Why then is it not mentioned? It is a vicious circle. The reason is that the only usable statistical data we have are those on military expenditure, and this expenditure is a result of the civil-military decisions. We cannot seriously attribute the military budget to the military and the GNP to the civilians. The figures available do not require and do not permit the intro-duction of any theory of the state and cannot therefore allow any progress to be made in the determination of wars but can only lead to numerical tautologies.

Quantification of diplomatic history
and ideology of the integration of knowledge

More modest and more clearly defined, at first sight, is the approach of the quantitativists who examine and account for diplomatic history.

By compiling huge registers of 'facts' (not always based on the *New York Times* index) and discovering correlations between all sorts of historical series in the field of international relations that can be associated with numbers (i.e. on the basis of national statistics), it is possible to verify certain ideas stated by historians in asides that are not always 'empirically based' in the statistical sense. The number of states worthy of appearing in the international system, the number of treaties of alliance or neutrality, the number of treaty violations, the number of conflicts, the number of crises, etc., are treated like data. They are processed and used to produce correlations and regularities, which one hopes are significant. The first example we have analyzed is particularly liable to criticism because it deals with an enormous subject (violence) over an enormous space of time (the world between 1400 and 1900). However, since it was a caricature, it made it possible to define the essential point of the whole approach. Even in more refined studies, which are thus apparently of a certain analytical interest, the historical material has to be subjected to the same breakdown of the significant units as one performs in synchronism or in the very short current term with the system of nation-states and, by bringing the data together, 'new facts' have to be produced that are supposed (somewhat preposterously) to be the constants of long series of events.

What is the use of all this, this card-indexing of factual history? Certainly it serves to destroy history, which then disappears completely as a science of what was at stake in the interests of the forces that acted in some particular way at a given moment in the past and should, for that very reason, cease to exist equally completely as knowledge of the sequences of contradictions and conflicts remembered by those who took part.

This is not the real aim of this type of research. There is a much more positive and concrete objective, which is expressed in ideological form. For Singer, for example (one of the most brilliant representatives of this school), this history seen in terms of profit and loss serves to 'increase the theoretical

integration of knowledge' and 'thus to bring about better
predictions' from which will emerge 'fewer policy disagree-
ments for us', because 'a greater number of value conflicts
will be transformed into prediction conflicts'. This means in
effect 'liberating our conflicts from our preferences'.[12] The
'we' here represents the same thing as the 'you' in the previous
example, i.e. the group of states that are treated as persons and
for whom, by destroying their past considered as an obscure
ideology, we would facilitate access to some liberating psycho-
analysis in the form of analytic accountancy, and access to
the wisdom of those who know how to distinguish phantasms
from reality.

For a historian of ideas, it is obvious that this approach
corresponds to the ideology of *détente* in which the 'we' is
composed primarily of two camps, East and West, the USSR
and the United States, and that the praiseworthy objective is
peaceful coexistence. For a Marxist analyst, however, it is
clear that the approach enables an ideological community,
specific to the new transnational group of the dominant classes
and their supporting classes, to be founded by confusing the
records of the history of each people's struggles. The epistemological problem is quite different, however. When all is
said and done, an ideology that represents the power of the
dominant groups of the world bourgeoisie should possess a
certain scientific effectiveness somewhere.

However, regarding the precise point in question, it has
to be admitted that the approach overall ends up as a system
for explaining the causes of violence that leads nowhere.
Wars are implicitly treated as consequences of a misunderstanding of the history of conflicts between nation-states. One
is referred back in time to the psychosociological problem
of 'misperception', and history is alleged to be only an
immense misunderstanding that needed American quantitativism in order to emerge from its indistinct dramas. The
old puritanical hatred of the tyrannical and cynical games
of the Europe that existed at the time of the Congress of
Vienna reappears in its own style.

We particularly wish to stress this treatment of history
because we intend to submit for discussion the idea that it is
precisely this approach that we need to reject in order to make
useful progress today towards an understanding of the
struggles in the modern world.

The extraordinary claim of the quantitativists will never

succeed in confusing the 'habit of thinking operationally' with the historian's demand for accuracy and the ability to produce clear and productive concepts.

It is obvious that the quantitativists have not usually had to hold serious discussions with Marxists because their polemic was waged with 'traditionalists' who only wished and were only able to oppose them with arguments of common sense.[13] As to the more critical of the quantitativists themselves, even if they are capable of enumerating much more completely than we have done here the vices of form and the absurdities of the mania for quantifying,[14] the only outcome they envisage is a greater precision in the development of concepts and methods.

To Singer's remark ridiculing the disquiet of the traditionalists faced with quantification, 'There is nothing hard about adding up apples and oranges as long as it is a matter of fruit', we believe that we can easily reply: 'There is no point at all in adding up fruit when it is a question of an understanding how the pip grows inside the mature fruit.'

Notes

1. Deodato Ribeira, Georges Menahem, Michel Dobry and Janet Finkelstein have contributed to the preparation of this chapter.
2. To 'discover' with Collins ('Foreign Conflict Behaviour and Domestic Disorder in Africa', APSA paper, 1969), for example, that 'foreign violence is related to conditions of domestic disorders more so in African states than elsewhere', is surely only to restate in a kind of new bureaucratic language that African frontiers divide ethnic groups, which provides opportunities for an imperialist power to foment trouble and intervene in a particular kind of way. It is not the motives of the research worker that we are concerned with but only the perception of the political powers.
3. See Mario Bunge, *A Clarification of Meaning*, pp. 17 et seq.
4. IPRA Studies in Peace Research, *Proceedings of the International Peace Research Association Fifth Conference*, 1975, p. 186.
5. Stuart Rice, *Quantitative Methods in Politics*, 1928.
6. What is called 'frontal response' by Paul Vieille in *La féodalité et l'État en Iran*, Paris, Anthropos, 1975.
7. Frank H. Denton and Warren Phillips, 'Some Patterns in the History of Violence', *Journal of Conflict Resolution*, Vol. 12, 1968, pp. 181–5.
8. Quincy Wright, 'The Escalation of International Conflict', *Journal of Conflict Resolution*, Vol. 9, 1969, p. 434.
9. Thomas Schelling, *Strategy of Conflict*, 1960.
10. Alan Newcombe and James Wert, *An International Tensiometer for the Prediction of War*, Canadian Peace Research Institute, 1972.
11. According to Bunge, op. cit., 'the consequences by the antecedent generally with the addition of efficient causes and mutual actions; e.g. forces modify the state of motion of bodies but the motion exists first'.
12. J. D. Singer, 'The Incomplete Theorist. Insight without Evidence', in Klaus Knorr and James N. Rosenau (eds.), *Contending Approaches to International Politics*, Princeton, N. J., 1970, p. 65.

82 Alain Joxe

13. For this debate, see in particular Hedley Bull, 'International Theory, the Case for a Classical Approach', *World Politics*, April 1966.
14. See in particular Marion J. Levy Jr., ' "Does it matter if he's naked", bawled the child', and Robert Jervis, 'The Cost of the Quantitative Studies in International Relations', Knorr and Rosenau, op. cit.

The specific contribution of peace research to the study of violence: typologies

Chair in conflict and
peace research,
University of Oslo

Johan Galtung

Introduction

In spite of the importance of the phenomenon, no typology
of violence exists yet, and the present author has yet to
encounter two researchers who use the same definition. Two
rules, however, would enable the elaboration of this typology
(or classification, which is a synonymous term):

1. Clear rules must be established as to what is included in
   the set.
2. The set must be divided into subsets that are (a) exhaustive,
   (b) mutually exclusive and (c) based on a *fundamentum
   divisionis*.

Based on criteria (a) and (b), the typology is defined in
extension; based on (a), (b) and (c), it is defined in intension
as well.

There are, then, three tasks to be done: a relatively clear
concept of violence has to be established; some meaningful
dimension has to be introduced into this set establishing
subsets, and finally, more trivially, one should check that all
things referred to as 'violence' according to the definition fall
into one and only one of these subsets. It may pay to reflect
first on what that dimension would possibly be and then use
some intuitions in that direction to build up a corresponding
definition of violence, then back to the dimension again,
revising it and so on, in some kind of hermeneutical circle.

A good typology of violence should meet two criteria:

First, conceptualize violence in a way that brings under the
concept of violence phenomena that have something very
important in common, yet are sufficiently disparate to
make the classification, at least in some cases, non-trivial.

Second, subdivide violence along a dimension that is theoretically important in the theory of violence, permitting

us to say something not only about the differences between the types, but also about the relations between the types. These two criteria are related. Imagine that we are interested in building a theory of violence. One basic question would be: 'What is the cause of violence?' Is there any advantage in being able to formulate sentences such as 'Type A of violence seems to be the cause of type B, which again seems to be a cause of either type A or type C'? In other words, is there any advantage to making a theory of violence of which a major part can be formulated using types of violence as basic elements?

The answer seems partly to be yes, at least in the sense that it may be worth trying. Research is also some kind of a game: 'Here are the elements I am going to use, let me see how far they can bring me in gaining deeper insights starting with the relations among them alone.'

What has been said so far essentially boils down to the following: the definition of violence has to be related to the typology of violence, and the typology of violence has to be related to the kind of theory of violence one has or tries to create.

On the other hand, there is the first criterion mentioned above: the phenomena brought together under that heading must also have something very basic in common. As a point of departure one might say that this 'something basic' is destruction; at a higher level of abstraction maybe the formulation 'anything avoidable that impedes human self-realization' might be used.[1] It should be noted though that the latter is anthropocentric as a concept: it excludes violence done to non-human life, to matter, perhaps also to the man-made environment. That limitation, however, we are going to accept to start with—as human beings we should be granted a certain right to be particularly motivated to understand the conditions of our own destruction.

But, if we now are at least relatively free to choose our definition and typology, we have two perspectives to guide us. According to the first one, violence as a concept should make our social reality transparent in significant directions. According to the second one, the types of violence should be useful as a basis for theory-formation. These are two different criteria, and the basic meta-criterion is whether they are compatible. If not, some mutual adjustment will have to take place.

We have to proceed with some care, for the very simple reason that 'violence' is a highly emotional term. As a concept it unifies such disparate phenomena as wars, torture, homicide, etc. Violence is generally seen as bad, as something to be rejected. That immediately opens for us two possible pitfalls: (a) excluding from the definition of violence anything one does not reject; (b) including under the definition of violence anything one does reject. What does one do about that?

This touches on the general area of research psychology and motivation, and research should be judged on its own terms; it is the result that counts, not the motivation.

The negative approach:
some typologies to be rejected

Let us now proceed by looking at some typologies that are not to be recommended, at least not according to the principles enunciated above. Two typologies, probably the best known ones, would be aggressive versus defensive violence, and intended versus unintended violence, giving rise to some kind of ranking of forms of violence, starting with the 'worst' forms—intended aggressive violence, unintended aggressive violence, intended defensive violence—and ruling out the fourth combination as relatively meaningless. This typology focuses the attention on 'who started' and the relation between the actor and the violent act.

We have chosen these two dichotomies as examples in order to illustrate the point that, in any typology, a paradigm including some perspectives and excluding others is already implicit. For something to be 'started' there has to be nothing of it before. Further, for something to be 'intended' there has to be somebody who intends, who wills the violent act, presumably the actor, possibly acting through others. But this means that violence is related to the idea of an actor, who may or may not intend the act—there has to be an actor somewhere.

Both positions are dramatic, as is seen very clearly when one adds their negations. See Table 1.

Type I here is what might be referred to as 'classical violence', and it is only within that type that the two dichotomies, aggressive versus defensive, and intended versus unintended,

TABLE 1. A first typology

	Violence as event	Violence as permanent
Violence as action	Type I	Type II
Violence as non-action	Type III	Type IV

really make sense. I shall refer to it as direct violence. Correspondingly, Type IV would be the pure case of structural violence, for if there is no actor, yet a permanent state of violence that cannot be said to be natural (in the sense of being 'unavoidable'), the violence must be somehow built into the social structure. Types II and III then are intermediate types: in Type II that permanent state of affairs (e.g. keeping people below subsistence level) is maintained deliberately, and in Type III the structure hits suddenly (e.g. in the form of traffic accidents).

Let us now go back to the two dichotomies that gave rise to Type I, and hence indirectly to the four types given above. Obviously, this focuses the attention on the worst case, the aggressor. The concept is oriented towards the subjects rather than the objects of violence, the actors rather than the victim, possibly focusing on the guilt and motivation of the actors rather than on the domain and scope of the destruction of the victims.

Within this subject-oriented perspective research would then tend to zoom in on the characteristics of the aggressive actor. Thus, an actor-oriented perspective at the intersocietal level may be combined with a structure-oriented perspective at the interclass level—as in the idea that international aggression is linked to the internal contradictions of a society. But this is too narrow as a focus; it does not also steer the attention towards relations between the actors as a possible cause of violence, nor towards violence in and by itself.

Let us then look at two other well-known but also unsatisfactory approaches. They are more neutral where the first criterion is concerned, since they are only concerned with typology-formation, not with the definition of violence; but they are not neutrally useful where theory-formation is concerned.

The first is a division that played a certain role in the early days of peace research, between the conceptions of violence (or peace, conflict, etc.) held by the psychologist, the social psychologist, the sociologist, the economist, the anthropologist, the political scientist, the international relationist, the historian, the specialist in international law, the criminologist, the military man, etc. From the circumstances that two types of violence differ in the sense that one is the concern of discipline A and the other of discipline B (e.g. war and criminal violence in the sense of domestic law), there does not follow anything useful in such sentences as 'Type A relates to type B in the following manner'. This is a typology not of violence but of the social sciences, and a collection of incompatible concepts. It is thus to be rejected straight off.

The second is a more advanced typology that has played and plays a considerable role, not entirely unrelated to the preceding one, but more sophisticated in terms of the level of social organization at which the violence is expressed: intrapersonal violence, interpersonal violence, intergroup violence (with interclass as a special case), intersocietal violence (with international as a special case).

'Interpersonal conflict' is relatively unproblematic as a concept, but 'intrapersonal violence' seems debatable. We would argue in favour of its inclusion, particularly given the approach to violence as anything avoidable that impedes human self-realization, or 'personal growth' if one prefers that term. The example is chosen also because it shows the relation between conceptualization and typology-formation; the moment we include that type we can formulate some basic sets of hypotheses: (a) the fundamental cause of all violence is intrapersonal violence, and the others derive from that; (b) the fundamental cause of all violence is interclass violence, and the others derive from that. The two formulations make the most sense if the word 'conflict' is used instead of 'violence'. Obviously, the two statements above can be exemplified through (vulgar) Freudianism and Marxism respectively.

Hence we are here dealing with a typology that permits theory-formation, relating the levels vertically; but it does not facilitate any horizontal theory-formation, relating types of violence at the same level, since it makes no distinction between types at the same level. The theories formulated with it would tend to be reductionist, placing the causal burden on one level at the expense of the others, and that is too dramatic epistemologically.

Vertical theories, with a single-level emphasis, can be seen as power strategies used by the specialists in one or more of the social science disciplines operating at that level, thereby trying to maximize their own relevance, presenting themselves as specialists in the roots and causes of all types of violence.

The positive approach: some suggestions

We shall now proceed, taking as point of departure the idea of violence as 'anything avoidable that impedes human self-realization'. We shall interpret 'human self-realization', in turn, as satisfaction of human needs, and make use of the list in Table 2.

There is hardly any limit to the number of comments that could be made about this list, most of them critical—but that will be by-passed in this context.[2] The list serves our purpose: to give an image of what can be meant by 'doing damage to man'. In each case it can be argued that, if the need is not satisfied, then there will either be some kind of human disintegration (somatic for the first cases, human for the social needs) or there will, in general, sooner or later be some kind of social disintegration simply because the failure to satisfy the needs may lead to revolts. Some of these needs are even referred to as rights in the list, since they have been crystallized into the human rights tradition, precisely, it seems, because people have tended to fight for them. However, we have also added, at the end, ten needs of a more ephemeral character: we think they are basic, but they constitute neither a *conditio sine qua non* for continued individual existence, nor for continuation of the social order.

In the table there are three horizontal spaces that divide the list into four parts, corresponding to four types of violence when the needs are not satisfied: (a) 'classical' violence; (b) poverty, deprival of basic material needs; (c) repression, deprival of human rights; and (d) alienation, deprival of higher needs.

The first category includes sudden bodily destruction at the hands of some actor who intends to exercise violence, in other words direct violence to the human body. It might also include psychological violence.

To proceed to the second category all that is needed is to ask the question (of a preceding paragraph) why there has to be an identifiable actor for something to be defined as violence—violence can be done to the human body in other

TABLE 2. Basic needs, material and non-material

Category	Needs or rights	Goods
Survival	*Individual*: against accident, homicide *Collective*: against attack, war	Security
Physiological	*Input*: nutrition, air, water, sleep *Output*: movement, excretion	Food, water
Ecological	*Climatic*: protection against climate *Somatic*: protection against disease, health	Clothes, shelter Medication
Social	*Community*: love, sex, offspring *Culture*: self-expression, dialogue, education	Schooling
Freedom	Right to travel and be travelled to Rights of expression and impression	Transportation Communication
Politics	Rights of consciousness-formation Rights of mobilization Rights of confrontation	Meetings, media Parties Elections
Legal	Rights of due process of law	Courts, etc.
Work	Right to work Need for creativity, self-expression in work	Jobs
Relation to society	Need for understanding the conditions of one's own life Need for activity, for being subject, not only object, client Need for unprogrammed time, for new experience, intellectual, aesthetic	
Relation to others	Need for togetherness, belongingness, friendship, solidarity, support Need for well-being, happiness, joy	
Relation to self	Need for self-actuation, realizing potentials Need for a meaning of life, a sense of purpose	
Relation to nature	Need for access to nature Need for some kind of partnership with nature	

ways as well. That opens, as the first category of structural violence, structurally conditioned poverty.

To proceed to the third category all that is needed is to ask the question why this violence necessarily has to be done to the human body to be characterized as violence. That opens, as the second category of structural violence, structurally conditioned repression, or 'repressive intolerance'.

To proceed to the fourth category all that is needed is to ask why the violence has to be of the kind associated with repressive regimes (and declared to be infraction of human rights in important documents). That opens, as the third category of structural violence, structurally conditioned alienation or 'repressive tolerance'—for it is repressive but also compatible with a low level of structural violence of the second type, repression as such.

Thus violence has been defined in terms of what kind of damage it does to man; in other words, this is a clearly victim-oriented approach. But poverty, repression and alien-ation may be the consequences of deliberate action of some-body. And does this not mean that the dichotomy direct/structural developed in the preceding section actually cuts across the four types just given, yielding a total of eight? Strictly speaking, yes. In practice, however, we feel that the cases just mentioned are so exceptional that it is justified to identify direct violence with the first type in Table 2, and structural violence with the other three. This is particularly true because the mechanisms seem to be about the same for all three types of structural violence: exploitation (vertical division of labour), autonomy, fragmentation and marginal-ization. Whereas the first type is a shared concern all over the world, one might hypothesize that the geography of poverty coincides with the geography of the periphery of world capitalism; repression is a widespread category except for some of the smaller, liberal capitalist countries, and alienation is above all a shared characteristic of industrial countries.

Let us now submit this concept of violence to the negation test. The negation of violence is, in a trivial sense, absence of violence; in a broader sense it is 'peace'. Since this is the key term in 'peace research', it is obvious that peace researchers have a stake in how it is conceptualized. Not many researchers today seem content to conceive of peace as the absence of classical violence alone; it is probably only in Western culture, and only recently, that it is trivialized in the direction of 'absence of large-scale violence between states'. Typically, this is an élitist concept; élites generally do not suffer from poverty, repression and alienation to the same extent as do non-élites (whereas war is a more shared condition). To designate as peace a state rampant with poverty, repression and alienation, however, is a travesty of the concept of peace. Peace as the negation of violence is defined as follows: absence of 'classical' violence and absence of poverty and absence of repression and absence of alienation. In other words, some kind of utopian condition. Peace, as goal-setting, should have the property of being not necessarily easily obtainable (e.g. by paper accords and signatures).

Let us then proceed to the other criterion: the feasibility of theory-formation. To engage in that the concept of direct violence has to be subdivided, too, and just as for structural violence a division into three types seems useful: (a) vertical direct violence directed against the top, 'revolutionary violence', fights for liberation, in other words direct counter-violence; (b) vertical direct violence directed against the bottom, counter-revolutionary violence, violence for oppression, in other words direct counter-counter violence; and (c) horizontal violence, which does not take place within a vertical structure.

Having said this, one may now build on a classical adage in peace thinking: the idea that violence breeds violence. Four theorems stem from this.

First, direct horizontal violence leads to direct horizontal violence. And a corollary is that 'preparations for direct violence lead to preparations for direct violence', which is a basis for one of the theories of arms races, the action-reaction theory[3]. This theorem, blind to structure and ignoring verticality, fails to grasp the most significant events of our times.

Second, structural violence leads to direct counter-violence, which leads to direct counter-counter violence. The first theorem merely directs the attention to certain features of the East-West conflict, the second to many features of the North-South conflict. It also follows from the general idea, as hypothesis, that structural violence in the form of repression and alienation will also, sooner or later, lead to direct counter-violence, one way or the other. But the idea can also be used the other way.

Third, direct horizontal violence leads to structural violence. Wars of conquest can be used to set up structures characterized by exploitation, penetration, fragmentation and/or marginalization. Operated internationally, and built around economic dimensions, this translates into capitalist imperialism: a division of labour between the producers of raw materials and manufacturers, the penetration of the periphery by means of bridgeheads, the fragmentation of the periphery into countries with little interaction among them (and the countries into districts, and into economic sectors with low levels of interrelation), and exclusion of the periphery from participation in the real centres of decision-making.[4]

Fourth, structural violence leads to structural violence. Poverty may lead to repression and repression to alienation, sometimes via interludes of vertical direct violence. These relations are less explored, but typologies should also point to possibilities that have not, so far, been the subject of much investigation. Imagine now that one combines all these 'equations' into a history that runs about as follows: direct violence was used to establish structural violence, then there was direct counter-violence (to destroy that structure), counter-revolutionary violence set in but was defeated, the net result being a new actor capable of exercising direct violence, also establishing successive types of structural violence, and increased capacity for direct violence, which in turn led to increased capacity for direct violence on the other side—and so on. All four partial theorems are here combined into something that, when elaborated, might read like the history of a part of our century in the North Atlantic part of the world. This history says nothing about the mechanisms or means of direct violence, the nature of the military hardware and software, but in a sense that belongs to the trivia of peace studies. More important is the effort to conceptualize chains of violence, providing more depth and more extension to the old saying 'violence breeds violence'. But if violence breeds violence, where does the 'first violence' come from, or, differently phrased, what is at the root of the violence? Perhaps there is something very Western in this question, in the idea of tracing things back to some identifiable 'root', to a first mover. Obviously, what came first, direct or structural violence, is a chicken-and-egg problem, unless one assumes that there was once an ideal state without any form of violence (Paradise).

Even without such cosmological assumptions, however, the question is meaningful, and broadly speaking three classes of answers may be indicated.

The first approach could be classified as horizontal theory in the sense discussed in the preceding paragraph, simply remaining content with the cycles indicated above, each one operating on its own level. Each case of violence, between persons, groups and societies, would be explained in terms of another case of violence at the same level. The causal chains should be constructed as hypotheses with a very open mind: direct violence may be followed by direct or structural violence, structural violence by direct or structural violence (of any kind), and so on. This, then, can be done at the global and/or domestic levels—and will, in general, lead to a relatively high level of insight.

The second approach could be classified as vertical theory, theory formation across levels. There are very important theories in this category, e.g. the idea of displacement or projection of intrasocial violence to the intersocial level. There is a Marxist version of this idea: that domestic structural violence in the form of the contradictions in capitalist formations leads to direct violence abroad in order to get new sources of raw materials and new markets, or to efforts to obtain the same by setting up, by various means (technical assistance, war reparations, etc.) international structures with the mechanisms of structural violence already built into them. In other words, capitalism at home leads to imperialism abroad, and the Chinese extension of that dictum: revisionism at home leads to social imperialism abroad. According to this view of violence both are tantamount to aggression, although of a type poorly understood by international law.

And there is the liberal version, the idea that leaders try to deflect social energy that may go into domestic direct violence, directed against them, onto the international level by engaging in 'adventures' abroad, whether of the direct or structural variety, or both. No doubt these vertical theories are important, and we hope to have shown that they are considerably enriched when the concept of violence is extended so as to include structural violence, perhaps particularly by including the concept of structural aggression.[5]

What about reversing these vertical theories? Can direct violence, or the threat of direct violence at the international level, lead to structural violence domestically? It certainly can; this is where the whole theory of the garrison state enters the study of violence. A country that prepares for large-scale direct violence must create a society more isomorphic to the structure of a modern army, where economic, political and cultural life is concerned. In doing so there may also be bursts of direct violence in either direction.

Correspondingly, a country embedded in structural violence, e.g. capitalist or social imperialism[6] internationally will usually have to reproduce that structure internally. If it is in the periphery of the structure there will be, generally speaking, bridgehead formations of one kind or another leading to (or making use of) steep vertical gradients inside the country. If it is in the centre, however, there is also the possibility that structural violence globally is served by a low level of structural violence internally, using structures characterized by high levels of mass political participation and well-distributed welfare. But the country may also have the periphery on the inside, Third World pockets in the midst of plenty (the African, American Indian and Chicano elements in the United States, for instance), in which case structural violence globally may very well lead to direct violence domestically.

The third approach is also, strictly speaking, a vertical theory, but it is of a different kind. It is the old search for the roots of violence 'in the minds of men', or in their bodies, biologically embedded. This is where aggression theories, of instinct or territorial varieties, etc., would enter the picture. No doubt, this leads outside the concept of violence as defined—outside the formula 'violence breeds violence'. But, if the search is for something more innate, it should not only be for the roots of direct violence, but also for the roots of structural violence—for instincts/drives/inclinations towards domination as well as destruction.

What should be pointed out is that there are obvious links between this type of approach to the question of where violence comes from and vertical theory: the conditioning theory and the trigger theory[7].

According to the conditioning theory man is born *tabula rasa* where violence is concerned; but certain structures or experiences may build into him violent inclinations in a society replete with structural violence, or direct violence, where violence is presented in a concentrated, 'telescoped' fashion through the mass media.

According to the trigger theory inclinations towards destruction and/or domination are latent and may be triggered into action by special external stimuli, some of which, if not all, may be classified as belonging to the categories of direct and structural violence.

These two theories may be said to differ in the same way as the major approaches to linguistic behaviour: according to the former, man is neutral but programmes of violence may be built into him through learning from the environment; according to the latter, man is already programmed in the direction of violence of either type.

According to the former, the basic cause is still in the structure; according to the latter, the roots of violence are deeper, possibly non-eradicable (although they can be maintained at a latent level). The former view may be used to justify direct violence to end structural violence and to justify granting power to 'experts' in structural transformation, leading—or so they promise—to non-violent structure; the latter view may be used to justify either kind of violence as a defence against direct violence, since it is an indelible part of the human condition. Thus, both views may lead to the use of direct violence. May peace research be the study not only of violence but also of how to overcome violence with non-violent means, e.g. non-military defence and non-violent revolution!

The basic difference, however, is that the second view often leads to inactivity and fatalism and the first to some type of action, the idea being that structures are easier to change than human action. It is easy to see, from what has been presented in this paper, what kind of action that would be: efforts to overcome exploitation through equity (and/or self-reliance), overcome penetration through autonomy (and self-reliance), overcome fragmentation through solidarity, and overcome marginalization through participation. Translated into more concrete terms, this means work towards some kind of world where each part is a centre, and where a great range of the needs in Table 2 is satisfied.[8]

Possibly this points towards a world where a large number of relatively small units are tied together in a network of global interdependencies. In such a world, the four mechanisms of structural violence might be counteracted, even to some extent eliminated. And thus the fundamental hypothesis could be tested: is it true that, if these mechanisms are negated, then structures are no longer violent, leading to endless chains of structural and direct violence? Or could it be that, if the instruments of direct violence, called arms (in a broad sense, including the social organization of the army), are eliminated, then they only reappear in some other form, because nothing has been done to the conflict formation built into the structure?

Conclusion

With that question we prefer to stop. The point is not what the answer might be, but that it is possible to formulate the question with the typology used. If the reader will permit a mixture of three languages: the *problematique* is *fassbar*, and that is the minimum one should request, not an answer. The rationale of the definition and the typology would be based on the contention that both criteria set forth in the introduction to this chapter are met at the same time—to a fair extent.

Notes

1. This is the formulation used in my 'Violence, Peace and Peace Research', *Essays in Peace Research*, Vol. I, pp. 109–34.
2. See Galtung et al., *Measuring World Development* (World Indicators Program No. 2), and Johan Galtung and Anders Wirak, *Human Needs, Human Rights and the Theory of Development* (World Indicators Program No. 10), University of Oslo, 1974 and 1976.
3. The other theory being the Eigendynamik idea, that the source of an arms race is found within the country itself, a tradition particularly associated with the many excellent studies carried out by Dieter Senghaas.
4. Johan Galtung, 'A Structural Theory of Imperialism', *Journal of Peace Research*, 1971, pp. 81–117.
5. Johan Galtung, 'A Structural Theory of Aggression', *Journal of Peace Research*, 1964, pp. 95–119, and *A Structural Theory of Revolution*, Rotterdam University Press, 1974.
6. Johan Galtung, *Social Imperialism and Sub-Imperialism: Continuities in the Structural Theory of Imperialism*, University of Oslo, 1975. (Mimeo.)
7. Johan Galtung, 'Is Peace Possible?', *Essays in Peace Research*, Vol. I, Copenhagen, Christian Ejlers, 1975, pp. 140–9.
8. For a United Nations document using this type of wording, see the Cocoyoc Declaration of 1974.

The specific contribution of peace research to the analysis of the causes of social violence: transdisciplinarity

Professor, University
of Bremen (Federal Republic
of Germany)

Dieter Senghaas

The analytical problem with which we shall deal in this short paper has an empirical and normative dimension. The empirical dimension refers to the contribution of the various social sciences to the analysis of social violence. Peace research has been part of these activities. Despite a considerable amount of theoretical and empirical research on social violence in the past ten years, one may normatively ask what peace research should or would have to contribute to the analysis of social violence. In fact, there have been certain gaps and deficiencies in past contributions to the analysis of social violence.

In the following I shall briefly try to delineate the achievements of the past research on social violence and then try to outline certain research issues that should de dealt with in the future.

Some achievements of past research on social violence

The internationalization of all types of violence in the past few years has led to a considerable differentiation in the analysis of social violence. Since manifest violence is not only experienced within one's immediate environment, regardless of where one is situated in international society, and since such manifestations have a particular news value, the number of human beings directly or indirectly exposed to the various types of violent events in the world is likely to be much larger today than ever before. In addition to this type of experience there is a growing feeling that it is not only manifestations of direct violence that have to be conceptualized as violence but also those social conditions under which people are being harmed or killed because of the prevailing social order. The latter experience has found its expression in the concept of institutional or structural violence within peace research. Structural violence is observable wherever people are living under unjust social conditions and are, therefore, deprived of the chance to realize their human potentialities. Such structural violence occurs both in intrasocietal conditions and within international society at large and, in many cases, it is the result of a particular interlinkage of internal and international factors, including deprivation and premature death.

If we, for heuristic purposes, differentiate direct from structural violence and internal (intrasocietal) from international (intersocietal) violence, the result will be four problem areas in which research has been done with differing emphasis in the past few years. These problem areas can be separated from each other only for analytical purposes; in reality they are highly interlinked.

A great deal of research has been concentrated on the analysis of direct manifest violence within the intersocietal or international context. This is especially true with regard to traditional peace research as it was developing in the 1950s and until the middle of the 1960s, and it is still observable, particularly in the discipline of international relations and in most of the studies of military strategy. To a large degree this research can be labelled as causes-of-war research, and its take-off was very much determined by the catastrophic experience of the Second World War. That type of research was above all induced by the basic patterns of the Cold War, and its practical aims have been conflict avoidance, conflict resolution and conflict management within the context of the East-West conflict formation.

The abundance of local wars in the postwar period has, especially since the 1960s, caused a shift in major research issues from the basic Cold War patterns towards the actual conditions of local wars, whether these have been instigated by the big powers of East and West or whether they have had more of an autonomous, local character.

These local wars or warlike conflicts very often bear the character of civil wars and, along with broad research activities geared to the analysis of intrasocietal outbreaks of violence within highly industrialized societies, the analysis of direct manifest internal violence may be conceived of as the second major focus of violence research within the past few years. This type of research has particularly produced analyses based on behavioural-science approaches.

In the course of the past ten years the analysis of structural violence conditions within international society has had a tremendous take-off. Research on asymmetrically structured international dependency relations, on the unequal international division of labour, on mechanisms of exploitation, etc., has been very prominent in peace research. For a very long time the major projects of that type of research have been concentrated in Latin America; under different labels this research has, however, meanwhile spread all over the world. Its major focus is the analysis of the structure of international society and the typical centre-periphery relations within that structure leading to the systematic enrichment of the centres and to tremendous misery in the peripheries. The recent political and diplomatic dispute on a new international economic order has made this academic research politically very relevant and salient.

If my assessment of the contemporary research situation is correct, I would argue that most of the research on intra-societal structural violence conditions has been concentrated on those cases and areas in which such structural violence has developed into manifest political violence. The analysis of latent violence structures in the metropoles has been very much restricted to the analysis of regional disparities, i.e. on centre-periphery relationships within the metropoles. Only a very small minority in the social sciences and an even smaller minority in peace research have worked on basic questions occurring in the analysis of total social orders like the capitalist or socialist ones. The abstention of most scholars from dealing with such basic philosophical and normative questions may be a reflection of the prevailing and immovable status quo within the East-West conflict formation. Of course, the picture looks different in the case of scholars from developing countries, where the options for different social orders (capitalism or socialism) might become very salient once the prevailing status quo is broken down. But, in general, it is to be observed that the question of what kind and what type of structural violence are systematically developed within prevailing capitalist and socialist social orders has not been one of the major focuses of research in the social sciences and peace research.

It has already been argued that the four mentioned research areas cannot be hermetically separated from one another; in the research actually done many interrelationships and interlinkages among these four areas are discernible. This applies particularly to the type of research that is engaged in systematically analysing the question of how concrete direct violence emerges out of conditions of structural violence, be it within societies or between societies. The interconnectedness of internal and international violence (both of the direct and structural type) as a potential research area is evident.

From a glance at these four research areas and particularly at the available research results it is clear that a certain scientific progress in the analysis of social violence is today far more differentiated than ever before. This observation, I think, is true both with respect to the empirical-analytical research on the conditions, causes and determinants of violence and with respect to the political and philosophical assessment of violence as a social and political phenomenon. The long-prevailing conceptualization of violence as social disorder, or violence as a societal dysfunction, has meanwhile been replaced by a very differentiated analytical and philosophical perspective, from which an evaluation of social violence in terms of its progressive or regressive functions becomes possible. The problematique of violence and counter-violence fits into this context, too, although it has to be stressed that this problematique is scientifically insoluble, since it is part of the contradictory positions of political interest out of which violence and/or counter-violence are defined as such. What is considered, from one perspective, as a peaceful condition, e.g. the specific structure of the prevailing status quo, may easily be considered as the very expression of structural violence by those suffering from this status quo and, hence, as something that can be changed. If social systems in such a context prove to be inaccessible to social change and collective learning processes and, if their power structures are highly petrified, then social and political violence, paradoxical as this may sound, very often turn out to be the only means of social communication. Looking back at the past twenty years, I think this observation is statistically irrefutable.

Research perspectives for the future

So far I have been emphasizing the general achievements of the most recent research on violence as a social phenomenon. To summarize my observations, these achievements consist particularly in the conceptual differentiation of conditions of structural violence from those of direct violence within an internal and international setting. Furthermore, they consist in systematic reflection on the interrelation between various types of violence within these areas. And finally they consist in the discussion of the social and political functions of violence within social orders.

The specific achievements of the empirical-analytical research projects of the past few years on social violence consist in the very detailed analysis of particular determinants of the social conditions out of which and within which violence potentials become manifest; they consist, furthermore, in the very differentiated analysis of the very process of violence manifestations, i.e. of the escalation dynamics of violence within an interaction pattern; and they consist, although to a smaller degree, in research on the ending of violent conflicts, i.e. on the transition from the stage of violence escalation to the process of de-escalation and to a new kind of status quo as the basis of social peace.

The strength of this research lies in the fact that it has produced very detailed analyses with regard to individual aspects of the violence syndrome. In this context the following research areas could be listed:

1. Research on human nature and the individual personality, particularly research on the causes of the individual's propensity to aggression.
2. Research on the role of large interest groups.
3. Research on dominant élites and class structures as the societal basis of social violence.
4. Research on the functions of mass media and public opinion in the development, the spreading and the ending of violent actions.
5. Research on the attributes of national systems and cultures and their role with respect to the production and spreading of violence.
6. Research on the roles of governments and bureaucracies, of national strategies, and of decision-making processes in the handling of structural and direct violence.

7. Research on violence escalation processes emerging out
   of conflictive or antagonistic interaction patterns between
   social groups within and between societies.

No doubt knowledge of social violence has been expanded to
a considerable degree by this past research. The reasons why
people fall back upon violence, within what type of social
setting and with what aims, are today less opaque then ever
before. The research on the above-mentioned particular
research areas has made social violence quite a transparent
phenomenon.

Nevertheless, from the perspective of peace research as a
discipline that encompasses various disciplines, a considerable gap in the analysis of social violence has to be noted.
This gap consists in the hitherto missing feedback of already
available results, which so far have been peacefully co-
existing with each other without really being interlinked.
Thus what is missing is the co-ordination of already available
research results on the one hand and the initiation of a kind
of research to which individual social science disciplines
(like political science, sociology, social psychology, mass-
media research, etc.) would make specific contributions,
not on the basis of their already existing particularistic
expertise but from a more encompassing perspective. Such
an encompassing perspective can, however, be developed
only if violence is considered as a social phenomenon in
its totality. This would necessitate a research that is simultaneously engaged in the analysis of the societal conditions
of social violence, the manifestation processes of social-
violence potentials, the dynamics of violent conflicts, and
the overcoming of structural violence and violent actions, as
well as the role of conflict-resolution mechanisms. The
compartmentalization of the expertise of individual disciplines, by which the research scene has been characterized
so far, would definitely have to be overcome. Ideally, what
is needed are flow charts of violence structures and violence
processes which would make transparent the overall societal
context within which violence structures are built up and
violence potentials become virulent.

In a very superficial sense such research would be interdisciplinary. In reality, however, it has to be structured in
a transdisciplinary way. The difference between interdisciplinarity and transdisciplinarity is a very considerable one.
Interdisciplinarity eventually means the adding up of ana-

lytical issues, precisely as interdisciplinary research groups have usually been added up, with scientists from various individual disciplines and their particular expertise. In contrast to this, transdisciplinarity means overlapping expertise of different disciplines focused on new problem definitions, which convey to such a research a new identity that is essential, but rather the opening up of new analytical perspectives, which very often happens too slowly in individual disciplines, owing to various reasons, including the very basic reasons of the autodynamic growth processes of the sciences and the particular bureaucratic inertia characterizing every scientific activity after a while. Such more encompassing and comprehensive analytical perspectives are necessary in order to keep research from becoming routinized. Such routinization is very obvious in various particular disciplines, e.g. in individual psychology, where one and the same arguments with respect to the propensity of individuals to aggression have been exchanged now for many years, whereas a systematic feedback of the analysis of individual aggresiveness with the analysis of the societal conditions of social violence could lead that type of individual-psychological research onto remarkable new paths. Further examples could easily be quoted. What is decisive is the explicit research on the interrelationships, the interconnectedness and the interdependence of problem areas so far dealt with separately. But this will become possible only if scientists of individual disciplines are ready to acquire part of the expertise of neighbouring disciplines in order to be able to cope with new research problems on the basis of such a combined or transdisciplinary expertise. Compared with such a procedure, multidisciplinary or interdisciplinary projects in the conventional sense are not very promising. Within transdisciplinary projects interdependent feedback processes would not only be assumed or postulated, but would very explicitly, both in theory and empirical research, deal with the analysis of overall violence structures and violence processes, and their manifold feedback processes would become the very focus of research. These feedbacks are the indispensable linkage mechanisms and the junctures between psychological and social phenomena. Hence the actual problem with respect to the analysis of social violence is not the lack of interdisciplinarity in past research. The response to the challenge of so far insufficient research results must be the development of a manifold transdisciplinary expertise, which necessarily means a long debate beyond the borders of individual disciplines.

Methodological conclusions

Like most of the essential phenomena within societies, social violence is, as a rule, a redundantly caused phenomenon. Redundant causation, however, implies that the elimination of few violence-promoting factors will not necessarily lead to the elimination of violence as such. This, by the way, is one of the very fundamental reasons why militarized societies, behaving aggressively towards other societies, can only be deprived of their propensity to political violence within international politics through a catastrophic defeat.

In this respect there is, of course, a specific problem with those analytical and practical approaches that postulate the change of people's minds as a prerequisite for the elimination of violence potentials. It is perfectly true that no action, and particularly no change of action, is possible without being processed by human consciousness; from this, however, it cannot be deduced that societal facts may be changed simply by means of the spreading of enlightenment. The collective ability to learn is, in the majority of cases and particularly under conditions of shortage, not of such a nature that overall social violence potentials can easily be overcome by rational modes of conflict regulation.

A further methodological remark has to be added. The social sciences have usually clung very much to a conventional causality methodology. This conventional character is clearly discernible in the perennial search for independent, intervening and dependent variables. The causation of social violence, as the causation of most major social phenomena, cannot, however, be adequately dealt with by such simple and one-dimensional causality rationales. Causality can in most relevant areas of social life only be conceptualized as configurative, being built up by manifold feedback processes that as a rule do not allow an unequivocal characterization of individual variables as independent, dependent or intervening. The problem of configurative causality does not emerge as long as the analysis of social violence is restricted to a particular problem area and as long as one carefully abstains from analyzing the totality of the phenomenon. But if one dares to proceed towards such an analysis, one will necessarily have to get rid of the conventional methodology of causality. By implication the analysis will be, of course, more complex and also more difficult, but ultimately the results of such research will be closer to reality.

Peace research can make an important contribution to such research on social violence, since it is related to several disciplines without having inherited the particular routine characterizing old and well-founded disciplines. This is also the reason why peace research has both participated in past research on social violence and developed into an area from which some basic criticism of this past research has been emanating.

Part two

**The individual and society:
social sciences
and normative disciplines
in the study of violence**

In the second part of this collection we wanted to group four studies that bring together two pairs of articles by two specialists in two different branches of social sciences (social psychology and the sociology of communication) and two closely allied normative disciplines (criminology and social defence). The general theme of this section would be how to decipher in practical terms where censurable violence begins. Among the contributions there are of course subtle differences of opinion as to the role of the mass media and the predominance of psychological or historical determinants.

Social psychology, represented by Otto Klineberg, is itself interdisciplinary. His presentation is not intended to put an end to current debates, even if his own views are pronounced. He clearly distinguishes between violence and aggression. He discards Lorenz's theories on the inevitability of violence, based on the argument of biological continuity with animals. Animals are not as violent as men, and learning is a human factor all the more important where violence is concerned because man learns more easily from his successes than from his failures—a fact that makes the concept of exemplary punishment illusory. Violence is acquired; it is maintained by its representation in the media; it can constitute a subculture (machismo, vendetta); its relationship to the phenomenon of frustration, particularly of 'relative deprivation', whether relative to another society, another age or our hopes for the future, has been demonstrated. Most of the correlations, as well as many others that have been discovered in social psychology, show, according to Klineberg, that although we can speak of complex causality, we are still a long way from providing the model of the matrix.

James D. Halloran wonders whether the media, as a social phenomenon, should be considered a symptom or a cause of violence. In any case, the relationship between the media and violence is not what it is generally thought to be. According to existing research, the 'violence' presented on television is not in itself a determinant of more aggressive behaviour on the part of the viewers. It may be an influence only on individuals who are predisposed to violence because of their character or their socio-economic condition. The particular distortion by which Western journalism has adopted eruptive violent behaviour as the archetype of 'news'—at the expense of analysis and continuity of information—doubtless has effects on people's mentality, but these are complex effects. Perhaps habituation to 'news' legitimizes the recourse to external violence, but the constant display of violent and delinquent behaviour as a priority appears rather to help create, at least domestically, a consensus favouring the maintenance of order. It therefore is a factor of conformism and order rather than of disorder. The bombardment of television advertising is certainly a far greater factor of violence in so far as it is a permanent factor of frustration for the majority of the poor.

The criminological point of view is represented here by the Soviet criminologist, V. P. Shupilov. The problem of the criminologist is to formulate a distinction between delinquent and non-delinquent forms of violence. This implies a distinction between violence as a weapon for the political class struggle and violence that expresses only personal, selfish and asocial tendencies. In order to give the concept of 'cause' an objective content in the social sphere, Shupilov contends that 'the mechanism of human behaviour has not yet been studied fully enough, either from the sociological or the psychological angle, for the criminologist to rely entirely on the models elaborated by these sciences'. He must therefore submit to the imperatives of the historical approach and seek a unifying method that simultaneously encompasses the social and biological aspects of the personality and the individual, taking into account the element of 'chance' that constitutes man's character. The criminologist is thereby led to isolate what may be termed 'interacting individual-environment systems' and to develop a typology from these; it is this typology that acts to connect theory and practice. Shupilov concludes as a moralist, alluding to one of the poles of this typology by quoting Brecht, 'It is an unhappy country that needs heroes', and by the comment of the Soviet philosopher, A. Gulyga, on the Brecht quotation: unhappy is the country where moral conduct demands heroism.

Krzysztof Poklewski-Koziell studies the issue of the causes of criminal violence from the viewpoint of social defence, a doctrine developed since 1947 as a reaction against both traditional legal thought (crime is the freely decided act of an individual endowed with free will) and the opposite concept (which tends towards the abolition of the ideas of delinquency and punishment). This orientation, present at the United Nations since 1978 and currently institutionalized in the United Nations Institute for Research in Social Defence, is concerned not so much with research on the causes of violence as with the scientific elaboration of humane criminal policy. As it is normative, the concept of social defence insists fundamentally on the need to break through the 'circle of degradation': i.e. the hereditary transmission of poverty, social alienation and violence through the family environment. To this framework of complex social and historical causality implicit in the concept of social defence, we must now add the tenacious influence of both the state and society on the individual. While studies on the 'criminal personality' continue to be important, they must be complemented by the critical study of the violent functioning of institutions and even of the quality of penal sanctions that can themselves be causes of violence. The author launches a debate with those who hold simpler theories of criminology, accepted in the German Democratic Republic, namely that 'the causes of violent acts are exclusively elements of the past and consequences of the imperialist social order'. He doubts that there has been a real increase in offenses, a belief widely encouraged by the publicity given to sensational events. He also believes that social defence should enable us to resist the general view in favor of unequivocal causality and the value and effectiveness of exemplary punishment.

The causes of violence:
a social-psychological approach

Director of the International
Centre for Intergroup
Relations, Paris

Otto Klineberg

Introduction

There is a widespread impression that ours is an era of
violence, that we are witnessing an exceptional outburst of
violent behaviour throughout the world. Even a brief look
at historical data reveals, however, that previous generations
could have arrived at a similar conclusion with equal justice,
and at least this places our own situation in clearer historical
perspective.[1]

What is perhaps new is that the social sciences have
increasingly turned their attention to the problem, sometimes
at the request of national or international agencies, sometimes as a direct response to the impact of events. This paper
presents a critical summary of what has been attempted in
the field of social psychology.

A comment on the term 'violence' may be helpful by way
of introduction. As is well known, the companion term
'aggression' has been the subject of many meetings and long
debate, and there is still no agreement as to its definition.
Unesco, too, has been active in this direction, and in its
publication on understanding aggression the neurologist, José
Delgado,[2] states that human aggressiveness is a behavioural
response characterized by the exercise of force in an attempt
to inflict injury or damage to persons or property. The
sociologist Hinde[3] suggests that the term aggressive behaviour
should be usefully restricted to behaviour directed toward
causing physical harm to others. On the other hand, a Russian
writer, Kovalsky,[4] says that 'the word "aggression" obviously does not apply to the use of force by dependent peoples
to secure their inalienable rights to self-determination'. This
would lead us to the paradox that certain varieties of violence should not be considered aggressive.

There is another problem with regard to the definition of aggression. For some scholars it goes far beyond the behaviour that can be described as violent. One writer, Lauretta Bender,[5] for example, refers to the original meaning of 'aggression' as a tendency to go forward or approach an object. Allen[6] describes it as the will to ensure and to test our capacity to vigorously carry out either constructive or destructive acts. This approach would make the term 'aggression' so broad as to include everything subsumed under what psychologists have called 'activity drives', and therefore much broader than the term 'violence', which would then represent one form of aggression. One further distinction should be made. Even those who, like Lorenz,[8] identify aggression with a 'fighting instinct', universal in animals and man, also indicate that it can be sublimated (Lorenz prefers the term 'redirected') into relatively harmless channels, such as sport, scientific research, humour, and so forth. Violence may be redirected also against a substitute object if the one we would like to attack is not available; as for sport, that does come close to violence in a number of cases. Violence cannot, however, be truly sublimated. It remains, in Delgado's words, 'an exercise of force in an attempt to inflict injury or damage'; we might add, however, that it may also take the form of a threat to use violence unless one's aims are satisfied. This would mean that the taking of hostages, or the hijacking of aeroplanes, would be included in this definition.

Two other preliminary points require comment. The literature makes a distinction between individual and collective violence; the former includes homicide and related crimes, and has for the most part been the concern of the jurist and the criminologist; the latter, which is found in riots and revolutions, has more frequently been studied by the historian, the sociologist and the political scientist. The psychologist in his search for the causes of violence has looked at both varieties, which in any case are not always easy to separate. A second distinction is between instrumental violence (or aggression) carried out in a deliberate attempt to achieve particular goals, and, on the other hand, violence represented by impulsive reactions leading to riots, or accompanying street demonstrations or resulting from confrontation between students and police.[9] Any analysis of the causes of violence should keep these varieties in mind; otherwise our interpretations will fail to do justice to the complexity of the problem.

An aggressive instinct?

In spite of all that has been said and written about the explanation of violence in terms of an alleged universal instinct of aggression, it seems to me necessary to add a few words of comment, since this view continues to be expressed with some frequency. Robert Ardrey,[10] for example, author of *African Genesis, The Territorial Imperative* and *The Social Contract*, has stated in an interview: 'Personal violence seems part of human nature. . . . It is perfectly natural for a man to get mad at his wife and hit her over the head and kill her, or vice versa. We have always been dangerous animals.' This simplistic and extreme view might be dismissed as unimportant except for the fact that Ardrey's books are best-sellers, and that they therefore influence, or are at least responsive to, the opinions held by a large number of people.

The anthropologist Tiger[11] regards the whole issue as 'among the most tediously overdiscussed issues in the social sciences', since man must have both a biological endowment and extensive social experience, which includes formal or informal learning. He adds, however, that although human aggression leading to violence is not inevitable, it is easy to learn. This may be true, but it has never been demonstrated that it is easier to learn than, for example, co-operative, friendly and neighbourly behaviour. It is after all only a minority of people, even in situations of social upheaval, who engage in violent, antisocial behaviour. This was true in the case of student violence even at its height, as well as in the 'ghetto riots' in the United States. As for individual violence, no matter how high the homicide rates go, they never reach a majority of the population.

One of the most common arguments in favour of the inevitability of violence in human beings is that of biological continuity with other animals. This is the main thrust of the position taken by Lorenz, but one has the impression that much depends on which particular species of animal is used as a basis for comparison. In a symposium on the natural history of aggression (1964), which attempted to trace the evolutionary history of fighting behaviour in the animal kingdom, special attention was naturally paid to aggression in monkey and ape societies. A striking finding was that there was great diversity in the behaviour shown by different species; the greatest resemblance to human practices was found among baboons, which are by no means the closest to man biologically. With regard to chimpanzees, described as 'very close to man in many ways',[12] it appears that actual fighting, as compared with the use of threat or bluff, is relatively infrequent. These animals never fight to the death, and they have never been observed to form groups that make war on each other.

One of the conclusions reached in the extensive study in *Violence in America* is that 'nature provides us only with the capacity for violence; it is social circumstance that determines whether and how we exercise that capacity'.[13] This position appears to be a reasonable one. Violence is not universal, not inevitable, not instinctive; there are individuals and groups that show a great deal of violence, and other individuals and groups that show very little. Why? Can we say anything about the factors that give rise to violence in some cases and not in others?

Instrumental violence

One does not need training in psychology to realize that, if violence succeeds, there will be a great temptation to make use of it. This presents an agonizing dilemma to the responsible authorities. Should violence be rewarded, or should hostages be allowed to die? I have no answer to this question, but as a psychologist I am bound to add that positive reinforcement (reward for success) apparently is much more effective than negative (punishment for failure), and that the perception of one case in which the violence prospered seems to make a greater impression than one which fails and suffers the negative consequences. One learns from success more easily than from failure. This leads to the more general question of violence as a form of learned behaviour.

Violence as learned

Whatever other factors turn out to be operative, there can be no doubt that learning to be aggressive plays a major role. A boy may identify with and imitate his father; much research indicates that identification with the father and his values plays an important part in the learning of aggressive behavioural patterns. This is particularly true in those cultures or subcultures (see below) in which machismo or male assertiveness is regarded as proper, even as idealized, behaviour. A number of other 'learning' factors may enter.

Violence and the mass media

There is an extensive literature of research, conducted mainly by psychologists, dealing with the consequences of violence in the mass media, particularly television and the cinema, on tendencies towards violence on the part of the audience. The results show that usually the perception of violence does engender violence. An article by R. M. and D. E. Liebert[14] summarizes research in this field with the statement that the greater the level of exposure to television violence, the more the child is willing to use violence, to suggest it as a solution to conflict, and to perceive it as effective. They add that this conclusion has been reached repeatedly in more than fifty investigations over the past ten years in Europe and America. The authors add that television could be used in the opposite direction. The view that the vision of violence can reduce violence through catharsis, that is to say, by satisfying aggressive impulses through seeing others express aggression, is not supported by research.

The subculture of violence

The mass media do probably contribute to this violence, but to a large measure they reflect attitudes toward violence that are already prevalent. As has been stressed in an important book written jointly by an American sociologist and an Italian psychologist, Wolfgang and Ferracuti,[15] violence may become a way of life, an accepted mode of behaviour, sanctioned by folkways and conventional morality—in other words, a subculture. The reference to machismo above may be regarded as an example.

Regarding such subcultures in general, 'there is a patent theme of violence current in the cluster of values that make up the life-style of individuals living in similar conditions'.[16] Violence is expressed in a number of situations but by no means in all; it is not usually viewed as illicit and is therefore not accompanied by a sense of guilt; in fact, when such situations arise non-violence may be considered a counter-norm and condemned by the society in question.

The frustration-aggression hypothesis

A psychological theory that has aroused great attention was developed a number of years ago, and in its original formulation, now seen as overly simple, it held that aggression is always caused by frustration, and that frustration always leads to aggression.[17] An impressive array of evidence was collected, including materials from animal behaviour, ethnology, experiments which children, phenomena of prejudice and discrimination, crime and delinquency. In relation to the present topic, the most pertinent demonstration was that economic frustration, as represented by the level of real wages and the success of the cotton crop, was related to the frequency of acts of violence on the part of whites against blacks in the American south.[18] As the value of cotton went down, the number of lynchings went up. This phenomenon would fall into the category of reactive rather than instrumental aggression; no material gain resulted from this form of violence.

Most social psychologists would agree that frustration does increase the likelihood of violence, but that a number of other factors help to determine whether violent behaviour will really occur. A useful analysis has been made by Berkowitz[19] on the basis of extensive observation and considerable research. He makes an important distinction, for example, between two things that have frequently been identified, namely, frustration and deprivation: 'I would say a person is *deprived* if he lacks a goal object people generally regard as attractive or desirable, but is *frustrated* only when he had been anticipating the pleasure to be gotten from this object and then cannot fulfil this expectation.'[20] This in turn is closely related to what sociologists have called 'the revolution of rising expectations'. It is when things begin to improve that impatience develops, because the improvement appears too slow and too uneven.

Berkowitz agrees with what was said above about the major role played by prior learning in the development of violence, but correctly insists that other aspects should not be neglected. Frustration, as he defines it, is a painful occurrence: no one enjoys being thwarted. The greater the discomfort, the more likely is violence. (It has been pointed out, for example, that during most of the black riots, the summer heat was excessive). In addition, however, there must be a feeling that one has a degree of personal control over one's destiny; a sense of helplessness usually breeds apathy rather than violence. It is probably for this reason that blacks in the lowest socio-economic levels are the least militant. They are deprived but not frustrated. Militants, on the hand, have strong feelings that they can and should shape their destinies. Research has indicated that more violence is shown by blacks who have had a degree of education, which has awakened their appetites, who were born in the North (and therefore have less of a sense of helplessness), who have hoped and expected more, and are therefore more frustrated. There are also experimental studies that indicate that, when students are led to expect substantial rewards, they feel more frustrated at not receiving them that when no such expectation was present.

Another important concept in this connection is that of reference group. This is the group with which we may identify, or wish to join, or (most important) with which we compare ourselves, our successes and our failures. Research on American soldiers[21] yielded the perhaps not very surprising result that lack of promotion was much more frustrating to those who saw others round them being advanced that when there was little or no promotion. Sociologists speak of 'relative deprivation' to describe this phenomenon, which undoubtedly has great importance. To return to the question of the blacks who participated in the violent riots, Berkowitz is of the opinion that the reference group in this case was not the whites, but that unfavourable comparisons were made with other blacks, and that this contributed to social unrest. (This may be a partial explanation for the fact that in ghetto riots it is mainly black property that is destroyed). Can it be that gains at the upper levels have actually increased the potentiality for violence in the rest of the black community? On the other hand, it is possible that the careers of black Americans such as Ralph Bunche, Senator Edward Brooke, Justice Thurgood Marshall and others have given blacks a chance to identify with success, and consequently to reduce their frustration. Perhaps these two alternative possibilities help to explain why public-opinion surveys yield such a difference of opinion among black respondents as to whether there has been any real improvement on the part of the black population in general.

There is one other variety of relative frustration that may operate under certain conditions. One may compare oneself with others (the reference group) and experience frustration because of one's own inferior position. One may also compare oneself with what one has been before; reduction in socio-economic status has been shown, for example, to be related to increase of negative attitudes towards minority groups. Bettelheim and Janowitz state that 'ethnic hostility was most highly concentrated in the downwardly mobile group, while the pattern was significantly reversed for those who had risen in their social position'.[22] The conclusion of *Violence in America* includes the point that violence increases when there is socio-economic decline after steady progress; it is suggested that this may have played a part in recent black riots in the United States.

Rapid social change

Statistical studies of the frequency of violent outbursts in a number of nations over a period of years indicate that violence is related to rapidity of social change.[23] This may mean that such change brings with it new expectations, and as a consequence new frustrations leading to violence. It may also mean that a greater rate of change is associated with greater instability. Gurr summarizes a large number of quanti-tative studies as follows: 'violent conflict is greatest in developing nations, least in modern nations, intermediate in the least-developed, most "traditional" nations.'[24] This con-fronts the world, including the United Nations and its Specialized Agencies, with a dilemma. Change is wanted, requested; technical assistance (or technical co-operation) is accepted universally as desirable. To the extent that it contributes to rapid economic growth, it reduces violence; to the extent that it brings about social and cultural change, it apparently contributes towards its increase.

This is undoubtedly an oversimplification, since a number of other considerations also enter. It has been pointed out, for example, that there is more violence when there is no generally positive attitude towards the legitimacy of the government, a feeling that it is not responsive to popular (democratic) needs and wishes, a tradition of violence, popular values that support (and even reward) it, and discontent because of relative frustration. The effects of rapid change in preparing the way for violence may be facilitated or reduced, depending on the role of these and other factors. It would seem to be of value to supplement the important quantitative studies summarized by Gurr with a qualitative description of those cases in which rapid change has been associated with violence, and those in which it has not. Such a 'differential diagnosis' should help towards a better understanding of a very complex phenomenon.

The ethics of violence

There has been approval, at various times and places, of at least certain forms of violence, under at least certain conditions. The possible 'justifications', usually presented with evident sincerity, are too familiar to require a detailed listing at this point. They will be accepted or rejected by others depending on their own sincerely held convictions.

It is not the role of the psychologist to decide when violence is legitimate, but to investigate the readiness with which people accept violence, and the conditions under which they regard it as justified. This is the subject of a study by Kahn[25] of a representative sample of Americans on attitudes and values regarding violence. One set of questions related to 'violence for social control'; about two-thirds of the respondents state that the police should shoot but not to kill in handling a gang of hoodlums; almost as large a proportion advocated that same procedure in the case of ghetto riots; slightly less than half when there were disturbances by white students. In the case of 'violence for social change', a tremendous majority agreed that change was necessary but that it could be brought about fast enough without property damage or personal injury. There was, however, a minority of about 10 per cent with the view that 'protest involving extensive damage and some death will be required'.[26] Kahn points out that 10 per cent means a substantial number of people, and regards this finding as disturbing and 'sobering'.

Another variety of 'justification' for violence is the excuse

'I was just following orders, merely obeying my superiors'. As is well known, this is what was said by those who appeared at the Nuremberg Trials. More recently, the same excuse was heard from Lt. Calley, who was accused and found guilty of responsibility for the massacre at Mai Lai. A cross-section of Americans were asked whether Lt. Calley should have been brought to trial (34 per cent approved, 58 per cent disapproved) and whether he should have carried out the orders to shoot (61 per cent said yes, 29 per cent no).[27] The assumption that he was acting 'under orders' was sufficient to justify his actions as normal in the opinion of a majority of the respondents.

An important experiment designed to study this tendency to 'obey' under controlled laboratory conditions was conducted by Milgram,[28] and it has received considerable publicity, including television coverage, and has been widely acclaimed and severely criticized. It consisted essentially in creating a situation in which the subject, usually a student, was instructed by the experimenter (a prestige figure) to administer electric shocks of increasing intensity to other students who gave incorrect solutions to problems presented to them. Cries of anguish (recorded on tape) were heard by the subject, but he was still ordered to continue. There were some refusals, but a majority of the students (65 per cent) obeyed. A replication of this study in Germany by Mantell[29] showed a slightly higher percentage. The criticism of these experiments has come mainly because of the severe trauma experimented by the subjects, many of whom were greatly disturbed by the excessive punishment they were ordered to administer. The investigation has, however, been considered important because it reveals that even in 'democratic' societies violent punishment is justified if the orders to administer it come from someone who represents authority.

Other factors in violence

This paper will conclude with a brief mention of a number of other factors that have been considered by social psychologists as contributing to the likelihood of individual and collective violence.

Age and sex. Although there are a number of exceptions, in general violence is found most frequently among young males. There may be hormonal factors responsible for greater aggression among males,[30] but the cultural and subcultural pressures (machismo, for example) clearly play an important part.

Social class. This factor was mentioned in relation to ghetto riots, but in more general terms it can be said that the lower the socio-economic class, the more frequently does violence occur. It has been suggested, however, that in the most deprived groups, apathy and hopelessness may reduce violence.

Race or ethnic group. There can be little doubt that blacks in the United States have higher homicide rates than whites, even when due allowance is made for the fact that blacks are more likely to be arrested and convicted, other things being equal. (This situation is changing for the better.) There is no evidence, however, that this is due to genetic factors. As Wolfgang[31] has pointed out, the social, economic and political disparities between the races in the United States are sufficient to justify the expectation that blacks would be found to have a higher crime rate (including crimes of violence) than whites. Stereotypes regarding criminal behaviour among minority groups (Algerians in France, for example) require much more careful study than they have so far received.

Biological or physiological causes. There have been a number of attempts to correlate violent behaviour with hormone balance, encephalograms, blood chemistry, chromosome patterns, etc. There has as yet been no agreement regarding the part played by such factors.

Overcrowding. Research with animals has shown that the overcrowding of animals may increase the likelihood of violent behaviour.[32] Extrapolation to human beings remains doubtful, however, since the human experience of overcrowding is rarely as extreme as that artificially created in animal environments. There are, however, a number of writers who regard this as a most serious problem, and for whom the population explosion is potentially a greater threat to mankind than atomic war. Leyhausen, for example, writes: 'The only danger to man is men, too many men.'[33] This seems to me to be an exaggeration as far as violence is concerned. Overpopulation certainly has many unhappy consequences, but it has so far not been proved that violence is one of them.

Psychological characteristics. Wolfgang and Ferracuti[34] summarize the results of the application of personality tests to subjects who have commited acts of violence such as homicide. According to them the results obtained with the Rorschach technique and the Thematic Apperception Test are inconclusive. Personality characteristics that do emerge with some regularity include egocentrism and lack of emotional control; the individuals concerned are explosive, immature, unable to establish social contact, deficient in conscious control, with a strong need for the immediate gratification of impulses. So far these approaches have not added a great deal to our understanding of the causes of violence.

An obvious conclusion

It is impossible to find a single cause of all forms of violence. We are dealing here clearly with a multidimensional phenomenon, and our understanding of it demands that we keep many facets simultaneously in mind. The distinctions between violence that is individual or collective, instrumental or reactive, are evidence of the complexity of the problem. It may be possible some day to combine the various contributing factors into a causal matrix that will allow us to predict whether or not violence will occur, but that day has not yet arrived.

Notes

1. T. R. Gurr, *Why Men Rebel*, Princeton, N.J., Princeton University Press, 1970; *Violence in America. Report to the National Commission on the Causes and Prevention of Violence*, New York, Signet Books, 1969.
2. J. M. R. Delgado, 'The Neurological Basis of Violence', *International Social Science Journal*, Vol. XXIII, 1971, pp. 27–35.
3. R. A. Hinde, 'The Nature and Control of Aggressive Behaviour', *International Social Science Journal*, Vol. XXIII, 1971, pp. 48–52.
4. N. A. Kovalsky, 'Social Aspects of International Aggression', *International Social Science Journal*, Vol. XXIII, 1971, pp. 68–78.
5. L. Bender, 'Genesis of Hostility in Children', *American Journal of Psychiatry*, Vol. 105, 1948, pp. 241–5.
6. F. H. Allen, 'Aggression in Relation to Emotional Development', *Proc. Int. Conf. Child. Psychiatry* (London, Lewis), 1948, pp. 4–11.
7. L. B. Murphy, *The Widening World of Childhood*, New York, Basic Books, 1962.
8. K. Lorenz, *On Aggression*, London, University Paperback, 1967.
9. L. Berkowitz, 'Frustrations, Comparisons and Other Sources of Emotional Arousal as Contributors to Social Unrest', *J. Soc. Issues*, Vol. 28, 1971, pp. 77–92.
10. R. Ardrey, Interview in *Psychology Today*, Vol. 6, 1972, pp. 73–85.
11. L. Tiger, 'Introduction', *International Social Science Journal*, Vol. XXIII, 1971, pp. 9–17.

12. J. Van Lawick-Goodall, 'Some Aspects of Aggressive Behaviour in a Group of Free-living Chimpanzees', *International Social Science Journal*, Vol. XXIII, 1971, pp. 89–97.
13. *Violence in America*, op. cit., p. 777.
14. R. M. Liebert and D. E. Liebert, 'War on the Screen: A Psychological Perspective', in *La Communication et la Guerre*, Brussels, Bruylant, 1974.
15. M. E. Wolfgang and F. Ferracuti, *The Subculture of Violence*, London, Tavistock, 1967.
16. Ibid., p. 140.
17. J. Dollard et al., *Frustration and Aggression*, New Haven, Conn., Yale University Press, 1939.
18. C. I. Hovland and R. R. Sears, 'Minor Studies of Aggression: VI, Correlations of Lynchings with Economic Indices', *J. Psychol.*, Vol. 9, 1938, pp. 301–10.
19. Berkowitz, op. cit.
20. Ibid., p. 79.
21. R. Merton and A. Kitt, 'Contributions to the Theory of Reference Group Behaviour', in R. Merton and P. Lazarsfeld (eds.), *Continuities in Social Reasearch*, Glencoe, Ill., The Free Press, 1950.
22. B. Bettelheim and M. Janowitz, *Dynamics of Prejudice*, p. 596, New York, Harper and Row, 1950.
23. Cf. *Violence in America*, op. cit., and T. R. Gurr, 'The Calculus of Civil Conflict', *J. Soc. Issues*, Vol. 28, 1972, pp. 27–48.
24. Ibid., p. 37.
25. R. L. Kahn, 'The Justification of Violence: Social Problems and Social Solutions', *J. Soc. Issues*, Vol. 28, 1972, pp. 155–76.
26. Ibid., p. 165.
27. H. C. Kelman and L. H. Lawrence, 'Assignment of Responsibility in the Case of Lt. Calley', *J. Soc. Issues*, Vol. 28, 1972, pp. 177–212.
28. S. Milgram, 'Behavioural Study of Obedience', *J. Abn. and Social Psychol.*, Vol. 67, 1963, pp. 371–8; and 'Some Conditions of Obedience and Disobedience to Authority', *Human Relations*, Vol. 18, 1965, pp. 127–34.
29. D. Mantell, 'The Potential for Violence in Germany', *J. Social Issues*, Vol. 27, 1971, pp. 101–12.
30. L. Tiger and R. Fox, *The Imperial Animal?*, New York, Dell, 1971.
31. M. E. Wolfgang, *Crime and Race: Conceptions and Misconceptions*, New York, Institute of Human Relations, 1964.
32. G. M. Carstairs, 'Overcrowding and Human Aggression', in *Violence in America*, New York, Signet Books, 1969.
33. P. Leyhausen, in *The Unesco Courier*, August–September 1970.
34. Wolfgang and Ferracuti, op. cit.

Mass communication:
symptom or cause of violence

Director, Centre for Mass
Communication Research,
University of Leicester,
United Kingdom

James D. Halloran

In recent years there has been abundant evidence, ranging from government-sponsored inquiries and research to expressions of concern in the media and elsewhere, and to the formation of pressure groups, that the alleged relationship between the mass media and violence is considered by many people to be important and problematic. Much of what is now being said about television has been said before about the other media, and throughout history innovations in communication technology have frequently been blamed for producing social disruption. Nevertheless, the protrayal of violence by the media, particularly by television, is increasingly seen as a major social problem, particularly in Western Europe and North America.

People complain, they group together and plan collective action in the hope that this will lead to a solution, usually a censorious one, to the problem as they see it. Whether or not the concern is justified is a different matter. The evidence suggests that the process of influence, the role of the media and the nature of violence are not understood and that, consequently, the problem is inadequately defined. In view of this, the solutions put forward are not likely to be appropriate.

The approach to the problem outlined in this paper is essentially a social-scientific one. A social scientist must never take the definitions of problems and expressions of concern at face value.

The problem of media violence should be studied in relation to other institutions and to violence in society as a whole, and it should be set within the appropriate social, political and economic frameworks.

People often talk about media violence and violent behaviour almost as though there were no other sources of violence in society. They seek net, convenient, uncomplicated answers that illustrate simple causal relationships. Once having identified a fixed point of evil, external to self, they use this as a scapegoat, and this helps them to maintain their own particular view of self and society.

Assuming that the media/violence relationship is worth examining, then the first thing to do is to remove the media from the centre of the stage.

Violence may be categorized in several ways; for example, we may make a distinction between collective or political violence and personal or individual violence. If we accept this distinction and look at collective violence from a historical perspective, we shall see that it is much more normal, central and historically rooted than many would have us believe. Tilly has written:

Historically, collective violence has flowed regularly out of the central political processes of western countries. Men seeking to seize, hold or realign the levers of power, have continually engaged in collective violence as part of their struggles. The oppressed have struck in the name of justice, the privileged in the name of order, and those in between in the name of fear.

Much of what we now accept, take for granted and enjoy, is the outcome of violent action in the past, although this will now have been fully legitimated, and the media, together with educational and other institutions, will have played a part in the legitimation process.

Most people think of violence, in both the collective and individual senses, in terms of assassinations, murders, riots, demonstrations, assaults, robberies, rapes, acts of vandalism, and so on. In fact, for many this sort of 'illegitimate' behaviour represents the totality of violence. But there are others who adopt a different and wider approach and include in their definition war, capital punishment, corporal punishment and certain aspects of penal practice, police behaviour and school discipline. A still broader definition might include poverty, deprivation, economic exploitation, and discrimination. In fact, society may contribute to violence by the seal of approval it gives to certain forms of violence, particularly those that have been legitimated in the name of social control.

Research and discussion on media violence should not be confined to 'illegitimate violence' as this is defined by most of those who express concern about media violence.

Many of these people, feeling that they have a firm stake in the established system, loudly condemn 'illegitimate violence' to protect the existing order and thereby their own position or vested interest. There is, of course, a difference between legitimate violence and legal violence. The former depends on consensus. Legal violence is not necessarily legitimate.

When violence is examined within the appropriate historical and cultural contexts, we can see many examples of how it has been culturally, and even subculturally, defined.

The roots of violent behaviour obviously differ from country to country. For example, in the United States it has been suggested that the 'frontier factor', the patterns and extent of immigration, the War of Independence, the industrial revolution, urbanization, rapid social change and mobility, unprecedented prosperity and affluence, the class system and relative deprivation—some of these unique to the United States, some common to several countries—have all played a part in contributing to the present situation in that country.

The media are not mentioned in the above list, and it is worth noting that in the United States and elsewhere few of those who have systematically and scientifically studied violent behaviour have cited the media as a major cause. They find the roots of such behaviour elsewhere.

In a report to the National Commission on the Causes and Prevention of Violence in the United States—claimed to be 'the most comprehensive, authoritative study of violence ever published'—we may read that although many factors impinge on what is a complex process, there is considerable evidence that supports the assumption 'that men's frustration over some of the material and social circumstances of their lives is a necessary precondition of group protest and collective violence', and that 'probably the most important cause of major increases in group violence is the widespread frustration of socially deprived expectations about the goods and conditions of life men believe theirs by right. These frustratable expectations relate not only to material well-being but to more intangible conditions such as security, status, freedom to manage one's own affairs, and satisfying personal relations with others'.

The above passages from the report to the National Commission are couched mainly in terms of group or collective protest or political behaviour, but they are applicable *mutatis mutandis* to individual behaviour as well. Studies of the violent behaviour of delinquents and criminals show that in many cases there is a lack of appropriate or legitimate ways of problem-solving at a variety of levels. In addition to the economic level, these include the search for identity and satisfactory interpersonal relationships. Those whose opportunities to respond to the demands of life are severely limited and who can visualize no other solution may resort to violence. Violence may come to be regarded as an alternative—perhaps the only—road to success, achievement and status which they have been led to believe society values so highly.

The above comments are not meant to provide a comprehensive explanation of violent behaviour, for there are several other approaches, each with its own emphasis. The main intention is to place the media/violence problem in perspective.

It should be noted that the Report of the United States National Commission[1] quite rightly does not absolve media institutions and practitioners from their responsibilities. Although television is not regarded by the Commission as a principal cause of violence in society, both the nature and amount of violence on the small screen are roundly condemned. However the Commission did not really face up to the media implications of its own conclusions about relative deprivation and frustration, which were referred to earlier, although there was a reference in the report to 'additional complications (which might) arise from the high visibility of both violence and social inequalities'.

Let us assume that we are dealing with a commercially oriented, industrialized urban society where advertising plays an important part in media operations and in the economy generally. Deprived groups in society are reminded, by a daily bombardment, of what is available to others, what is said to be theirs for the asking, yet what they certainly do not possess and, moreover, are not likely ever to possess. There are, of course, other powerful agents of frustration operating at a variety of levels, from the interpersonal to the environmental, but it would be foolish to ignore the possibility that the media, in their normal day-to-day operations, by the presentation of these norms and values, may increase expectations unrealistically, aggravate existing problems, contribute to frustration and consequently to the aggression and violence that may stem from this.

This, however, is not the sort of relationship people

normally have in mind when they speculate or pontificate about the link between the media and violence.

The condemnation of media content is highly selective. Not all forms of media violence are condemned, any more than are all forms of violent behaviour. In passing, it is interesting to note that quite a number of those who regard media violence as a serious problem not only tend to be aggressive in the way they express this, but also adopt a somewhat negative and punitive approach to several other social issues. They favour the death penalty, corporal punishment and tougher discipline generally. They also exhibit racist tendencies, and oppose penal and other social reforms. Overall, they tend to be conservative, conformist and authoritarian, even though this does not apply by any means to all those who at some time or other have expressed concern about the media portrayal of violence.

Although those researchers whose work centres on violent behaviour and violence in society have not found the media to be a major source of violent behaviour, others—those whose main focus has been the media and violence—have been more inclined to indict the media. On the whole, most of these researchers are psychologists who have addressed themselves directly to some form of hypothesized relationship between the media's portrayal of violence, on the one hand, and violent or aggressive behaviour on the other. In many cases, their work has been commissioned and is financially supported for this specific purpose.

The United States Surgeon-General's million-dollar, twenty-three-project research programme on television violence[2] represents the biggest and most expensive, if not the most sophisticated and co-ordinated, exercise in this area. As the findings and interpretations of this research programme are frequently quoted by those who claim that a causal link (media violence=violent behaviour) has been established, despite the many criticisms levelled against the individual projects, we must obviously look at what the Report has to say.

In view of the way it has been used to prove a case against television, it is surprising to find that the Surgeon-General's Report is really quite cautious in its conclusions. It refers to a preliminary and tentative indication of a causal relation between viewing violence on television and aggressive behaviour, operating only on some children who are already disposed to be aggressive and only in some circumstances. It is also recognized that both the heavy viewing of violence and violent or aggressive behaviour could be the joint product of some other common source. They could both be symptoms of a wider condition.

This last point confirms our own research on television and delinquency,[3] carried out in the United Kingdom some years before the Surgeon-General's work. In this research, it was also found that the television-viewing patterns of the delinquents did not differ significantly from those of their non-delinquent peers from the same socio-economic background. Neither were any significant differences in television viewing and preferences discovered when the media behaviour of aggressive and non-aggressive teenagers in the north-east of England were compared.

These and other studies led us to state, some years ago, that no case had been made where television (or the other media) could be legitimately regarded as a causal, or even as a major contributory factor, of any form of violent behaviour. A more recent conclusion, following a survey of work in this country and elsewhere (including research from the United States) is that it has still not been established that the mass media have any significant effect on the level of violence in society.[4] In fact, the whole weight of research and theory in this field would suggest that the mass media, except just possibly in the case of a small number of pathological individuals, are never the sole cause of such behaviour. At most they play a contributory role, and that a minor one.

We should not be surprised at this; rather, we should be surprised at the persistence with which researchers still look for simple cause-and-effect relationships. In the strict sense we shouldn't really be asking questions about the effect of television. We rarely ask such questions about other institutions, such as the family, religion or education.

Two points need to be made with regard to the above comments. First, they refer for the most part to studies that conceptualize the problem in terms of imitation, increased aggression, attitude change, and so on. These represent what may be termed the conventional approach, which, so it is argued here, is based on an inadequate understanding of the media, of violence, of the communication process, and of the nature of society.

Secondly, most of the conventional research—the results

of which are often used to support the causal argument—has been carried out in the United States. The United States is different from the United Kingdom and other countries in a variety of ways, particularly with regard to the nature and amount of violence both on the screen and in society at large. What obtains in one country need not obtain in another.

More to the point, however, is the possibility that this work, or at least certain interpretations of it, does not even hold in the United States. It has been criticized on several grounds (theoretically, conceptually and methodologically), particularly for the lack of clarity and consistency in the use of such concepts as violence and aggression. In many cases, the operationalization of the concepts is also very questionable. There is likely to be a substantial gap between behavioural, verbal and attitudinal responses in a laboratory and antisocial aggression or violence in the home or street. The major weaknesses in the experimental laboratory work are the artificiality in the setting, the type and time of the measurements, and the nature of the 'victim' (e.g. dolls, balloons, recipients of electric shocks, etc.). Moreover, it is by no means always clear what is really being measured. Validity is low. Generalization to antisocial behaviour in real-life situations must be very suspect indeed. Survey work—the results of which, so it is claimed, point in the same direction as those from the laboratory work—is more realistic but is not susceptible to causal explanation.

Perhaps the last word on this highly controversial topic should be given to George Comstock, and who has been closely and supportively associated with the Surgeon-General's research and its follow-up over the last few years. Writing in late 1976, Comstock, fully aware of the convergence of the different research approaches, reports as follows:

It is tempting to conclude that television violence makes viewers more antisocially aggressive, somewhat callous, and generally more fearful of the society in which they live. It may, but the social and behavioural science evidence does not support such a broad indictment. The evidence on desensitization and fearfulness is too limited for such broad conclusions at this time. The evidence on aggressiveness is much more extensive, but it does not support a conclusion of increased antisocial aggression. The evidence does not tell us anything about the degree of social harm or criminal antisocial violence that may be attributable to television. It may be great, negligible, or nil.[5]

There is no intention here to absolve those who work in the media from their responsibilities—the gratuitous insertion of violence for kicks or profits is to be deplored. But deploring the portrayal of violence is one thing, and linking it with violent behaviour is another, entirely different matter.

Violence and deviant behaviour, particularly in their extreme forms, are extensively covered by the media in most Western societies. There is nothing new about this practice, nor about the style or manner of presentation, unless it is that it is not quite as sensational as it once was. Yet it could be that because of the nature of our fragmented, plural, industrial society, where many believe mediated culture plays as increasingly prominent part in shaping our values and behaviour, media portrayals of violence and deviance may have more important social repercussions today than they had in the past.

Some years ago an American sociologist, Marshall Clinard, writing on 'The Newspaper and Crime', argued: 'By continually playing up crime, it is likely that newspapers are important in making us a crime-centred culture. As a result crime often seems more frequent than it is.'

Although this claim and others like it are rarely accompanied by hard supporting evidence, it is not unreasonable to hypothesize that what people read in the papers, hear on the radio and see on television might influence their views about the nature and extent of violence in our society. Some years ago studies carried out in the United States[6] indicated that public estimates of the amount and type of crime in the community were more closely related to newspapers reports than to the actual amounts of crime as recorded by the police.

The media help to set the social/political agenda. They select, organize, emphasize, define and amplify. They convey meanings and perspectives, offer solutions, associate certain groups with certain types of values and behaviour, create anxiety, and legitimate or justify the status quo and the prevailing systems of social control.

But the media, of course, do not work in isolation. What we should really study is the mix, the interaction or inter-relationship between media experiences on the one hand, and non-media or situational experiences on the other. These will differ from issue to issue, from person to person, from country to country, and so on. For example, we know from our research on race relations and racial conflict[7] that the media may have a disproportionate influence in conveying meanings and perspectives where personal experience is lacking. Our work on the media and race showed that, over a seven-year period, the media portrayed coloured people essentially as a threat and a problem, and that this was reflected in public attitudes. Here we have a clear example of the media exacerbating conflict and reinforcing, if not actually creating, social problems. Our research also shows that the coverage by the British media of the hostilities in Northern Ireland is another example of conflict exacerbation.

These questions bring us to even more fundamental ones. What is news? Do the mass media create new 'facts' by making non-news news? Must the negative, deviant, violent or sensational always predominate? On the whole, the way the news about violence and related issues is presented by the media make it unlikely that the facts will be placed in meaningful context or that the issues behind the story with regard to offence, victim or official agency will be adequately covered.

It is often argued by those working in the media that, when events are reported, it is natural to focus on the immediate case. This may be true, but it provides a poor base from which an adequate understanding of the problem can be developed.

The formation of sound social policy depends on knowledge of changes in the development rate and distribution of the relevant events, but policies more frequently are formed in reaction to certain extreme cases. The media deal in extreme cases.

One of the reasons why the media portray situations as they do is that they operate within a socio-economic system where readers and viewers have to be won and kept. The presentation of violence and related phenomena have become vital in this connection.

For the daily news media, persons, events and happenings (particularly negative ones) are the basic units of news. One reason for the concentration on events is the 'publication frequency' of the media themselves. Events are more likely to be picked up by the media working to a daily publication cycle if they occur within the space of one day. For example, a demonstration is a possible news event, while the development of a political movement over several years does not have the correct 'frequency'.

The concentration on events itself makes some aspects of a story more likely to be regarded as newsworthy than others. The issue of violence, for example, is directly related to the visible forms of events on the streets. But this preoccupation with events and incidents tends to exclude consideration of background development and of the issues involved.

One of our research projects,[8] which focused on the media coverage of a large political demonstration, an anti-apartheid demonstration against a tour of the South African rugby team, provides a good illustration of some of the foregoing points.

In this research, differences among the various media in the treatment of the demonstration were obviously detected, but we were also able to show a more important and fundamental similarity among practically all branches of the media. In all but one case, the story was interpreted in terms of the same basic issue that had originally made it news, namely the issue of violence. Yet violence need not have been central—in fact, it was not central. The 'set' of violence was used because, together with the other implications of news values, it was the logical outcome of the existing organization of the news process, and of the assumptions on which it rested.

As indicated earlier, these news values are an integral part of professional news selection and presentation as this has developed within our particular socio-economic system. No matter what lofty ideals are claimed, the numbers of readers, listeners and viewers, and the economics of advertising play an important part in shaping these values and the news which they underlie.

What, then, are the results of this form of news presentation? One interpretation is that the way the media deal with these situations may lead to labelling, to the association—perhaps unjustifiable—of certain groups with violent behaviour, and possibly to the acceptance of violence as a legitimate way of dealing with problems or as a necessary form of retaliation.

In the case of the demonstration project, given the climate of public opinion at the time of the research, the largest negative presentation was almost bound to devalue the case of the protesters. Moreover, in the long run, this might increase rather than reduce the risk of violent behaviour. Because of the way the media operate, a minority group may have to be violent before there is any chance of its case being presented to the general public.

Whether we are dealing with student demands for reform in the universities, anti-apartheid marches, antiwar demonstrations, drug-taking, alcoholics, homosexuals, prisoners' unions, racial questions or strikes, the account will be largely isolated from antecedent conditions and convey little understanding of either root causes or aims. In fact, the whole presentation is likely to be fragmented and out of context.

Research has shown that, in reporting violence and deviance, the media exaggerate, sensationalize and stereotype, and that public perceptions derived from these presentations may modify or even create the behaviour in question. For example, the images of drug use obtained from the media, so it is claimed, have influenced court and police behaviour, and in turn this has influenced behaviour in such a way as to make it conform with the stereotypes. The stereotypes were fulfilled, the behaviour—previously marginal—became more central and more frequent, and this was followed by further (reinforcing) social reaction. The problem was confirmed at a redefined level, and all sides behaved as they were 'expected' to behave.

At a different level, the overall effect of this type of presentation of deviance and social problems could be to eliminate or play down alternative conceptions of social order. The news-selection process, therefore, may have an ideological significance for the maintenance of the status quo of power and interest by managing conflict and dissent in the interest of the establishment.

This represents a more complex and indirect approach to media influence than is normally postulated, but surely the study of the media in this way is much more valid and rewarding than the relatively simple-minded causal stimulus-response approaches that have been frequently, if unproductively, utilized in the past.

But these newer approaches do not provide all the answers. For example, the labelling-amplification approach mentioned earlier, although useful and interesting, does not account for deviant behaviour—still less for the initial deviation. It also has a limited application, for it does not apply equally to all forms of deviant behaviour, some of which are clearly visible. Furthermore, people do have experiences other than media experiences and, although the agenda may be set by the media, the ability of the public selectively to use and interpret what the media make available should not be underestimated.

Generally, media violence is viewed negatively, and is criticized or condemned because of its alleged disruptive effects. But the media, in their portrayal of violence and deviance, may serve a 'positive' function by acting as an instrument of social control and by maintaining the status quo. The function may be regarded as positive from the standpoint of the establishment, although not necessarily from the standpoint of other groups in society who are seeking change.

The media may reinforce the status quo by maintaining a 'cultural consensus'. It is possible that the media coverage of violence could enhance normative consensus and community integration. Where people have little first-hand knowledge of violent crime they are likely to depend on the media for most of their information. The media inform, bring to light, create awareness, redefine the boundaries of what is acceptable and what is not, and structure perceptions of the nature and extent of violence. In doing this they bring people together in opposition to disorder, reinforce a belief in common values, facilitate the imposition of sanctions, and strengthen social control.

Although many of the hypotheses that stem from this approach have still to be put to the test, there is nothing new in the view that regards violence as a catalyst. Marx, Durkheim and Mead all stressed the unanticipated functions of crime in creating a sense of solidarity within the community by arousing the moral and aesthetic sentiments of the public. More recently, Lewis Cose developed a related idea when he argued that not only criminals but law-enforcing agents also may call forth a sense of solidarity against their behaviour. In certain circumstances the use of extra-legal violence, particularly when exhibited under the glare of television cameras, and made highly visible to the public at large, could lead to awareness, indignation and revulsion, which might result in the rejection of a hitherto accepted practice. It has been suggested that the media coverage of racial disturbances in the southern states of the United States in the early 1960s is a case in point.

After seeing racial disturbances in the streets on their television sets, some people may reach for their guns in the name of law and order; others may learn a lesson or two that they will put into practical use when their time comes, and still others—as the hitherto invisible or partly visible becomes clearly visible—may be jolted out of their apathy and stirred into social action directed at the roots of the problem. Here, as in other situations, different people take different things from the same message. There are no easy decisions for the responsible broadcaster in deciding what to present and how to present it in situations like this. In reminding broadcasters of their responsibilities, we must also recognize their difficulties and try to understand their problems.

In the last few pages we have been dealing with non-fictional media material, but George Gerbner, one of the most prominent mass-communication researchers in the United States, is much more concerned with fictional material.[9] He would agree with some of the criticisms made earlier in this paper, particularly those that focus on attitude and behavioural change and the stimulation of aggression. According to Gerbner, television is essentially different from the other media, and research on television requires an entirely new approach: 'The essential differences between television and the other media are more crucial than the similarities . . . the reach, scope, ritualization, organic connectedness and non-selective use of mainstream television make it different from other media of mass communications.'

Gerbner argues that television should not be isolated from the mainstream of modern culture because 'it *is* the mainstream'. It is 'the central cultural aim of American society', a 'major force for enculturation (which permeates) both the initial and final years of life as well as the years between'. His interest is not so much in individual programmes or specific messages as in 'whole systems of messages' and their consequences for 'common consciousness'.

He sees little point in making the conventional distinction between information and entertainment. He regards entertainment, particularly television drama, as highly informative—'the most broadly effective educational fare in any culture'—and maintains that all of us, whatever our status or educational background, obtain much of our knowledge of the real world from fictional representations. Television entertainment provides common ground for all sections of the population as it offers a continuous stream of 'facts' and impressions about the many aspects of life and society: 'Never before have all classes and groups (as well as ages) shared so much of the same culture and the same perspectives.'

This is not just a speculative exercise on Gerbner's part, for he supports at least part of his case with some of the most impressive systematic analysis of television content ever carried out. Naturally, he recognizes and accepts that content analysis by itself tells us nothing definitive about the viewing public's reactions to the content. He claims, however, that his studies of the public, although as yet in their early stages, demonstrate quite clearly the ability of television to cultivate its own 'reality'. In all the cases studied, heavier viewers had versions of social reality that squared more with 'the television world' than did the versions of the lighter viewers.

Gerbner's work, then, provides support for the main themes of this paper, namely that television is not without influence (Gerbner would put it much more strongly than this), but that the nature and directions of the influence are not as commonly supposed.

Gerbner, then, is certainly worried about television's portrayal of violence, but this is not because of its potential for disruption or even change, but because it might function to legitimate and maintain the power and authority of the establishment. Change is more likely to be impeded than facilitated as television demonstrates the values of society and the rules of the game 'by dramatic stories of their symbolic violations'. In this way, it serves the social order of the industrial system.

Gerbner sees television violence as the simplest and cheapest dramatic means available to demonstrate the rules of the game of power, to reinforce social control, and to maintain the existing social order. He supports this view with data from his research, suggesting that the maintenance mechanism seems to work through cultivating a sense of danger, risk and insecurity. This leads, especially for the less powerful groups in the community, to acquiescence to and dependence upon established authority. It also facilitates the legitimation of the use of force by the authorities in order to keep their position.

Gerbner states that 'media-incited criminal violence may be a price industrial cultures extract from some citizens for the general pacification of most others. . . . Television—the established religion of the industrial order—appears to cultivate assumptions that fit its socially functional myths'.

Violence and its portrayal by the media clearly serve specific social functions, although these will differ from country to country, as will the nature and extent of media violence. The Finnish scholar, Veikko Pietilä, comparing television violence in the United States and the Soviet Union, shows that in the two countries it is presented in different contexts and serves different functions.[10]

In the Soviet Union, televised violence tends to be presented in historical, societal and collective contexts, whilst in the United States the emphasis is on individually-oriented aggression, which is frequently linked to personal success, achievement and private property. In the United States, one of the main aims is to create excitement and attract and keep an audience in a fiercely competitive system where profits have to be made. In the Soviet Union, according to Pietilä, the purposes are more often propagandistic and educational.

Pietilä comments on both the commodity (box office) and ideological functions of televised violence in the United States. He asks if television violence represents a vital aspect of the essential nature of this society, because a core element in its history and development has been individual success by means of violence or aggression. This form of violence is deeply rooted in the society, and the media portrayal of violence is a manifestation of this state of affairs that ought not to surprise us.

Pietilä confines this type of speculative analysis to capitalist societies and refers to television content contributing 'to the directing and regulating of social progress in such a way that the existing order and form of these societies is protected'. We saw that Pietilä's research indicated that televised violence in socialist societies is different in content and context from that in capitalist societies. Not surprisingly, he argues that media violence functions in different ways in the two countries. However, at another level, it serves both systems by reinforcing the existing order. At this level the system is the message in both countries.

Enough has been written to illustrate one of the main aims of this paper, which is to suggest some of the social and political consequences that may possibly stem from the ways in which the media deal with violence and related phenomena. We are not in a position to make clear, definitive statements, supported by evidence, on the precise role of the media in the areas and directions outlined. The necessary research has not been carried out. Moreover, even if the recommended research were carried out, the neat, simple, packaged, convenient, unequivocal answers sought by so many are still not likely to be forthcoming. The nature of the problem is not susceptible to this type of answer. The process is too complex.

I am convinced that it will be more profitable to explore the avenues of inquiry outlined in this paper than to persist in the much simpler conventional search that attempts to establish causal links between media violence and real-life violence.

In spite of the problems, we have enough information now to know where to start if we wish to reduce violent behaviour in our societies. The final report of the United States National Commission on the Causes and Prevention of Violence called in 1969 for 'a reordering of national priorities and for a greater investment of resources—to establish justice and to ensure domestic tranquility'. The emphasis was on social reform and increased expenditure to facilitate the achievement of essential social goals. The needs and the priorities are still the same, and are likely to remain that way for some time.

Notes

1. H. D. Graham and T. F. Gurr (eds.), *The History of Violence in America. A Report to the National Commission on the Causes and Prevention of Violence*, Bantam Books, 1969.
2. *Television and Growing Up: The Impact of Televised Violence. Report to the Surgeon General*, United States Public Health Service, from the Surgeon General's Scientific Advisory Committee on Television and Social Behaviour, United States Department of Health, Education and Welfare, 1972.
3. J. D. Halloran, R. L. Brown and D. C. Chaney, *Television and Delinquency*, Leicester University Press, 1970.
4. D. Howitt and R. Dembo, 'A Subcultural Account of Media Effects', *Human Relations*, Vol. 27, No. 1; D. Howitt and G. Cumberbatch, *Mass Media Violence and Society*, Elek, 1975; R. Dembo, 'Critical Factors in Understanding Adolescent Aggression', *Social Psychiatry*, No. 8, 1975.
5. G. Comstock, *The Evidence of Television Violence*, Santa Monica, Calif., Rand Corporation, October 1976.
6. *Final Report of the National Commission on the Causes and Prevention of Violence*, Washington, United States Government Printing Office, 1969; 'Patterns of Violence', *The Annals of the American Academy of Political and Social Science*, March 1966.
7. P. Hartmann and C. Husband, *Racism and the Mass Media*, Davis-Oynter, 1974; P. Hartmann, C. Husband and J. Clark, *Race as News: A Study in the Handling of Race in the British National Press from 1963 to 1970*, Paris, Unesco, 1974.
8. P. Croll, 'The Nature of Public Concern with Television with Particular Reference to Violence', unpublished paper, Centre for Mass Communication Research, Leicester, United Kingdom.
9. G. Gerbner and L. Gross, 'Living with Television: A Violence Profile', *Journal of Communication*, Spring 1976.
10. Veikko Pietilä, 'Notes on Violence in the Mass Media', *Instant Research on Peace and Violence*, No. 4, Tampere Peace Research Institute, Finland, 1976.

Methodological problems in the study of violence from the standpoint of criminology

Department Director in
the All-Union Institute
for the Study of the Causes
of Crime and the Elaboration
of Preventive Measures,
Moscow

V. P. Shupilov

Many centuries ago scholars, meditating upon the mysteries of the universe, put forward the notion of 'social physics'. It was expected that this science would enable the behaviour, not only of society as a whole but of each individual, to be appraised and predicted with mathematical precision. Centuries went by before it became clear that the processes at work in society are governed by their own laws, which can be discovered only if a special approach and a special methodology are applied.

In order to study complex social phenomena one must have a particular interest in methodological problems, for methodology and method are the tools by means of which the scientific problems of knowledge can be solved. The modern scientist is equipped with the method of dialectical materialism, which seeks to discover the objective laws of social life.

When a criminologist, who is investigating criminality and its causes in order to prevent it, begins to study violence, he finds that he is confronted with a phenomenon much broader and more complex than is the subject of his immediate scientific concern: criminality—that is, all acts recognized as socially dangerous and criminally punishable in a given society at a given time.

The use of force is the characteristic mark of the particular categories of crimes that, in criminology, are classed as crimes of violence. Crimes of this sort include murder, rape and the infliction of bodily injury, which are distinct from crimes committed out of negligence or offences against property (theft, misappropriation, embezzlement) and so forth, but the use of force is characteristic of violence in general.

The use of force may be either direct or indirect. It should be noted that in legal science (criminal law) considerable attention is paid to the study of the indirect use of force. However, as in the case of crimes of violence, it would be wrong to restrict the definition of violence to the use of force. From the methodological angle, this would mean that we would merely describe the phenomenon formally and overlook its real substance, its material and determinant basis. This is obvious to a criminologist who studies the social laws that affect the occurrence of criminal behaviour.

In sociological literature, violence is regarded as a form and, at the same time, a means of people's social activity. It is observed that violence serves the practical interests of social groups.[1]

The social content, the political purport and the aims of violence are directly dependent on the social relations it reflects and defends. The study of the history, conditions and forms of the revolutionary and liberating process has shown that violence may be an important weapon in the struggle against aggression and enslavement and thereby serve the interests of the progressive development of society[2]. At the same time, violence may also be of a markedly destructive character. For the criminologist this destructive character of violence is principally reflected in violent crime.

In elaborating methodological approaches to the study of criminality, the criminologist endeavours to clarify the relation between the social and the individual aspects, between cause and effect, and between the single, the particular and the general.

It is always difficult to distinguish the common element —to identify the quality that is unchanged in a given subject. In the analysis of social violence, this stable, constantly present quality must be socially significant. A world war and an ordinary act of street vandalism, a social revolution and a racial conflict are particular instances of the general notion of violence. Since the notion of social violence may embrace phenomena the form, magnitude, significance and aim of which differ widely, it is important to distinguish criminal offences from other forms of social violence. In works on the subject it is frequently assumed that all forms of violence can be put under a single head as phenomena of the same order.[3]

Distinguishing criminal offences from other kinds of social violence means differentiating between violence as a weapon of class and political struggle, and acts of violence as an expression of the personal aspirations of the individual pursuing his own personal aims and attempting, through crime, to overcome the contradictions between the public interest and his personal interest.

The class struggle runs through the entire history of the development of society, right from the break-up of the primitive community:

Freeman and slave, patrician and plebeian, landowner and peasant, foreman and apprentice, in short, the oppressor and the oppressed, were constantly in a situation of mutual antagonism and carried on a relentless struggle, whether covertly or overtly, always ending in the revolutionary reorganization of the entire social edifice or in the total destruction of the warring classes.[4]

In order words, the efforts of classes and social groups to further their interests give rise to a struggle which finds expression in three main forms: economic, political and ideological. Violence is one of the means by which this struggle is carried on; in many cases it is 'the weapon which a social movement uses to pave the way for itself and shatter fossilized, lifeless political forms'.[5]

We do not, of course, intend to discuss the role of violence when resorted to as part of a political struggle. This is not a matter for the criminologist.

In no society known to us have criminals formed a particular class or even an isolated social group. Members of all the social strata of the population are, to a greater or lesser extent, liable to turn to crime.[6]

Crimes are committed by people in an attempt to further their personal interests. These interests may lie in any number of directions. They do not always correspond to an endeavour to attain what in criminology has come to be called a rational aim. Acts of violence sometimes appear in a sense to have been committed 'for their own sake', since they cannot be ascribed to such motives as profit, vengeance, and the like. An irrational motive for acts of violence may be due to nervous strain or a crisis, and it may point to deep inner conflicts in the development of the personality of such offenders.[7]

Thus criminality differs from other forms of social violence in the nature of the interests pursued, the social content and the political objective. It is important to take account of these differences when elaborating methodological approaches to the study of the causes of violence.

The category of causality reflects one of the most general and fundamental laws of the objective world. This law extends to all phenomena and processes of nature and society, including those that are of a stochastic nature and respond to the laws of statistical processes.

In modern science causality is understood as a form of relation in which an event A gives rise to an event B. When causality is defined in greater detail, reference is usually made to such elementary attributes of causality as: (a) change (emergence) of objects and phenomena and (b) the sequence of events in time. None of these attributes depends necessarily on the knowing subject and his idea or sensual qualities. This accounts for the objectivity of the content of the notion of causality.[8] From the methodological standpoint, however, in the study of such social phenomena as violence and criminality, it is necessary to bear in mind the subjective aspect of the notion of causality and to take account of all the minute details of the dialectical correlation between the objective and the subjective.

In the theory of criminology it is rightly emphasized that causal dependence in social matters is, as a rule, multivalent. Each cause gives rise to a number of effects, and each effect is the result of the operation of several causes and conditions. This multivalence is manifested in each particular act of causation and in criminality as a whole. There is also a specific probability side to the multivalence of the causal connection. It lies in the fact that, where any condition is changed, even where the cause remains the same, a different result is obtained. This accounts for the differences in the behaviour of different people who are affected by the same cause.[9]

At the same time, it may be noted that the cause of a particular crime is an individual variant of a more general phenomenon. The cause of a social phenomenon (including such a social phenomenon as criminality) is the recurrent pattern; and in order to perceive that pattern we must turn from the individual to the social, since the fortuitous element in individual behaviour is subject to the law of the life of the whole. The laws governing the life of society are contingent upon the objective laws of social development.[10]

Some criminologists are sceptical as to the desirability

of studying the causes of criminality.[11] It seems to us, however, that the study of the causes of criminality not only helps to build up our theoretical knowledge of criminology, thereby assisting its quantitative growth, but also improves the quality of criminological science. Attempts to construct theories by manipulating facts without getting at the causal mechanism of phenomena inevitably end with the breakdown of such theories. The history of criminology offers a number of examples of this. At this stage in the development of science, however, there are also objective difficulties due to the fact that the mechanism of human behaviour has not yet been studied fully enough, either from the sociological or from the psychological angle, for the criminologist to be able to depend entirely on the models elaborated by these sciences.

It is, therefore, an important methodological principle to adopt a historical approach to criminality. One of the leading theorists in the methodology and methods of criminological research, V. V. Pankratov, rightly considers that the historical approach is not universal—indeed, no individual method is, for there is no such thing as a universal method. The historical approach establishes the historical character of the laws themselves and the fact that their emergence is related to the emergence of new phenomena and the disappearance of phenomena the existence of which these laws express.[12]

The historical approach is even more important when one is studying socio-political violence, for the latter is essentially a socio-historical category arising at a particular stage in historical development, which is associated with the splitting of society into antagonistic classes and the formation of the state with its inherent attributes of power: army, police and laws. The nature of violence cannot be correctly understood unless we adopt the historical approach.

The causes of a specific act performed by an individual are to be found in all the individual's character traits, in which there may be no direct perception of the general social background of a particular form of violence. One of the most important issues in criminology is the relationship between the individual and the social, and between the personality and the social environment.

We know that man is to a certain extent a bio-social being: social because he has a social nature and biological because the living human organism is the vehicle of this nature. Every person has a definite individuality. A person's individuality finds expression in natural inclinations and mental properties. The entire content of the consciousness—views, judgements and opinions—has an individual colouring; and these, even when shared by different people, always have a certain personal element. The personality is man viewed not only from the standpoint of his general properties and traits, but also from the angle of his specific individual social, spiritual and physical qualities.[13]

If we are to comprehend the various forms of behaviour of the personality, including both law-abiding and law-breaking behaviour, the personality must be described systematically. This means more than enumerating the individual features and attributes of the personality. It means isolating a certain elementary structural unit, which, with one variation or another, can be observed at all levels of activity. If a fragmentary approach is adopted and if the principle of systematization is not observed, attempts will be made to derive the causes underlying criminal behaviour solely from the psycho-physiological properties of the individual, or else a one-sided sociological view will be taken, so that it is forgotten that the sociologist is chiefly concerned with the most general, commonly encountered and constant features of the personality acquired in the socialization process. As emphasized in works on sociology, the personality interests the sociologist not as an individuality, but as a depersonalized personality and as a social type.[14]

If the 'behaviour' of classes, nations and social groups is socially determined, which in our view is of direct relevance to the study of the causes of social and political violence, then, when we are trying to understand the behaviour of a particular human individual we must take into account the extremely complex interaction between the social and the biological.[15] In defining this interaction, a monistic conception of man, which rejects the opposition of the biological and the social in human development, is of great importance.

The originators of the monistic approach maintained that the very nature of man is the product of history and that, in changing nature, which is outside him, man at the same time changes his own nature. These ideas are borne out by the way in which modern science is developing. A fair amount of information has been amassed that indicates that the development of the human organism is affected by the social conditions of man's existence.[16]

At the same time, the formation of those qualities of man that are defined as social does not take place outside the human organism or apart from the process of man's biological development, but in the actual course of this process. When we go into the question of the indirect effect that the biological and the social exert upon each other, we abandon the dualistic approach to the study of man, and we begin to see the process of man's development as a single process within which all the various human properties are formed and developed.[17]

To elaborate an integral, logically connected and coherent conception of the causes of violent behaviour by individuals, we must first define the relationship between the social and the biological correctly.

In our search for the causal connection between acts of social and political violence, the subjective personality factor should be taken into account, though here the investigator comes up against what we consider a more complex problem, that of the relation between general, particular and isolated causes in the process of historical development.

A basic stage in social development, such as the transition from feudalism to capitalism, is governed by objective laws that are independent of human will and consciousness. But we cannot correctly understand specific historical events and instances of social and political violence unless we take the part played by personality into account. As Marx points out in a letter to L. Kugelmann:

History would be of a very mystical character if 'chance occurrences' played no part in it. These chance occurrences are certainly part and parcel of the general course of development, being counterbalanced by other such occurrences. But acceleration and deceleration depend to a great extent on these 'chance occurrences', which include such a 'random' factor as the character of the people originating a movement.[18]

The study of acts of social and political violence will also be of a mystical character if the personality factor is totally disregarded.

The development and improvement of methods of investigating the personality of those who commit individual acts of violence raise the problem of the classification of the personality according to type—a problem often dealt with in criminological works.[19]

In criminology the notion of personality type is understood as meaning all the important traits of character that are manifested in relation to social phenomena and are assimilated by man from the social environment.

The notion of the social environment covers all the objective conditions that go to make man what he is. The social environment is created by individuals themselves, but under certain conditions that are independent of their will. It cannot be regarded as existing apart from individuals. At the same time, it provides the objective conditions for their activity.

Criminologists cannot classify individuals alone. An attempt to classify only factors in the individual's environment will also be of little use. One solution might be to 'synthesize' the individual and his conditions, to try to distinguish interacting 'individual/environment' systems and to classify such systems.

A particular environment produces a particular type of individual and, as a rule, a particular type of personality, when selecting what he will do, gets into certain situations only, since that type of personality of itself constitutes the chief element in such situations. In other words, the individual limits the diversity of the effects of the environment on him, and is formed by these 'selected' influences. The process is objective and dialectical. It gives rise to a particular 'individual/environment' system.[20]

The complex of enduring inner motives and purposes of action and the form taken by the wishes and aspirations of the individual under the influence of education and adaptation to the social and ecological environment together form what we call character. When the criminologist is dealing with traits that are of definite significance in criminological classification, such as acquisitiveness, domination and egocentrism, or their opposites, he works on the assumption that people are not made like that but become so as a result of some modifying factor and because they have adapted to the conditions imposed by various important social and psychological requirements.

There is nothing new in the assertion that everyone has more or less the same basic social and psychological requirements and motives for action. It has frequently been pointed out that the individual needs to be sure of social stability and an assured standard of living, emotional contact with others, some sort of new experience, recognition, self-fulfilment and so forth.

By means of its socializing institutions, society endeavours to form the character of individuals and encourage certain motives and values so as to harmonize, as far as possible, with the living conditions of the social group to which the individual belongs. And criminological classification certainly does not sidestep the question of what means, depending on the values accepted in society, are the most effective in meeting the social and psychological requirements of the individual.

In this aspect of the matter, classification may rightly be said to serve as a connecting link between theory and practice.

While drawing attention to the importance of taking account of social and psychological requirements when analysing the violent behaviour of individuals, we would at the same time emphasize that, when analysing social and political violence, what is termed historical or social necessity should be taken into account. It is an important principle that:

If this man is removed, there will be a demand for someone to replace him, and such a person will be found. He may be more or less successful, but in time he will be found. It was a mere chance that Napoleon, who was a Corsican, was the military dictator who was needed by the French Republic, exhausted as it was by war. But had there been no Napoleon, his part would have been played by someone else. The proof of this is the fact that, whenever such a man has been needed, he has been found, cases in point being Caesar, Augustus, Cromwell and so on.[21]

In one of his articles on the moral basis of science,[22] the philosopher A. V. Gulyga quotes the following two remarks from the play *The Life of Galileo*, by Bertolt Brecht: 'ANDREA: It is an unhappy country in which there are no heroes. GALILEO: No, it is an unhappy country that needs heroes.' Commenting on these remarks, Gulyga observes that man is obliged to conduct himself morally, but 'unhappy' (unstable, liable to disintegrate) is that 'country' (social system, society as a whole) where moral conduct demands heroism. One can and must count on the 'heroism' (intelligence, conscience, fortitude) of man (scientist, politician, etc.) but mankind will only be able to sleep secure when a system of social relations has been established that rules out the catastrophic development of events.

Notes

1. V. V. Denisov, *Sociologija nasilija* [Sociology of Violence], p. 10, Moscow, Izdatel'stvo Političeskoj Literatury, 1975.
2. Ibid., p. 11.
3. *Violence in America. Historical and Comparative Perspectives. The Complete Official Report to the National Commission on the Causes and Prevention of Violence*, p. xvii, The White House, The New American Library, 1969.
4. K. Marx and F. Engels, *Sŏcinenija* [Collected Works], Vol. 4, p. 424. (Russian edition.)
5. Ibid., Vol. 20, p. 189.
6. D. Hardman, 'Historical Perspectives of Gang Research', *Journal of Research in Crime and Delinquency* (Ann Arbor, Mich.), Vol. 4, No. 1, 1967, p. 15.
7. V. N. Kudryavtsev, *Pričiny pravonarušenij* [Causes of law-breaking], p. 208, Moscow, Izdatel'stvo Nauka, 1976.
8. I. Z. Naletov, *Pričinnost' i teorija poznanija* [Causality and Theory of Knowledge], p. 11. Moscow, Mysl, 1975.
9. N. V. Kudryavtsev, *Pričinnost' v kriminologii* [Causality in Criminology], p. 9, Moscow, Juridičeskaja literatura, 1968.
10. V. V. Pankratov, *Metodologija i metodika kriminologičeskih issledovanij* [Methodology and Methods of Criminal Research], p. 29, Moscow, Juridičeskaja literatura, 1972.
11. N. Morris and J. Hawkins, *The Honest Politician's Guide to Crime Control*, p. 30, Chicago, 1970.
12. Pankratov, op. cit., p. 19.
13. *Osnovy Marksistsko-leninskoj filosofii* [Fundamentals of Marxist-Leninist Philosophy], p. 438. Moscow, Izdatel'stvo političeskoj literatury, 1975.
14. E. V. Sokolov, *Kul'tura i ličnost'.* [Culture and Personality], p. 170, Leningrad, Nauka, 1972.
15. P. N. Fedoseev, 'Problema social'nogo i biologičeskogo v filosofii i sociologii' [The Problem of the Social and the Biological in Philosophy and Sociology], *Voprosy filosofii* (Moscow), No. 3, p. 70, 1976.
16. B. F. Lomov, 'Sootnosenie social'nogo i biologičeskogo kak metodologiceskaja problema psihologgi' [Relationship of the Social to the Biological as a Methodological Problem of Psychology], *Voprosy filosofii* (Moscow), No. 4, 1976, p. 84.
17. Ibid.
18. Marx and Engels, op. cit., Vol. 33, p. 175.
19. *Ličnost' prestupnika* [The Personality of the Criminal], pp. 46–57, Moscow, Juridičeskaja literatura, 1975.
20. Pankratov, op. cit., p. 19.
21. Marx and Engels, op. cit., Vol. 39, pp. 175–6.
22. A. V. Gulyga, 'Možet li nauka byt' beznravstvennoj?' [Can Science be Immoral?], *Priroda* (Moscow), No. 12, 1975, p. 47.

The study of violence from the perspective of social defence

Deputy Editor,
Panstwo i Prawo, Warsaw

Krzysztof Poklewski-Koziell

In her work *On Violence* Hannah Arendt[1] recalls the comment of Georges Sorel sixty years ago: 'The problems of violence are still very obscure.' She adds that his finding remains as true today as it was then. Whether she is right of not, her remark emphasizes the impressive scope of the very notion of violence, and the complexity of a number of its aspects, with which many of the illustrious names in modern philosophy, from Engels and Bergson to Sartre, have tried to deal. The remark can also be seen as a challenge to all those interested in the matter.

Study of this problem now falls under the competence of various specialties, which means that the borderlines must be very carefully drawn, if somewhat flexible none the less.

With few exceptions, violence is a phenomenon that is harmful to society, and it therefore provokes a defensive reaction. Generally, this reaction takes the form of penal sanctions provided for in criminal law. It is thus impossible to investigate how the problems of the causes of violence and research in this field can be approached from the perspective of social defence, without explaining the general viewpoint of this theory regarding crime and its perpetrators.[2]

While social defence, like other theories in the field, aims at ensuring society of the best possible protection against crime, it provides for a new conception of means adapted to this end. Social defence is a reaction against various doctrinal excesses, such as, for example, the purely legal conception, according to which a crime is an act freely decided by an individual endowed with reason and free will or, on the other hand, demands tending to abolish classical penal law, including the notions of delinquency and punishment.

Since the First Congress on Social Defence in San Remo in 1947 and the foundation, in 1949, of the International

Society, which has organized seven congresses and has its own journal (*Les cahiers de défense sociale*), the principal goal has been to elaborate and implement a coherent system of criminal policy, based on scientific research and representing humane tendencies:

As a cohesive system, it should be able to avoid any summary legislation that might be adopted in the wake of sensational events.

Drawing its inspiration from the results of scientific investigation, it seeks out the aid of other specialties and encourages co-operation among jurists and sociologists, criminologists and psychologists, judges and other experts.

As a humane system, it contributes to the humanization of penal law and all anticrime activities; it demands that the personality of the offender be taken into consideration, as well as his chances for reintegration into the community. The most important real steps forward do not consist in the signing of treaties, such as those concerning human rights (so frequently violated), but in enabling every individual to make himself heard, whatever his quality: political or sexual dissident, member of a racial minority, prostitute or prisoner serving a life-term. Social defence adjusts the rules of its system to this reality.

The notion of criminal policy mentioned above creates a link between the doctrinal side of social defence and its practical aspect. The latter was implemented in 1948, when a social-defence section was organized within the United Nations Secretariat. It is obvious that no organ of the United Nations can adopt specific doctrinal principles. This is also clearly implied in the contents of the *International Review of Criminal Policy*, published by this section, and by the labours of the conferences of the United Nations on the prevention of crime and the treatment of offenders.

The difference between social defence as a doctrine and as a criminal policy dealing directly with concrete problems is also evident in the discussions of the International Society for Social Defence. I have in mind here the round table on criminal policy[3] (Paris, 22–23 March 1974), which defined criminal policy as both 'a science of observation' and 'an art and a strategy'. The first conception implies a broad investigation of the situation in a particular country, with an approach going beyond that of comparative law. The whole structure of the state must be studied in depth—not just its laws, but also its police, prosecutors' offices, courts and penal system. Scientific research should show how these various mechanisms really operate. The second conception depends on the facts; once they are established and scientifically analysed, it then becomes necessary to act normatively and to take practical measures. It is clear that both aspects of criminal policy imply an analysis of the causes of criminality and the taking of a stand on it.

In this chapter violence is considered to be included in the concept of criminality, and we suppose that the attitude adopted towards offences generally results in a criminal policy concerning violence as well. Furthermore, I consider that any trend in criminal policy accepting some of the fundamental principles of social defence as defined above can be assimilated into the field, thereby permitting me to examine various research projects and debates from the perspective of social defence, even though they may not fit the theory in its narrowest definition.

F. H. McClintock,[4] for example, distinguishes the following classes of violence: I, Instrumental violence, (1) crimes against property (theft, etc.), (2) sexual violence (rape, etc.), (3) resisting arrest; II, interpersonal violence; III, destructive and spectacular violence (at local, national and international levels); IV, ideological and political violence (at local, national and international levels); V, disturbances of public order. The main thing is to point out the differences between instrumental violence and the other sorts, especially the impulsive forms.

It can hardly be claimed that social defence has developed a particular programme of research into the causes of violence. But when social defence insists, for example, on the general necessity of breaking the circuit of degradation, that is, the hereditary transmission of poverty, social alienation and violence, it can be logically deduced that social defence classifies unfavourable family environment among the causes of youthful violence. In any case, social defence is interested in violence as an offence neither of a political nor ideological character, although the border between what is political and what falls under common law is often blurred. Some think that various common forms of violence are manifestations of revolt against society. It is interesting to note that they are frequently probably right.

The approach to criminality in general is doubtlesly

conclusive for approaches to the causes of violence. It is therefore especially interesting to read in this respect the foreword to the third edition (1975) of Jean Pinatel's *Criminologie*,[5] a basic work that sheds some light on the significant development of attitudes about criminology:

The third edition of this book comes out at a decisive moment in the history of criminology. For the last few years, in fact, the challenge of criminality has been constantly worrisome, while prison mutinies are proof of the difficulties that are the rule in the domain of social reaction. When events develop in this manner, society must be secreting powerful 'criminalogenic' stimuli that cause latent and hesitant tendencies to erupt in many subjects. Given these conditions, it is not astonishing that sociological criminology is experiencing a new leap forward. Henceforth, what counts is the study of social reaction.

Throughout his career, Pinatel has worked on the theory of the 'criminal personality'. I believe he is right today, as he was yesterday. It would be a mortal sin against the rationalization of criminal policy to overlook the strictly personal characteristics of the criminal. Still, the principal novelty that marks our period is the hold of the state and society on the life of the individual, the well-documented trend towards subordination of the individual's interests to the community's, at the same time as, paradoxically, human rights are expanding, as we have noted.

The question of causes is particularly difficult to isolate in research with specific social goals. As opposed to the blank slate with which chemists and physicists begin their labours, we want to discover the causes of a phenomenon that we judge *a priori*—in order to simplify—socially negative, thereby prejudicing to some extent the scientific objectivity of our effort. We are seeking means to help us defend society. Hence the risk of a confusion that would be unthinkable in other spheres. Measures aimed at preventing the very existence of a phenomenon or at reacting against it, especially through penal sanctions, can provoke further violence if they are badly applied.

Observation of public bodies in operation has a significant effect on attitudes regarding the use of violence. Let us say, to simplify, that the state does not set a good example for individuals.

Consequently, it is instructive to recall another aspect

of the development of criminology. In the United States, E. H. Sutherland[6] and his followers have sharply criticized traditional criminology because it has focused on the permanent prison population, unfortunate deviants and psychopaths, and overlooked individuals who commit offences no less harmful to society, but who are more difficult to identify. Thus the concept of 'white-collar criminals' was formed: criminals who are well adjusted to society, act like business men and cleverly avoid penal sanctions. But it would seem as if even more ought to be demanded of criminology: this field must take an interest in the acts of bureaucrats, leaders and states that would be considered crimes if they were perpetrated by ordinary citizens. It is not a question here of accusations explicitly made against certain authoritarian states before, during or shortly after the Second World War nor of an international jurisdiction involving the responsibility of states, but of everyday 'official' violence, tortures, oppression and persecution.

In this respect, Jacques Verin[7] has shed light on some extremely interesting criminological aspects of international immorality and the danger of promoting the belief that two distinct types of criteria exist for evaluating behaviour: one applicable to individuals and the other to states and groups. The 'law-making culture' becomes alien to the citizen and the law itself is devalued. The mass-media 'demythify' authority, show that the members of the international community practice the law of the jungle and lead the individual to ask himself: 'If they can achieve their goals using such means, why can't I?'

The citizen can be scandalized not only by what takes place on an international level, but also by the various expressions of public violence in his own country. Police brutality and the situation in prisons come particularly to mind in this connection. Sometimes, when circumstances favour a frank presentation of facts, people suddenly become aware of what penal institutions really are (in spite of the almost unanimous adherence of governments to the United Nations minimal rules). The 1972 report in the United States on the Attica Correctional Facility,[8] where thirty-nine people died, and the press campaign organized in France after the riots of 1973 are noteworthy, and attention must also be paid to the continual alarms raised by such organizations as Amnesty International. The British Association of Police

Officers armed its members with great reluctance, aware as it was that the mere presence of an instrument of violence risks in itself provoking violence.

The administration of penal justice naturally implies recourse to a number of coercive measures related to violence. But we are speaking now of violence as a cause of other violence. What must we think of draconian sentences handed down by courts applying a primitive conception of crime prevention, flying in the face of justice and any rational criminal policy? The expression 'institutional violence' is perfectly suited to violence in public activities, especially as used by S. C. Versele[9] to reveal the reaction mechanism it triggers or as used by Rosa del Olmo[10] in Venezuela, when she criticizes the traditional criminology of the Latin American countries and considers that individual acts of violence are the result of the institutional and structural violence that is the rule in this region.

To seek out the causes of a phenomenon, it is advisable to have a thorough knowledge of the phenomenon. When the man on the street is questioned about violence, he states that it has expanded considerably. But specialists are less positive, and it would seem that we urgently require statistical research.

J. Selosse[11] states that, while violent acts are tending to increase slightly in absolute figures, this increase is out-stripped to a greater or lesser extent in some countries by the rise in criminality in general and by the almost universal increase in crimes committed for motives of profit.

E. Harremeos[12], summing up the labours of the Conference of Directors of Criminological Research Institutes (Council of Europe),[13] came to some rather surprising conclusions. There is no formal proof of a worldwide growth in criminal violence in relation to the general rate of increase of crime. The concern displayed by public opinion with regard to the rise in violence may be partly attributable to the mass media's interpretations of spectacular events, like hold-ups, hijackings and the taking of hostages.[14] It is currently impossible to analyse scientifically the manifold and complex problems that are at the roots of violence (the role of instinct, the importance of environment, social conditioning, a feeling of frustration), owing to a lack of essential concrete data.

An entirely different attitude consists of not recognizing such complexity and such a multitude of factors to be at the roots of violence. The emphasis placed on the importance of the past and the influence of the imperialist social system in the study of the causes of violence, for example, are fundamental principles of criminology as practised in the German Democratic Republic. Let me quote a passage from the collective work, *Gewalt- und Sexualkriminalität* ('Violence and Sexual Criminality'): 'It can be established that the causes of violent acts and sexual aggressions are exclusively elements of the past and consequences of the imperialist social order.'[15]

The Social Defence Section of the United Nations Secretariat has been renamed the Crime Prevention and Criminal Justice Section, which should not affect the quality of its aims and efforts. I have always favoured the creation of a United Nations organ similar to the World Health Organization, which would serve as a data bank, an international documentation centre on criminality, and where experts would closely follow methods practised and would recommend the abolition of measures that had become obsolete or even criminogenic. It is known that too frequently progressive principles are proudly proclaimed, while reactionary policies are quietly applied. Thus, another important task of this impartial international organization would be to keep track of contradictions of this sort. The French journal *Études polémologiques*, besides listing the armed conflicts that are waged all over the world, catalogues 'minor domestic expressions (micro-conflicts) of world violence'. A social defence organization could follow this example and publish every year data on capital and life-imprisonment sentences meted out in every country, indicating the kind of crime involved.

I would be glad to make available to this specialized agency of the United Nations the results of in-depth research systematically conducted in the Criminology Department of the Institute of Legal Sciences of Warsaw.[16] The Journal *Archives of Criminology* provides, as well, empirical data on violent acts, showing their complexity and the multitude of possible causes. Frequent cases of psychopathy, various personality disorders, the influence of a family environment leading to criminality at an early age, alcoholism—these are just a few examples that prove the necessity of treating each case individually and of refusing presumptions prejudicial to the violent man. A second conclusion follows, about the inefficacity of very severe penalties. It is all the more difficult to make society accept this truth, in so far as public opinion generally calls for the law of 'an eye for an eye'. Extensive research carried out by Podgorecki[17] and his sociologist collaborators, based on questionnaires, points out particularly the following, relevant to the matter under consideration: Polish public opinion is indulgent towards alcoholism, but strict with regard to violent crime (though this frequently stems from alcohol abuse).

The Fifth United Nations Congress on the Prevention of Crime and the Treatment of Offenders (Geneva, September 1975)[18] expressed its concern about the problem of violence, of which it adopted a very broad definition. Drawing from the conclusions of the Universal Declaration of Human Rights and of various United Nations resolutions—for example, the 'anti-torture' General Assembly Resolution 3218(XXIX) of 1974—and of numerous documents of the four preceding congresses, the congress approached violence in diverse aspects. Section 3 of the report deals with the new role that the police and other institutions responsible for the respect of the law seem to give themselves; Section 4 concerns the treatment of offenders, particularly with regard to the set of minimum rules for the treatment of prisoners adopted by the United Nations. Document A–10158, 'The Analytical Summary by the Secretary General on Torture and Other Cruel, Inhuman or Degrading Treatment or Punishment in Relation to Detention and Imprisonment', was distributed to participants.

Let us mention here also General Assembly Resolution 3348(XXX) of 9 December 1975, two months after the congress, which sets out the detailed position of the United Nations on torture and other cruel or degrading treatments or punishments, with reference to a specific case: the protection of human rights in Chile. Of greatest interest to us is Section 1, which studies the development of the forms and dimensions of criminality, and the recommendations adopted in the spirit of social defence. In particular, it was stated (Doc. A/Conf. 56/3, pp. 27–88) that in recent years the problem of violence has become a matter of great concern. In the most developed countries and in certain developing countries, violent acts, including homicides, assaults, rapes and robberies, are increasing rapidly[19]. Information on the victims, a relative novelty in criminology, attests not only to an increase in the number of victims, but also to the cruel physical and mental suffering they undergo.[20] In many countries of the world, violence is creating a growing feeling of insecurity, which even surpasses the real risks and provokes great anxiety among the residents of some big cities.[21]

As a phenomenon, criminal violence has an extremely heterogeneous character. The relationship between increasing violence, on the one hand, and industrialization, urbanization and the resulting anomy, on the other, is rather complex and indirect. Industrialization and urbanization are not in themselves causes of violence. The rise in the incidence of violent behaviour should be considered in the more general context of the social problems facing contemporary societies in the different parts of the world.

Consequently, the above-mentioned congress adopted the following conclusions and recommendations (Section 1):

Violent behaviour in general should be seen in the broader context of social problems (unemployment, discrimination against different ethnic groups, barriers preventing attainment of a certain social status). Discussion has shown the lack of scientific information on this problem.

In many respects, violent behaviour seems to express a crisis of social policy and social infrastructure in the contemporary community. Individuals who see possibilities for progress and success steadily closing before them rationalize their violent reactions and aggressiveness through a personal perception of social justice. This leads to violent subcultures, particularly dangerous for the young.

Alcohol abuse and violence generally go together, especially among the young, who, under the influence of alcohol, frequently commit mischief and gratuitous vandalism.

The mass media can be a conditioning factor. Confronted with images of violence in its most brutal and sadistic forms, sensitivity is sometimes dulled, particularly among the very young, who are thus led to accept more easily resort to violence in a conflictual situation. The mass media should be used to teach the public to react in a socially acceptable manner when faced with these situations.

Research should be undertaken to determine if a relationship exists between development and violence (disintegration of traditional community rules and values, shortcomings of social and economic structures, etc.).

To what degree does violent behaviour reflect the failure of
national policy for youth? What real part do young
people play in the taking of decisions aimed at solving
major national problems?

The cultural organizations of the United Nations should
study proposals for the establishment of an international
convention providing minimum guidelines for the content
of mass media programmes aimed at children or adolescents.

At the end of this study of violence from the perspective of
social defence, I am seeking arguments to help me overcome
a feeling of powerlessness tied to doubts. Why expand
research on such an enigmatic topic? Is it necessary to
propose something other than a better society, economy or
family? To my mind, continuation of research would be
justified even if it only brought forth one result: to make
known the faults and oversimplifications evident in official
activities, in public declarations and in the general attitude
of those whom we call honest men. So long as judges set
themselves up as dispensers of retribution, so long as they
believe, along with the vast majority of public opinion, in
the deterrent value of punishment, so long as violence is
committed by police, prison guards and, in a sense, by legislators, we have a lot of work to do.

Notes

1. Hannah Arendt, *On Violence*, New York, Harcourt, Brace and World,
   1970.
2. M. Ancel, *La défense sociale nouvelle (Un mouvement de politique
   criminelle humaniste)*, 2nd ed., Paris, Éditions Cujas, 1966; and the
   same author's, *La Défense sociale, vingt-cinq ans après*, written for
   Panstwo i Prawo [State and Law], Warsaw, translated into Polish and
   published in No. 4, April 1976, pp. 47–56. Cf. K. Poklewski-Koziell,
   'Social Defence versus Traditional Attitudes towards Criminality',
   International Review of Criminal Policy (United Nations), No. 30,
   1972, pp. 22–7.
3. 'Table ronde internationale de politique criminelle', *Cahiers de Défense
   Sociale* (Paris), No. 2, 1975, pp. 77–97.
4. F. H. McClintock, *Crimes of Violence*, London, MacMillan, 1963;
   and 'Phenomenological and Contextual Analysis of Criminal Violence',
   in *Violence in Society. Collected Studies in Criminal Research*, Vol. XI,
   reports presented to the Tenth Conference of Directors of Criminological
   Research Institutes (1972), Council of Europe, 1974. Cf. also N. Christie,
   'Definition of Violent Behaviour' (XXIIIrd International Course in
   Criminology, Maracaibo, Venezuela, 28 July–3 August 1974). (Typescript.)
5. J. Pinatel and P. Bouzat, *Traité de droit pénal et de criminologie*, Vol. III,
   3rd ed., Paris, Librarie Dalloz, 1975.

6. J. Vérin, 'La criminologie et l'immoralité internationale', *Revue de science criminelle et de droit pénal comparé*, No. 3, July/September 1971, pp. 745–50.

7. J. Vérin, 'L'efficacité de la prévention générale', *Revue de science criminelle et de droit pénal comparé*, No. 4, October/December 1975, pp. 1061–8; and his *Banditisme et prison* (XVᵉ Congrès Français de Criminologie : Aspects modernes du banditisme), Clermont-Ferrand, October 1975. (Typescript.)

8. *Attica. The Official Report of the New York State Special Commission on Attica*, New York, Bantam Books, 1972.

9. S. C. Versele, *La violence institutionnelle* (XXIIIᵉ Cours international de criminologie, Maracaibo). (Typescript.)

10. Rosa del Olmo, 'Les limitations dans la prévention de la violence', *Revue de droit pénal et de criminologie*, No. 6, March 1975, pp. 511–27.

11. J. Selosse, 'Statistical Aspects of Violent Crime', in *Violence in Society*, op. cit.

12. E. Harremoes, 'L'activité du Comité européen pour les problèmes criminels du Conseil de l'Europe 1966-1974', *Revue de science criminelle et de droit pénal comparé* (Paris), No. 2, April–June 1975, pp. 327–42.

13. C. Debuyst, 'Etiology of Violence', in *Violence in Society*, op. cit.

14. O. N. Larsen (ed.), *Violence and the Mass Media*, New York, Evanston, London, Harper and Row, 1968.

15. *Gewalt- und Sexualkriminalität*, Berlin, Staatsverlag der Deutschen Demokratischen Republik, 1970, collective work, p. 23. Cf. E. Buchholz, *Sozialistische Kriminologie. Ihre Theoretische und Methodologische Grundlegung*, 2nd ed., Berlin, Staatsverlag der Deutschen Demokratischen Republik, 1971.

16. Dobrochna Wójcik, 'Mlodociani sprawcy rozboju' (English summary) [Young Adults Convicted of Robbery], *Archiwum Kryminologii* [Archives of Criminology] (Warsaw), Vol. V, 1972, pp. 151–90. 'Ostrihanska Zofia. Wielokrotni recydywisci' [Persisting Recidivists], *Panstwo i Prawo* [State and Law] (Warsaw), No. 8, August 1976.

17. A. Podgorecki, *Poglady spoleczenstwa polskiego na moralnosc i prawo* [Morality and Law as seen by Polish Society], Warsaw, Ksiazka i Wiedza, 1971.

18. Fifth United Nations Congress on the Prevention of Crime and Treatment of Offenders, Geneva, 1–12 September 1975, Section I. A/Conf.56/3.

19. On the increase of criminality in general, see R. Hacker, *Agression et violence dans le monde moderne*, Paris, Calmann-Lévy, 1972; Sandra J. Ball-Rokeach, 'The Legitimation of Violence', in J. F. Short and M. E. Wolfgang (eds.). *Collective Violence*, Chicago and New York, Aldine Atherton, 1972; F. Ferracuti, *Present State of Knowledge on Crimes of Violence* (paper presented at Commonwealth Caribbean Conference on the Treatment and Prevention of Crime and based in part on F. Ferracuti and G. Newmann, 'Assaultive Offences', Chap. 5 of D. Glaser (ed.), *Handbook of Criminology*, Rand McNally, Chicago, 1974); L. Dupont and T. Peters, 'L'image de marque du hold-up et ses implications pour une politique criminelle', *Revue de droit pénal et de criminologie* (Brussels), No. 2, November 1974, pp. 93–129; M. E. Wolfgang and L. Curtis, 'Criminal Violence: Patterns and Policy in Urban America', *International Review of Criminal Policy* (United Nations), No. 30, 1972, pp. 7–11; G. D. Newton and F. E. Zimring, *Firearms and Violence in American Life* (A Staff Report to the National Commission on the Causes and Prevention of Violence), 1970; D. Oehler, 'Criminal Violence and its Control in the Federal Republic of Germany', in E. M. Wise and G. O. W. Mueller (eds.), *Studies in Comparative Criminal Law*, Springfield, Ill., Charles C. Thomas, 1975.

20. H. C. Kelman, 'Violence without Moral Restraint: Reflections on the Dehumanization of Victims and Victimizers', *The Journal of Social Issues*, Vol. 29, No. 4, 1973, pp. 25–61.

21. L. Lenke, 'Criminal Policy and Public Opinion towards Crimes of Violence', in *Violence in Society*, op. cit.

Part three

Social and economic violence

In his study of the relationship between violence, on the one hand, and economic and social development on the other, Rasheeduddin Khan first recalls the major theories of the causes of violence, based on the legacy of Weber and Parsons. Then, within the framework of analysing liberation movements and, in a general way, social movements, he criticizes the abuses of the concept of 'modernization', which among other things hinders treating the interventionist policy of the United States as a factor of violence. He also draws up a typology of correlations among violence, politico-economic systems and the situational context, placing in this last category such specific processes as the different types of decolonization and the development of socialism. Finally, recapitulating the different approaches that link violence to change, or conflict (violent or non-violent) to change, he proposes in his own right a typology of the patterns of the use of force by states, linked to two complementary conceptual approaches: accumulation/distribution (the economic dimension) and bureaucracy/mobilization (the political dimension). With regard to violence in developing countries, he states clearly that neither development nor underdevelopment is a cause of violence in itself. Rather, it is 'maldevelopment' that results in the transformation of traditional feudal or tribal élites into new exploiting classes that reinforce inequalities. Quoting a recent empirical study that found that 'economic inequality begets political violence', he concludes that the major cause of violence in the developing countries of Asia, Africa and Latin America is rooted in the politico-economic system.

Pierre Spitz attacks the silent violence of famine caused by political and social structures. Men who work the land produce food and, theoretically, have a power of life and death over others. Yet it is they who die of hunger while no one starves to death in offices or cities. Basing his argument on the harsh analysis made by Necker of the scarcity experienced by France in 1775, Spitz demonstrates that any true analysis of famine manifests a bipolar pattern: haves/have-nots. This pattern is not only for revolutionaries. Without wanting to overturn the 'sacred right of property', as did Babeuf's later concept of agrarian reform, Necker thought in bipolar terms and sought a way of controlling the effects of dispossession by controlling the flow of grain in such a way as to avoid the violent reaction of the starving to this structural violence.

Moving to the international level, which is governed by the same bipolarity, Spitz examines Indian famines, which seem to be closely related to the moment when India began exporting grain. Similarly, the famines of 1926–31 in Upper Volta were related to the forced increase in production of non-food cash crops such as cotton, which destoyed rich and balanced peasant economies. He also presents material on the unsuccessful policies followed first by the League of Nations and later by the United Nations, and denounces the 'green revolution' of the 1960s for increasing the gap and dependence between developing and developed countries as well as between the exploited in both the countryside and cities in relation to dominant local élites. At the same time, he contends, in order to avoid revolts and to temper the extremes of famine, the rich countries distributed food aid, which slowly transforms peasantries into dependent populations. He demonstrates that, since 1955, for the most lucid economists, policies of 'foreign aid' to developing countries have been little more than elements of a policy of security, and he concludes by quoting Tolstoy: 'Here is the cause of the futility of the efforts made by those who, without changing their relationship with the people, wish to come to their aid by distributing the riches which have been taken from them.'

Pierre Mertens draws up an exhaustive indictment of the constant violence, usually ignored, that is inherent not only in the normal functioning of totalitarian and repressive regimes, but in the democratic ones themselves. Beyond the law (which is often violence side by side with noble but rarely applied principles), institutional violence encompasses all the abuses that permit us to define as 'violent' the legitimate counter-violence that can erupt either in democracies or in countries subject to the economic power of democracies. Mertens criticizes certain ideologies of 'non-violence', which, ignoring the causes of violence, condemn only its manifestations and can even equate Ho Chi Minh with Hitler—a 'humanistic' judgement that ended in the 'hysterical indifference' with which the bombings of Viet Nam were regarded.

Political violence, economic violence, intellectual and cultural violence—even when implemented in forms which imply no immediate physical violence—are necessarily accompanied by the organized repression of institutional counter-violence. Mertens devotes a part of his study to the law's evasions in the definition and treatment of political offenses, as well as to torture in democracies. In a world of flagrant social injustice, he concludes, perhaps no more violence is needed to abuse the status quo than to maintain it.

Finally, according to Elise Boulding, the pathologies of sex roles that lead to violence are inherent in societies structured by 12,000 years of the patriarchal tradition. The androgynous ideal, found in both Buddha and Jesus, is not about to culminate in a relationship between the sexes that is not dominated by male violence. It is the patriarchal structure of the family that constitutes the principal form of violence committed against women. It legitimizes the role of the woman as an object and, particularly, the female role as the object of violent behaviours, among them rape and prostitution. The author also studies women as agents of violence, whether indirect, through their role in the upbringing of violent males, or direct, by their enlistment in armies and repressive organizations. She reminds us that the lower rate of female criminality appears to correspond directly to women's lower status and that, with true equality, i.e. as many opportunities as men to commit offences, women would tend to commit as many crimes as men, albeit a smaller proportion of violent crimes. Recalling the objectives of the International Tribunal on Crimes Against Women during the International Woman's Year, she concludes that women need a transitional phase to share equally with men the roles of soldier and policeman—even at the price of an increase in female violence—so as to put an end to the patriarchal model.

Violence
and socio-economic development

Professor of Political Science
and member of the Indian
Council of Social Science
Research, New Delhi

Rasheeduddin Khan

Towards a definition of violence

Violence is a term that suffers from a surfeit of meanings. Even a cursory glance through the rapidly proliferating literature on the subject is enough to show the bewildering medley in which the concept is entrapped.

In a recent study violence has been defined as 'the exercise of physical force so as to inflict injury on or cause damage to persons or property; action or conduct characterized by this; treatment or usage tending to cause bodily injury or forcibly interfering with personal freedom'.[1] This is obviously the commonly assumed, personalized, criminological and lexicographical meaning of the term. Some indication of the modern usage of the term can be obtained by reflecting on the fact that 'violence is itself a symbol and a metaphor', as indicated in phrases like 'violent crime' (physical assault or threat thereeof), 'violence in the streets' (provocation, demonstration, police violence, partisan counter-violence, internal war), 'external war', 'violence to oneself' (suicide, alcoholism, drug addiction, etc.), 'violence at the wheel' (killing by vehicular accident), 'violence in the media' (a syndrome: news or fiction of violence stimulating further violence), 'non-violent violence' (the paradox that personality may be destroyed by indirect methods as much as by physical brutality), 'social violence' (or what Herbert Marcuse and R. D. Laing call 'repressive toleration').[2] Then there is a lot of discussion and inquiry these days about 'violence in groups', 'violence in mobs,' and 'violence in subcultures' as part of the macro-study of 'violence in society'. But in each case, as Mackenzie bemoans, 'one looks uncertainly for an operational definition'.[3]

Social psychologists, like Neil Smelser in his *Theory of*

Collective Behaviour,[4] regard violent behaviour as a 'pathological deviation' that generates balancing forces to maintain the structural-functional equilibrium in society. Political sociologists, like Ted Robert Gurr,[5] on the other hand, maintain that 'political violence' is a 'normal' phenomenon and that, as part of the 'self-adjusting conflict' situation, it contributes to the eventual maintenance of societal equilibrium.

A major focus on violence today is on the aspect of it that is called 'political violence'. The causal linkage between politics, power and violence is self-evident. This is what C. Wright Mills underlines when he propounds succinctly: 'All politics is struggle for power, the ultimate kind of power is violence.'[6] And this is what Mao means in his oft-quoted aphorism that political power 'flows out of the barrel of a gun'. Karl Marx maintained that the state is an instrument of oppression in the hands of the ruling class, and Max Weber also postulated that violence is a 'means specific' to the state, and that the state alone possesses the 'exclusive source of the right to use violence'.[7]

Typology of violence

While differentiating between violence used by the state or its agents (police, military, bureaucracy, etc.), which Fred H. von der Mehden calls 'establishment violence' (i.e. use of violence as a deterrence to deviant behaviour of the citizens for the maintenance of domestic tranquillity),[8] and violence used by the masses and the classes, Gurr suggests a three-tier typology for the latter: (a) turmoil, a relatively spontaneous, unorganized political violence with substantial popular participation including violent political strikes, riots, political clashes, demonstrations, localized rebellions: (b) conspiracy, a highly organized political violence with limited participation, including organized political assassination, small-scale terrorism, small-scale guerrilla wars, *coups d'état*, mutinies, etc.; and (c) internal war, a highly organized political violence with widespread popular participation, designed to overthrow a regime or dissolve the state, and accompanied by extensive violence, including large-scale terrorism and guerrilla wars and revolutions.[9]

However, Johan Galtung is the only known social scientist who provides systematic and multidimensional typologies of violence. His first typology is represented in the following diagram.[10]

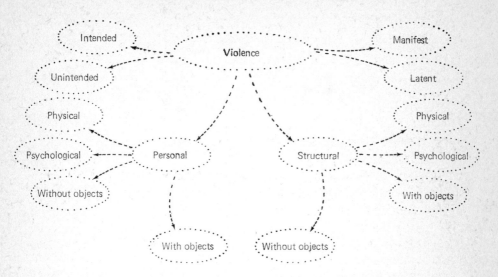

Galtung's first systematic and multidimensional typology.

His second typology appears on page 89 of this book.[11]

Galtung identifies 'inequality', particularly inequality 'in the distribution of power', as the 'general formula behind structural violence'.[12] The study of social structure and, beyond that, social stratification, is necessary in order to comprehend structural violence. In this connection 'most fundamental are the ideas of actor, system, structure, rank and level'.[13] Galtung suggests that examples of structural violence (which can be traced back to personal violence in their prehistory) are an exploitative inegalitarian caste system or a race society.[14]

Theories of the aetiology of violence[15]

This brings us to the question of the aetiology of violence—that is, the causality pattern of the origins and consequences of violence. The relevance of this, particularly in structural violence, is all too apparent. In recent years, a whole school of 'conflict theorists' has emerged, who draw their classical inspiration, directly or obliquely, from the writings of Marx and Engels on the one hand, and Weber and Parsons on the other.

There are five well-known theories of the aetiology of violence that need to be mentioned in this connection:

1. The frustration-anger-aggression theory, developed with empirical evidence by John Dollard.[16]
2. The concept of relative deprivation, by Gurr.[17]
3. The J-curve principle, of Davies.[18]
4. The Feierabends-Nesvold theory of social change and systematic frustration.[19]
5. The theory of modernization causing violence in transitional societies, by Samuel Huntington.[20]

For our purpose, a bare statement of the major postulates of the five theories will be sufficient, followed by a brief critique of the major theoretical assumptions.

1. Dollard[21] maintains that the primary source of the human capacity for violence appears to be the frustration-aggression mechanism. The anger induced by frustration is a motivating force that disposes man to aggression.

2. Relative deprivation is defined by Gurr as 'a perceived discrepancy between men's value expectations and their value capabilities.[22] Value expectations are the goods and conditions of life to which people believe they are rightfully entitled. Value capabilities are the goods and conditions they think they are capable of attaining and maintaining, given the social means available to them. Deprivation-induced discontent is a general spur to action. The aetiology may have the following pattern: the primary causal sequence in political violence is, first, the development of discontent, second, the politicization of that discontent, and finally, its expression in violent action against political objects and actors.

3. Davies attributes a revolutionary outbreak to the frustration that results from a short-term decline in achievement following a long-term increase that generated expectations about continuing increase. He holds that, contrary to Marxian expectations, or even the assumptions of Alexis de Tocqueville and others, revolutions do not occur during periods of prolonged, abject or worsening situations of social deprivation. On the contrary, revolutions occur during periods of relative prosperity and improvement. Thus, Davies postulates

a J-curve where the discrepancy between 'achievement' and 'expectations' becomes intolerable.

4. Feierabends and Nesvold have developed the hypothesis of 'systematic frustration', which, they argue, is applicable to any analysis of aggregate, violent political behaviour within social systems. 'Systematic frustration' is defined as frustration collectively experienced within societies. As an extension of the basic hypothesis of frustration-aggression, they advance four general hypotheses for empirical investigation: (a) systematic frustration at any given time is a function of the discrepancy between present social aspirations and expectations on the one hand, and social achievements on the other; (b) present estimates (i.e. expectations of future frustrations or satisfaction) determine the level of present frustrations or satisfaction; (c) uncertainties in social expectations (i.e. whether the future will bring disaster or salvation) in themselves increase the sense of systematic frustration; (d) conflicting aspirations and conflicting expectations provide another source of systematic frustration.

5. Huntington argues that the causes of violence and instability in the emerging countries of Asia, Africa and Latin America are to be found in the lag between the development of viable political institutions and the processes of social and economic change. Accepting the three-tier paradigm of societies as developed by the structural functionalists—traditional, transitional and modern—Huntington argues that the first and the last are less prone to political violence and instability, and the transitional societies are the most prone. Revolutionary upheavals, military coups, insurrections, guerrilla warfare and assassinations are a common feature of transitional societies. Huntington rejects the 'poverty thesis', according to which it is not poverty and backwardness but the desire to become rich and modern that breeds violence and instability.[23] He recalls that, in modernizing countries, violence, unrest and extremism are found, more often than not, in the wealthier parts of the country and society rather than in the poorer. He states that some measure of economic growth is necessary to make instability possible.[24] Not far from the ideas of Feierabends and Gurr, Huntington asserts that social mobilization is much more destabilizing than economic development. Urbanization, literacy, education and the mass media

expose the traditional man to new possibilities of satisfaction. However, the ability of a transitional society to satisfy these new aspirations increases much more slowly; consequently a gap or lag develops between aspirations and expectations. This gap generates social frustration and dissatisfaction, which lead to demands on government and the expansion of political mobilization and participation to enforce those demands. The lack of adequate political institutions makes it difficult, if not impossible, for the demands to be expressed through legitimate channels and to be moderated and aggregated within the political system. Hence, the sharp increase in political participation leads to political instability and violence.

A critique of the theories of the aetiology of violence

By way of a general and specific critique of these five theories, the following comments may be made.

All the theories presume a normative situation that implies a 'stable political system' at each level of socio-economic development, i.e. in the three-tier paradigm: traditional, transitional and modern. Further, a higher premium is attached to 'political stability' than to 'change' (social and economic). Regarding the phenomenon of 'change', these theorists suggest that 'change' without upsetting the 'system' is 'legitimate', 'normal' and 'functional'; but 'change' involving a radical recasting of socio-economic relations and a shift in the locus of power and, more particularly, the modalities of such a change, are conceived as 'pejorative', 'non-legitimate', 'abnormal' and 'dysfunctional'.

The epistemological roots and heuristic parameters of these theories are not difficult to identify as ethnocentric. The entire perspective of the global phenomenon, the framework of the preferred future, the perception of ends and goals, and the stages of change and its realization, are set by value premises of the North Atlantic community.

Even the model of 'modernization' or 'political development' is a stereotype patterned on the historical experience of the West, with minor accretions and modifications to lend to an impression of universal validity. The term 'Westernization', which was earlier used rather unabashedly, has now been discarded. Yet, scrutinized more closely, 'modernization' appears to be the same old wine of 'Westernization' offered in a new bottle of contemporary jargon. Indeed, the concept of 'modernization' has been proposed by the structural functionalists, no less than by the behaviourists and even the post-behaviourists, as an alternative to what the Marxists call 'revolution'.

In these five theories there is no recognition of the basic global process, the process of decolonization, which permeates the life, society, economy and politics of the bulk of contemporary states and territories. More than 100 of the Member States of the United Nations today, accounting for more than two-thirds of mankind, are today faced with this stupendous challenge of creating a new identity out of the wreckage of the defunct colonial system. But this present and urgent reality is almost totally ignored in the esoteric wisdom of model-builders of social change, except for an oblique or indirect reference. Naturally, therefore, the nature, role and impact of the liberation movements remain at best relegated to the background. The role of ideology in mobilizing, articulating and activating people for change, upsurge and revolt is also underplayed, or mentioned in a pejorative way.

The frustration-anger-aggression theory and the concept of relative deprivation are more applicable to individuals, compact groups and subsegments than to numerically large segments or heterogeneous groups, and they are even less applicable to a society as a collectivity. These theories and concepts appear more as an extension of individual psychology to social levels, assuming a constancy of stimuli and response in two otherwise distinct categories, i.e. the individual as a unit and society as a collectivity.

The J-curve principle of Davies is valid in certain specific socio-political situations, but it seems wanting in universal applicability. Cross-national case studies of revolutions would refute some of its basic premises. It does help to explain the occurrence of *coups d'état*, particularly in a Latin American context, but is inadequate in explaining other revolutionary outbreaks.

The Feierabends-Nesvold theory and Huntington's 'gap' hypothesis are partially valid. 'Systematic frustration' is difficult to measure. Even if it can be gauged in quantitative terms, it is hard to work out a plausible calculus for establishing the nodal point where 'quantities' get transformed into a new 'quality'. In its generality it is ambiguous, and in its specificity it is neatly academic—a sort of 'laboratory formula' that cannot be tested at the 'production level'. Huntington's hypothesis overemphasizes violence in what he calls transitional societies, and overlooks the types of violence—both direct and structural—that are endemic in tribal and feudal societies on the one hand, and in developed industrialized ('modern') society on the other. The plural nature of modernized societies, particularly in federal polities with multi-ethnic and multi-strata complexities, gives rise to a different set of intergroup tensions, intergroup conflict and intergroup violence. The increase and recrudescence of student and youth, interracial and interdenominational violence modifies, if it does not refute, the 'universalist' assumptions of Huntington's thesis.

Patterns of structural violence

Economic and political systems, situational contexts and violence: a correlation

The division of the world into what may be called geographical dichotomies, i.e. either North and South in terms of economic-industrial-technological levels of development, or East and West in terms of ideological allegiances and military-economic combinations, is too broad, too loose and too undifferentiated, apart from the fact that it is unidimensional in approach.

It is territorial sovereignty (i.e. state, nation-state or multi-national state, as the case may be) that is, in terms of its multidimensional cohesion, socio-economic distinctiveness and political identity, and as a definite analytical unit of global problems, the most convenient, and an all-inclusive, category of study. This is so partly because of the nature and exercise of power and the sanction to back the exercise of that power by the state on citizens, groups, classes and masses, and partly because of the recognition accorded to states in international law, in the international economy, in international transactions and in a wide variety of regional, hemispheric and global activities in our modern, highly interdependent world. Therefore it will be more meaningful and analytically convenient to examine societal patterns also in terms of territorially determined political and economic systems.

Accepting the state (or territorial sovereignty) as a unit, we can relate societal patterns to two determining systems, i.e. a political system and an economic system, and to dominant situational contexts in which a country or people finds itself. Let us therefore define the three terms, economic system, political system and situational context, and then suggest a typology of violence correlating these three parameters.

The economic system can be characterized by at least six aspects: basic nature of the economy (subsistence, barter, money or credit); employment of the predominant part of the population in the primary, secondary or tertiary sector of production; the nature of production relations (tribal, feudal, capitalist-industrial, socialist-industrial); the aggregate GNP and per capita income; the communication pattern for goods and persons; and the stage of maturity in one of the three decisive economic-cum-technological revolutions, viz. the urban revolution, the industrial revolution or the automation revolution.[25] On these bases of socio-economic development, we might identify four types of economic systems:

Primitive: subsistence economy, tribal society, low technology, on the verge of urban revolution.

Traditional: barter economy, feudal society, intermediate technology, on the verge of industrial revolution.

Modern (capitalist): money-cum-credit economy, competitive, profit-oriented entrepreneurial post-industrial society, multinational-dominated global commercial transactions, undergoing the automation revolution.

Modern (socialist): money-cum-credit economy, co-operative-cum-centrally planned industrial society, on the verge of an automation revolution.

A contemporary political system may be identified by the orientation of the regime, the locus of power, the basis of legitimacy, the constitutional structure and political functions (authoritarian regime, liberal democracy, socialist democracy).

'Situational context' is a term used to indicate the general sociopolitical orientation in which a people or country finds itself today in terms of the major goals and concerns of internal (domestic) development. Tentatively, the following five 'situational contexts' may be identified: (a) colonial/liberation struggle, (b) post-colonial/nascent independence, (c) ex-colonial/neo-metropolitan, (d) socialism under construction, and (e) mature socialism.

The nature, types and manifestation of violence in each of the 'societal patterns' and 'situational contexts' are different and require specific comprehensive study.

A basic assumption is that violence is endemic in each
'societal pattern' and 'situational context'. Epigrammatically
one might even say that 'to be violent is human', even if
the converse is not true. It is a truism that no society and
very few human beings are bereft of all manifestations of
violence.

Decolonization and violence

A dominant feature of our times is what is known as decolonization. Decolonization represents a watershed in human
history. It is both the rejection of a dominant power structure
and the affirmation of a new awakening. The people in struggle,
in revolt, manifest a yearning for a new relation between man
and man and groups of men. But decolonization is not always
a complete or a completed process. Sometimes it is piece-
meal, fragmented, partly genuine, partly spurious, partly
accomplished, partly compromised. Whatever shape and form
it takes, decolonization nevertheless represents a decisive
break with the past, a step away from the domination of the
colonial masters and their indigenous agents.

Frantz Fanon, in his sentiment-charged book *The
Wretched of the Earth*,[26] sang the paean of the resurrection
of the downtrodden. Together with Sorel, Fanon remains
one of the most outspoken proponents of violence as a
catharsis of the enslaved people and as a catalyst of change.
He is one of the leading lights of the literature of rebirth
through commitment to violence.[27] Sorel proclaimed that
'a class can be resurrected through violence', and Fanon
asserted that 'individuals and peoples can become whole
again by participating in violent politics'.[28] This is certainly
reminiscent of Marx, with his classic formulation that 'class
constitutes itself only through conflict'.

Reflecting on the repercussion of violence in the colonial
education, Fanon says that, since violence was used in 'the
ordering of the colonial world, which has ceaselessly
drummed the rhythm for the destruction of native social
forms', therefore when the time comes, violence would be
used by the natives 'to wreck the colonial world'.[29]

Fanon's commitment to violence is as much euphoric as
prescriptive. 'The colonized man', he declares, 'finds his
freedom in and through violence.'[30] 'Colonialism is separatist
and regionalist . . . violence is in action all-inclusive and

national . . . violence is a cleansing force. It frees the native from his inferiority complex . . . and restores his self-respect.'[31]

Social change, conflict and violence:
Marxist and non-Marxist viewpoints

A systematic study of the relationship between social cohesion, social conflict and social violence has been attempted by Lewis Coser in *The Functions of Social Conflict*[32] and 'Internal Violence as a Mechanism for Conflict Resolution'.

Coser explains the social structural aspect of violence. He sees 'violence as serving social structures by furnishing mechanisms for conflict-resolution when established authority fails to accommodate to demands of new groups for hearings'.[33]

The interrelationship between violence and conflict is self-evident, according to Paul H. Conn.[34] 'The use of the term "conflict" with reference to political systems often brings to mind physical violence. Yet conflict may be violent and non-violent.'[35] Similarly, the relation between conflict and change is not too difficult to establish. To quote Conn:

Conflict in a society is most often the product of change. . . . Change often advantages some groups while disadvantaging others. . . . This is not to imply that conflict exclusively or even primarily arises from changing economic conditions.[36]

But, as is universally recognized, it was Marx who made the classic formulation linking change with conflict and conflict with violence, with philosophical profundity tempered by a vision of the future. Restating the Marxian theory that the state is an instrument of oppression and force used by the ruling class to keep the exploited classes in subjugation, Lenin writes in his classic *The State and Revolution*:

The state is a product and the manifestation of the irreconcil-iability of class antagonisms. The state arises where, when and in so far as class antagonisms objectively cannot be reconciled. And, conversely, the existence of the state proves that the class antag-onisms are irreconcilable. . . . According to Marx, the state is an organ of class rule, an organ for the oppression of one class by another, it is the creation of order, which legalizes and perpetuates this oppression by moderating the conflict between the classes. . . .

It is obvious that the liberation of the oppressed class is impossible not only without a violent revolution, but also without the
destruction of the apparatus of state power which was created by
the ruling class and which is the embodiment of this 'alienation'.[37]

Interpreting the Marxian concept of class struggle, Lenin
emphasizes that the 'contradiction' and 'struggle' take place
not only between classes within the same society and nation
(i.e. intrasocietal and intranational conflict), but also between
societies and nations (i.e. intersocietal and international
conflict).[38]

Reverting to the 'driving forces and forms of the national
liberation revolution', Lenin perceived what is known as the
national and colonial question as part of the wider world
revolutionary process. He propounded the thesis of the
alignment of class and social forces in the national liberation
movements. The national movements could not go beyond
the boundaries of bourgeois democratic movements, precisely
because, as Lenin put it, 'the overwhelming mass of population in the backward countries consists of peasants'. This
made him conclude that the 'peasants must make up the
main social basis of the national liberation movement'. Of
course, the importance of the alliance of the working class
and the peasantry was emphasized, together with the active
role of the national bourgeoisie in the national movement.[39]

Ho Chi Minh, while affirming that the principles of
Marxism-Leninism as applied to the national and colonial
question were triumphantly corroborated 'by the experience
of the people's liberation struggle in the East', recapitulates
the three guiding principles, viz.: (a) that the revolution in
the colonial and semi-colonial countries is a national-
democratic revolution, conducted by a very broad national
front uniting all the social strata and classes interested in
liberation from colonial domination; (b) that this revolution
is primarily a peasant revolution but conducted by the
alliance of the peasants with the working class, and is therefore
inseparable from the anti-feudal revolution with agrarian
reform as the chief objective; and (c) that the liberation
revolution in the oppressed countries and the proletarian
revolution in the oppressing ones must support each other.[40]

Because of a peculiar combination of forces, internal and
international, in many liberation struggles in Asia, Africa
and Latin America in the wake of decolonization after the

Second World War, guerrilla war became an important method of struggle. Naturally, therefore, 'the bulk of the work on guerrilla war, including the contemporary "classics" by revolutionaries like Mao, Guevara, Giap and Debray, has been more concerned with techniques of violence appropriate to stages of insurrection than with the outcomes for social change.'[41] Debray postulates: 'Guerrilla warfare is to peasant uprising what Marx is to Sorel.' He relates violence and uprising to change, and says that 'insurrection is a total political strategy for total change'.[43] Mao laid stress on national mobilization for fighting the internal and external enemy. For him 'rural revolution' is an act of violence because 'violence implicates and involves people'. It is reported that, refuting Bertrand Russell's suggestion to establish Communism without the dictatorship of the proletariat, Mao argued that 'this was not feasible historically and psychologically'. He stressed that the propertied classes did not change by persuasion or education. To change them, a resolute struggle and violence in a brief period of dictatorship of the proletariat 'were necessary to suppress the activities of counter-revolutionaries and to establish the authority of the formerly oppressed'.[43] For Lenin, Mao and Debray, 'under conditions of a specific kind, well-organized violence is the shortest distance between two points'.[44] This is in keeping with the Marxian line that violence and political revolution are intertwined, and that political revolution by itself does not create change but only expresses the transition from one economic system to another. It is the premise that leads to Mao's contention 'that the central task and the highest form of revolution is to seize political power by armed force and decide issues by war'.[45] It was Marx who said that the revolutionary role of 'force' is that 'it is the midwife of every old society which is pregnant with the new'.[46] Engels stressed 'the immense moral and spiritual impetus which has resulted from every victorious revolution'.[47]

Among the non-Marxist theorists of violence and revolution, Hannah Arendt and R. Dahrendorf have emphasized the linkage between violence and change. Arendt[48] considers violence as 'the instrument of direct intervention in politics' and therefore postulates that 'a theory of revolution can deal only with the justification for violence'. She distinguishes between violence as used for destroying existing power, and violence as the necessary prerequisite of change.

R. Dahrendorf[49] conceives of revolution as a rapid and violent political and social change. He attempts to correlate violence and change and suggests certain propositions.[50]

Lucian Pye,[51] Edward Shils[52] and Clifford Geertz,[53] among others,[54] representing the structural-functionalist-cum-behaviourist school of thought, have drawn attention to the prevalence of violence in the newly emergent states of Asia and Africa, constituting what they call the transitional societies (in the triple paradigm of traditional-transitional-modern societies). Their main contention is that the basic cause of internal violence is the lack of political integration because of ethnic, regional, linguistic or communal splits and divisions. Bienen points out that 'as people are being changed from traditionals into moderns . . . [their] sensitivity to being changed is a source of violence in transitional societies. . . . Since change produces more insecurity, there must be a quantitative increase in the degree of aggression and hostility within society'.[55]

It is suggested that the main features of the development process are six-dimensional, accounting ultimately for the performance of the system. Egil Fossum[56] lists the following three conceptual pairs comprising the six dimensions: (a) accumulation-distribution (economic dimension), (b) bureaucracy-mobilization (political dimension), (c) co-operation-autonomy (international dimension). Playing with these six dimensions, paired in three sets, Fossum identifies three models of development, with different permutations and combinations of the conceptual pairs as follows:

Model 1, liberal modernizing: accumulation first, distribution later; bureaucracy first, mobilization later; co-operation first, autonomy later.

Model 2, radical nationalist: accumulation first, distribution later, bureaucracy first, mobilization later; autonomy first, co-operation later.

Model 3, revolutionary socialist: distribution first, accumulation later; mobilization first, bureaucracy later; autonomy first, co-operation later.

He also suggests that the class character of the proponents of, and the driving force behind, each strategy would be: for Model 1, modern upper class and middle class; for Model 2, middle class, especially from co-operative structures; for Model 3, working class.

The main thrust of Fossum's argument is that there is

no single or all-exclusive model of development,[57] and further, that there are many deficiencies in the much advertised 'liberal modernizing model'[58]: (a) the assumption of collective goals and interest identity in society is untenable, resulting in a wrong conception of conflicts[59] and a quantitative way of reasoning; (b) the model assumes too restricted a concept of politics;[60] (c) the notion that politics is autonomous and that socio-economic factors enter almost exclusively as independent variables in the structure and functioning of the political system is misleading and lopsided; and (d) the exclusion of the international class structure and specific foreign actors as determining factors in the politics of poor countries is fallacious because there is no insulated national political system.

Relating the two conceptual pairs accumulation-distribution (economic dimension) and bureaucracy-mobilization (political dimension) in each of the three models of development to the phenomenon of violence, one can draw up different patterns of societal violence and individual violence. It is assumed that, in each of the models of development, there are structural characteristics contributing to the use of force by the state, in defence of the 'values' cherished and maintained by the politically dominant class.

Such is the total sway of states[61] in each of the models (in our contemporary world) that citizens everywhere are faced with the inherent limitation and challenge of living and working within a 'maximal state', a new leviathan. The nature of structural violence may vary from model to model, and more specifically within submodels, but no child or man can escape the bondage of the all-powerful modern state. Sugata Dasgupta writes: 'Societal violence lies not so much in the use of the bayonets but in what the bayonets protect.' This, according to Gandhi, is 'exploitation', and exploitation to him is the supreme form of violence.[62]

In a highly interdependent world, the international dimension in its twin aspects, co-operation and autonomy, impinges most significantly on the comprehensive development process. Let us look here briefly at some aspects that impede international co-operation, weaken the autonomy of states, and accentuate the structure of violence at the international level.

The dismantling of the Western colonial system (begun in the wake of the Second World War) and the structuring of 'one world' by multiple ties of interdependence may or may not have a causal relationship. Yet it requires emphasis that, precisely at the time when new states and the new nations of Asia, Africa and Oceania were gaining independence, the world became a perilously interlinked, interlocked politico-economic unity.

But what is surprising, as Fossum points out, is that 'the most important effect of the international structures . . . is the extent to which they (negatively) influence the possibility of attainment of desired values in the poor world, and values which the international system itself defines as important [such as] the striving for increased accumulation of wealth and the quest for education'.[63] Development is frustrated 'by the existence of the distributive mechanism inherent in the international structure. Implicitly . . . the amount of value taken out of the poor countries is far greater than what is invested in them'.[64] And to top it all, 'not only are socio-economic dimensions basically determined by the international structure and the big powers, but also the functioning of the political system itself. It decides which groups are allowed to take power. It defines the limits of their actions, often in conjunction with the most conservative national groups. . . . This is one of the vicious circles in which the poor countries find themselves'.[65]

Six major factors that act as heavy constraints on the positive and balanced development of the poor countries eager to reconcile the principle of economic growth with that of social justice are: (a) interpenetration of national economies by multinational corporations,[66] (b) a sixfold increase in twenty-five years (1950–75) in the volume of world exports and international transactions,[67] (c) the phenomenal growth of international capital flows, ranging from direct investments to shifts of liquid balances,[68] (d) the vigorous impact of international economic relations on national and (within nations) on sectoral economic relations; (e) the steep rise in oil prices, resulting in energy crises, inflationary conditions, economic disequilibrium and the erosion of the foreign-exchange balances, and (f) a world armaments race, resulting, on the one hand, in the spiralling of world military expenditure that diverts a significant proportion of world resources from aid to poor countries and from productive pursuits everywhere, and, on the other, in the ever-increasing expenditure by poor and developing countries on arms purchases and the diversion of their scarce resources from much-needed development to wasteful defence expenditures.

Conclusion: 'maldevelopment', a cause of violence

Patterns of structural violence can be analysed in each of the socio-economic systems and situations indicated above, with due regard to the specific factors that differentiate them; but here, for illustrative purposes, we shall focus on certain aspects of violence in the developing countries.

Looking more closely at this problem, it becomes necessary to rectify the common impression that violence is the by-product of the developmental process per se. The fact is that it is not development itself but the disequilibrium in development, or what may be described as 'maldevelopment', that results in tensions, conflicts and violence.[69]

Maldevelopment in the newly liberated, ertswhile colonial, poor and backward countries is the result of many forces. At the base is the appalling problem of poverty, inherited inequality and the lack of equal opportunity as a legacy of the tribal and feudal past. This legacy was prolonged by the colonial system, which not only allowed tribal and feudal hierarchies to survive and perpetuate unequal social relations that directly contributed to the perpetuation of poverty and kept the economies at low levels of performance, but also introduced a new form and higher level of exploitation, by transforming the indigenous traditional political and economic élite into an intermediate strata of collaborators in the colonial design of political domination and economic aggrandizement.

With the dawn of political independence, the dark night of poverty, inequality and exploitation has not vanished. On the contrary, in most parts of Asia and Africa, political independence has only transferred power to the dominant élite and, what is more, legitimized the political domination of the indigenous power élite in the name of the new national political order. The identity of class origin and the class interests of the political élite with the economic élite (the captains of business and industry and rich landlords) made the concentration of power and wealth in fewer hands quite a smooth and a 'spontaneous' operation. In any variant of authoritarian regimes, this process is facilitated, but even where 'liberal democracies' or constitutional governments have been established, the manipulation of politics and of economic policies and action to ensure the continuous hegemony of the incumbent élite groups and supporting classes has occurred within the framework of a parliamentary system,[70] electoral politics, a constitution and laws, if possible, or, if necessary, through extra-constitutional methods, the suspension of parliaments and rights, the subversion of the electoral process and so on.

The point to be noted is that the dominant competing parties in liberal democracies in Asia and Africa have more or less the same social and electoral base of support, and almost similar policy perspectives, the only differences being a change of leaders and minor divergences in political emphasis and policy priorities.

In an unequal society, fragmented by tribal, caste, class or other cleavages, the 'maldevelopment' that means unequal opportunities in the competition for jobs, services, educational and social facilities and so on, also aggravates group and class conflicts and accentuates individual frustration. While the rich have become richer and the middle class has expanded in many countries, the poor have either remained poor or, in some cases, become even poorer because of the increasing gulf between the 'haves' and the 'have-nots'.[71]

The links between economic inequality and political violence have been confirmed since Aristotle said that inequality was the 'universal and chief cause' of revolutions, and contended in *Politics* that 'inferiors revolt in order that they may be equal, and equals that they may be superior'. Centuries later Madison, in *The Federalist*, characterized inequality in the distribution of property as the 'most common and durable' source of political faction. Still later, Engels argued that political violence results when political structures are not synchronized with socio-economic conditions.

In a recent study called 'A Cross-National Test of Linkage between Economic Inequality and Political Violence', the authors[72] take a global sample covering forty-nine nations, for which data on the following indicators were available: personal-income inequality, political violence, affluence, social mobility, socio-cultural heterogeneity, rate of social change and population size. Noting that 'the political implications of inequality may vary dramatically from impoverished to affluent nations', they state that 'we have . . . broad theoretical agreement that economic inequality begets political violence'.

New opportunities and openings in the political system increase political mobilization and participation. Economic interests and disputes get politicized, resulting in tensions, conflicts and violence. Intergroup disputes acquire the form of interethnic, interlingual, intercommunal, intercaste, intertribe, intercultural, or interclass conflicts, pursued by methods ranging from peaceful demonstrations, non-co-operation and parliamentary battles to street fights, stabbings, strikes, riots and civil violence. Sometimes these situations are transformed by active radical parties into congenial soil for ideological extremism and political militancy.[73] Similarly, disputes and conflicts arising from regional disparities and economic imbalances within an administrative state or province can become focal points for militant mobilization. Regional and subregional movements, in many parts of the Third World, have resulted in violent conflicts that have rocked even stable governments.[74]

It is in this way that shortfalls in the performance of the system—indicated by indices like price rises, increasing unemployment and underemployment (even of educated and skilled personnel), inflationary conditions contributing to a decline in already weak purchasing power, failure to overcome famine or near-famine conditions, default in implementing land reforms and production-boosting schemes in agriculture and industry, failure to solve labour-management disputes peacefully and to maintain discipline in schools and colleges, an increasing impression of administrative inefficiency and corruption in the bureaucracy and among the political élite, and so on—become breeding grounds of discontent that are soon politicized and, transformed into militant demagogy, followed by large-scale conflict and organized violence.[75]

Notes

1. W. J. M. Mackenzie, *Power, Violence, Decision*, p. 39, Harmondsworth, Penguin, 1975.
2. Ibid., pp. 115–6.
3. Ibid., p. 142.
4. Neil Smelser, *Theory of Collective Behaviour*, New York, 1962.
5. Ted Robert Gurr, *Why Men Rebel*, Princeton, N.J., 1970.
6. C. Wright Mills, *The Power Elite*, p. 171, New York, 1956.

7. Max Weber, 'Politics as a Vocation', in H. H. Gerth and C. Wright Mills (eds.), Max Weber, *The Theory of Social and Economic Organization*, New York, 1966, in which he states that authoritative violence in the service of the state is a crucial concept in political theory, that the state is meant to exercise political power and that power is maintained only through force and violence. However, defending the right of the state to use force, he says that the state as a political structure upholds a claim to the monopoly of the legitimate use of physical force in the enforcement of its order (p. 407).

8. Fred H. von der Mehden, *Comparative Political Violence*, p. 37, New Jersey, 1970.

9. Gurr, op. cit, p. 11.

10. Johan Galtung, 'Violence, Peace and Peace Research', *Journal of Peace Research*, Vol. 6, 1969, pp. 167–91; diagram: p. 173.

11. Presented to the Unesco Interdisciplinary Expert Meeting on the Study of the Causes of Violence, Paris, 12–15 November 1975.

12. Galtung, op. cit., p. 175.

13. An interesting critique of Galtung's theory of violence is found in Jukka Gronow and Jorma Hilppo, 'Violence, Ethics and Politics', *Journal of Peace Research*, Vol. 7, 1970, pp. 311–20. They write, p. 312, 'Galtung's ethical vocabulary (violence, non-violence) is not rich enough to define violence adequately. . . . There are two basic ethical systems, *deontological ethics* (rule ethics) and *utilitarianism* (the ethics of consequence). . . . Galtung classifies violence according to the dimensions of the object of violence . . . [i.e.] on deontological ethics or on the means of violence . . . defining violence as a negative influence.' They conclude, p. 317: 'Violence does not seem to be a useful concept in the same sense as e.g. norm or power or social conflict.'

14. Galtung, op. cit., pp. 178–9, amplifies this as follows: 'That structural violence often breeds structural violence, and personal violence often breeds personal violence nobody would dispute—but the point here is the cross-breeding between the two. . . . It could be argued that an inegalitarian structure is a built-in mechanism of conflict control, precisely because it is hierarchical, and that an egalitarian structure would bring out in the open many new conflicts that are kept latent in a feudal structure.'

15. Material for this subsection has been drawn from the unpublished doctoral dissertation produced under my supervision by Gopal Singh, *Politics and Violence: A Study of the Gujarat Upsurge*, Jawaharlal Nehru University, Centre for Political Studies, 1976.

16. John Dollard, *Frustration and Aggression*, New Haven, 1939. See also Elton D. McNeil, 'Psychology and Aggression', *Journal of Conflict Resolution*, Vol. 3, June 1959, pp. 195–294.

17. Gurr, op. cit.

18. James C. Davies, 'Toward a Theory of Revolution', *American Sociological Review*, Vol. 27, February 1962, pp. 5–19. Also: James C. Davies, 'The J-Curve of Rising and Declining Satisfactions as a Cause of Some Great Revolutions and a Contained Rebellion', in Hugh Davies Graham and Ted Robert Gurr (eds.), *The History of Violence in America: Historical and Comparative Perspective*, Washington, D.C., 1969.

19. Graham and Gurr, op. cit., pp. 635–8.

20. Samuel P. Huntington, *Political Order in Changing Societies*, pp. 39–50, New Haven, Conn., 1968.

21. Dollard, op. cit., n. 21.

22. Gurr, op. cit., p. 13.

23. Huntington, op. cit., p. 41, writes: 'If poor countries appear to be unstable, it is not because they are poor but because they are trying to be rich. A purely traditional society would be ignorant, poor and stable. . . . It is precisely the devolution of modernization throughout the world which increases the prevalence of violence around the world. . . . Causes of violence lay with the modernization rather than with the backwardness.'

24. Ibid., pp. 52–3.

25. Henry Bienen, *Violence and Social Change*, Chicago, 1968, pp. 9–10.

26. Frantz Fanon, *The Wretched of the Earth*, London, 1965.
27. Cf. Gandhi, who emphasized the 'therapeutic results of non-violence'.
28. Fanon, op. cit., p. 33.
29. Ibid., p. 67.
30. Ibid., p. 73.
31. Cited in Bienen, op. cit., p. 21.
32. Lewis Coser, *The Functions of Social Conflict*, p. 111, Glencoe, Ill., 1956.
33. Ibid., pp. 22–4.
34. Paul H. Conn, *Conflict and Decision Making: An Introduction to Political Science*, New York, 1971.
35. Ibid., p. 4.
36. In support of this contention, Conn adds that 'it was the rise of trade and the merchant class, the growth of towns, and later the advent of industrialization which contributed to the end of feudalism in Western civilization. The changing circumstances led to conflicts between various groups, to the rise of an urban and eventually middle class, and to a redistribution of rewards within the society'.
37. V. I. Lenin, *The State and Revolution*, p. 154, New York, 1932. A. Rapoport, in his *Conflict in Man-Made Environment*, Penguin, 1974, writes, p. 151: 'From this conception it follows that, if there were no exploiters and exploited, there would be no need for the state, and Marx actually drew this conclusion.'
38. V. I. Lenin, *On Marxism*, p. 22, Moscow, 1970.
39. G. Kim, *Leninism and the National Liberation Movement*, p. 14, Moscow, 1970.
40. Ho Chi Minh, *On Lenin and Leninism*, pp. 84–5, Moscow, 1971.
41. Bienen, op. cit., pp. 41–3. He writes: 'For Mao, war and politics are inseparable; war is the politics of bloodshed. [Mao says that] the people will rise in protest even if leaders make compromises with oppressors. Debray [says] the revolutionary is forged out of fighting.'
42. Ibid., p. 43.
43. Ibid., p. 45.
44. Ibid., p. 46: 'Lenin harnessed his ideas about violence to a conception of social change . . . for him violence and social change were inseparable under certain conditions. . . . For Lenin, the aggravation of political crises and growing pauperization, famine and unemployment led to armed combat.'
45. Ibid., p. 70.
46. F. Engels, *Anti-Dühring*, p. 275, Moscow, 1945.
47. Ibid.
48. Hannah Arendt, *On Violence*, New York, 1970.
49. R. Dahrendorf, *Class and Class Conflict in Industrial Society*, Stanford, Calif., 1959.
50. Bienen, op. cit., p. 83, writes: 'Dahrendorf gives a number of propositions which relate violence and change: (i) the intensity and violence increase when political conditions for the organization of conflict groups are absent; (ii) the intensity and violence increase in proportion to the degree of superimposition of conflicts, either regarding the distribution of authority positions, or the distribution of status positions: (iii) the intensity increases as social mobility decreases; and (iv) the violence increases when the exclusion from authority positions is accompanied by absolute deprivation in social and economic terms; (v) the intensity increases when the exclusion from authority positions is accompanied by relative deprivation in terms of social and economic status.'
51. Lucian Pye, *Guerrilla Communism and Malaya*, Princeton, N.J., 1956; *Politics, Personality and National Building: Burma's Search for Identity*, New Haven, Conn, 1962; *Aspects of Political Development*, Boston, 1966; Lucian Pye and Sidney Verba, *Political Culture and Political Development*, Princeton, N.J., 1965.
52. Edward Shils, *Torment of Secrecy*, Glencoe, Ill., 1956; *Political Development in the New States*, New York, 1962.
53. Clifford Geertz (ed.), *Old Societies and New States: The Quest for Modernity in Asia and Africa*, New York, 1963.

54. See, for instance, Fred Riggs, 'The Theory of Political Development', in James Charlesworth (ed.), *Contemporary Political Analysis*, New York, 1966; G. Almond and J. P. Powell, *Comparative Politics: A Developmental Approach*, Boston, 1966; Karl W. Deutsch, 'Social Mobilization and Political Development', in Harry Ekstein and David Apter (eds.), *Comparative Politics*, New York, 1963; G. Almond and James Coleman, *The Politics of the Developing Areas*, Princeton, N.J., 1960.

55. Bienen, op. cit., pp. 51–2. The main contention is that 'the highest and lowest points of the modernity continuum will tend to produce maximum stability in the political order, whereas a medium position on the continuum will produce maximum instability'. And secondly, 'there is a connection between rates of change, the breaking up of traditional societies and increased violence'.

56. Egil Fossum, 'Political Development and Strategies of Change', *Journal of Peace Research*, Vol. 7, 1970, pp. 17–32.

57. A position reflected in the writings of authors listed in notes 51 to 54 above.

58. Fossum, op. cit., p. 18.

59. Fossum says on p. 18: 'the authors allow for conflict; conflict between different groups, parties, etc., and conflict between city and countryside, but not for conflict over the basic assumption of the system. The formula is: primary consensus, secondary conflict . . .'

60. On pp. 19–20, he says: 'What is defined as "political" has essentially to do with *distribution* and *control* . . . [but] it takes place *implicitly* through social structure. . . . This structure is a determinant of values. . . . It does the *controlling of behaviour* . . . and it does the *distribution of values*, social, economic and political.'

61. For a discussion of the nature of the modern state, see Rasheeduddin Khan, 'The Total State', *Seminar*, No. 172, January 1974, pp. 38–45.

62. Sugata Dasgupta, 'The Real Theme', *Seminar*, No. 121, October 1969.

63. Fossum, op. cit., p. 21. See also: Morton A. Kaplan (ed.), *Isolation or Interdependence? Today's Choice for Tomorrow's World*, Chicago, 1973.

64. Fossum, op. cit., p. 21.

65. Ibid., p. 22. See also Harry Madoff, *Imperialismens Politiska Ekonomi*, Stockholm, 1969; Paul Baran, *The Political Economy of Growth*, New York, 1967; André Gunder Frank, *Capitalism and Underdevelopment in Latin America*, New York, 1967; A. Rahman, Moonis Raza and Mohit Sen (eds.), *Imperialism in the Modern Phase*, Vol. II, New Delhi, 1977; J. Galtung, 'A Structural Theory of Imperialism', *Journal of Peace Research*, Vol. 18, 1971, pp. 82–117.

66. See Richard J. Barnet and Ronald E. Muller, *Global Reach*, New York, 1974; Tugendhat Christopher, *The Multinationals*, Penguin, 1974; Raymond Vernon, *Sovereignty at Bay*, New York, 1971; Frederick T. Knickerbocker, *Market Structure and Market Power: Consequences of Foreign Direct Investment by Multinational Corporations*, Center for Multinational Studies, Washington, D.C., 1976. (Occasional Paper No. 8.)

67. It exceeded $300 billion in 1973, with an average annual rate of growth of 10 per cent, which is much faster than the world-income rate of growth.

68. American direct investment flow in 1971 was approximately $4,800 million to developed countries and $1,200 million to developing countries.

69. Sugata Dasgupta, 'Peacelessness and Maldevelopment', in *International Peace Research Association. Proceedings II: Poverty, Development and Peace*, Netherlands, 1968.

70. The Indian experience is a good example of this situation. The Constitution provides the 'right to property' as a fundamental right. Conversely, the propertiless have no constitutional protection for the eradication of their 'propertilessness'. (See D. N. Dwivedi, *Economic Concentration and Poverty in India*, pp. 58–9, New Delhi, 1974.)

71. See: The Mahalonibis Committee Report, known as *Report of the Committee on Distribution of Income and Levels of Living*, Part I, Government of India, Planning Commission, New Delhi, 1964.

72. Lee Sigelman and Miles Simpson, 'A Cross-National Test of the Linkage between Economic Inequality and Political Violence', *The Journal of Conflict Resolution*, Vol. 21, No. 1, March 1977, pp. 105–28.

73. In India, twice in the last thirty years, organized attempts were made by Communist partisans to mount armed insurrection. The experiences of these episodes have relevance for many Third World countries. On the Telangana Communist armed struggle (1946–51) see Ian Bedford, *The Telangana Insurrection: A Study in the Causes and Development of a Communist Insurrection in Rural India, 1946–1951*, unpublished doctoral dissertation, submitted to the Australian National University, 1965; Romesh Thapar, *Storms Over Hyderabad*, Bombay, 1948; Raj Bahadur Gour, et al., *Glorious Telangana Armed Struggle*, New Delhi, 1973. On the Naxalite Movement (1967–75) see: Biplab Dasgupt, *The Naxalite Movement*, New Delhi, 1974; J. C. Johari, *Naxalite Politics in India*, Delhi, 1972.

74. The experience of regional and subregional movements in India reveals many aspects of relevance to the new states engaged in the process of integration and development. On linguistic movements see: Paul R. Brass, *Language, Religion and Politics in North India*, Delhi, 1974; and Jyotirindra Das Gupta, *Language Conflict and National Development: Group Politics and National Language Policy in India*, Bombay, 1970. On regional movements see: K. V. Narayana Rao, *Telangana: A Study in the Regional Committees in India*. Calcutta, 1972; Joan V. Bondurant, *Regionalism versus Provincialism: A Study in Problems of Indian National Unity*, Berkeley, 1958; Sher Singh, *The Case of Haryana and Hindi Region of the Punjab*, Rohtak, 1972; Rasheeduddin Khan, 'Territorial Reorganization', *Seminar*, No. 137, January 1971; 'Need for more Rational Restructuring of Federal Polity', *Janata*, Vol. 28, pp. 1–2, January 1973; 'The Regional Dimension', *Seminar*, No. 164, April 1973.

75. See Ghanshyam Shah, *Protest Movements in Two Indian States: A Study of the Gujarat and Bihar Movements*, Delhi, 1977; Gopal Singh, *Politics and Violence: A Study of Gujarat Upsurge* (unpublished doctoral dissertation), Jawaharlal Nehru University, 1976.

Silent violence:
famine and inequality

Director for Asia in the
project 'Food Systems
and Society', United Nations
Research Institute for Social
Development, Geneva

Pierre Spitz

> '*Virtually all civil institutions are intended to serve
> landowners. . . . It is as if a few men had shared
> out the earth among themselves and had then framed
> laws proclaiming their union and protecting them
> against the multitude, much as they would have
> constructed shelters in the woods to defend them-
> selves against wild animals.*'
>
> Necker, April 1775

The men and women who work on the land, who produce
the world's supply of cereals, tubers, oilseeds, vegetables,
fruit and meat, hold the lives of all human beings in their
hands, including those of the generations to come. In theory,
they have the power of life and death. How is it that, during
the last ten years, hundreds of thousands of men and women
who worked the soil of Asia, Africa and America, who
sowed the seeds, harvested the crops and minded the herds,
have perished for lack of food? How is it that they died of
hunger in those parts of the world, whereas most of the people
who do not produce foodstuffs were spared?

For, during the same period and in the same countries, no
one starved to death in ministries, banks or barracks. Might
it not be precisely because agricultural production is of vital
importance that those who work on the land in the poor
countries are robbed of the power that is theoretically theirs?
People who have thus become so powerless that they can no
longer be sure of having enough food for themselves from
one year to the next, or even from one season to the next, and
who die for that reason, bear witness to the fact that, as the
most downtrodden social group, they have lost the most
elementary of rights—the right to food, the right to life itself.

The crisis created by a famine reveals the workings of the economic and social system and affords an insight into the structural violence that has the effect of denying the poorest members of society the right to feed themselves in order to stay alive. The fact that, in times of famine, town-dwellers can still get something to eat while country people starve to death is a sign of the power relation between the urban population and the rural population. When a food shortage starts to make itself felt in the towns and there is a sharp increase in food prices, all the urban social classes are affected by the crisis, although of course to varying degrees: the poorest know that their very lives are threatened, whereas the others, at worst, run the risk of having their comfort affected, and may in fact merely be deprived of some luxuries. However, entrepreneurs, even if, personally, they do not suffer very severely, have to cope with the wage claims that follow in the wake of soaring food prices. The pressure that is then brought to bear on the government by the different social groups in the towns has all the more weight because the towns are the seat of political power. If the government is to stay in power, it must take effective action to check the rise in food prices through a combination of measures that will be determined by the prevailing situation. These include increasing the amount of food channelled from rural areas into the towns (which may create or aggravate a food crisis in the rural areas), stepping up food imports, exercising closer supervision over marketing practices and prices and, possibly, subsidizing foodstuffs intended for certain social groups (by instituting ration cards, cut-rate shops and even free issues).

Town-dwellers are therefore relatively well protected against famine, at least in peacetime, and it is for this reason that, when supplies are scarce, there is a mass exodus of country-dwellers towards the towns, to which they are lured by the hope of finding cheap food or some way of earning money, no matter how little.

The rush on the towns may be accompanied by different degrees of popular organization. During the great Bengal famine of 1943, which according to various estimates killed from one and a half to three and a half million people, the migration towards Calcutta consisted of a host of individual movements and did not develop into a dangerous form of group behaviour. There were very few riots and hardly any looting of shops. Food supplies were reserved for the inhabitants of Calcutta, and the thousands of dead strewn about the streets of Calcutta had all come from rural areas. Not a single inhabitant of Greater Calcutta died of hunger, while millions of people were suffering and dying of hunger in the country.[1]

In order to keep starving people from flooding into the towns, it has long been the practice in India[2] and in north-east Brazil[3] to organize rural work programmes in times of food shortages. In north-east Brazil the army took action not only to organize such emergency work camps, but also to prevent hungry peasants from entering the towns. In the Sahel, in 1973, 13,000 nomads were amassed at the camp at Lazaret, near Niamey, thus locating the victims outside the towns to avoid any trouble. In October 1974 the Indian army conducted search operations in the whole area around Calcutta Station and guarded the railway lines for miles around in an attempt to prevent the peasants fleeing from the famine from getting into the city. Country-dwellers are a threat to the authorities only when they head towards the towns. If they are physically dispersed, they are also socially divided.

In time of famine, all the urban social categories become united in the struggle against rising prices, but the situation is very different in rural areas. The richest farmers, even if they sell less, are compensated by higher prices; the poor peasants are forced to pawn or sell their farming equipment, animals and land in order to survive. A year of famine always corresponds to a rise in mortgaged lands and a merging of property, while the poor peasants join the ranks of landless agricultural labourers.[4]

These crises are the highlights in a long-term process of dispossession that is undermining the security of the poorest social groups so far as food supplies are concerned. Between 1961 and 1971 the number of agricultural labourers in India increased by 20.4 million (by 75 per cent), and in the same period the number of cultivators decreased by 15 million (by 16 per cent). In the Sahel region of Africa, famine is tending today to disrupt the collective patterns that were some guarantee of security for the family group, and to encourage more individual patterns of ownership, so enabling agrarian capitalism to develop. The most deprived members of the community lose their land, their means of independent supply. And so, by enhancing inequalities, famine helps to perpetuate the conditions for its recurrence.[5]

I do not propose to discuss the question of inequality in itself, but to examine the significance of various views on inequality within a nation, before considering those that have been expressed regarding inequalities between nations.

Landrights and the right to life: binary views on inequality

Land rights vary to a remarkable degree from one society to another and at different times and places. The history of land-tenure systems is marked by moments of tension and disruption attended by radical changes, owing to the pressure of forces that may be predominantly external (colonization, for instance) or predominantly internal. In the latter case, it is as though the social forces at work expanded within the frame of a particular structure until they found that they had to break through the frame in order to expand further. During the last two or three centuries the pattern of development between two elements of disruption has often been interpreted as a binary process reflecting the antagonism between the 'haves' and the 'have-nots', the former being 'landlords', who hold all the rights in land, and the latter being the agricultural labourers, whose only means of livelihood is their physical strength.

Such an interpretation gives a simplified picture of the situation, for two reasons. First, the principle that a landowner is invested with full rights is an elaboration of a European notion of property that was crystallized in Roman law and has been influenced by it ever since. Secondly, whatever the system of land tenure, the agrarian situation is far more complex in reality than is suggested by the antagonism between landowners and agricultural labourers. It is a web formed by various possible combinations of circumstances pertaining to types of land rights, degrees of control over means of production other than land, and differences in the size of properties and holdings.

However, an approach that highlights the simpler binary pattern has been—and still is—widely used by those who want to change the order of things. For instance, in France in the years 1795–96 the writings of Babeuf marked the beginning of revolutionary socialist action in Europe. He based his case on the notion of 'agrarian law' (i.e. reform), 'which never

reappears on the horizon of the centuries except in circumstances such as those in which we find ourselves: that is
to say, when there is a meeting of extremes' and a threat
of famine.

Babeuf came to the conclusion that there were only two
significant groups of people, the great landowners on the one
hand (including those who had seized land under the cover
of the 1789 revolution) and the poverty-stricken labourer on
the other. This concentration of wealth in the hands of a few,
which he denounced in the *Plebians' Manifesto*, would lead
inevitably to a 'general upheaval in the system of ownership',
'the revolt of the poor against the rich', the need for equality
('having been born equal, we intend to live and die as equals,
and we want genuine equality or death') and the sharing of
property and labour ('no more individual ownership of land;
the land belongs to no one, its fruits belong to everyone').

The line of reasoning that consists in exposing social
inequality in rural areas by highlighting the contrast between
the most well-to-do members of a community and the people
who have so little that they are in danger of starving to death,
may be motivated by extremely varied considerations. When
it is in tune with the hopes of the most deprived, we find that
the approach in question does not impoverish reality by
simplifying it but, on the contrary, marshals the facts in a
meaningful pattern around the two poles that mark out a
real field of investigation—namely, the study of the violence
generated by a fundamentally inegalitarian social structure.

The analytical studies on which action must be founded are
intended for the handful of leaders of a revolutionary movement; this is true, for instance, of the analysis of the classes
of rural Chinese society that was made by Mao Tse-tung
in 1926.[7] The size of the circle within which such studies are
circulated depends on many different factors and, in particular,
on the political determination of those engaged in the struggle.
If the circle is too large, there is a risk of weakening the
movement, for analytical studies may dampen revolutionary
ardour by revealing the complexity of the task to be
performed.

Conversely, the ruling class finds that, in order to maintain
and reinforce its dominant position, it is in its interest to
convey to the whole population, using all the information
media at its disposal, a picture of the situation that emphasizes
the great complexity of social co-existence, stresses the

interdependence of different groups, glosses over old and new conflicts and, in particular, refers to the bipolar illustration as if it were merely an oversimplified theory of impassioned rabble-rousers, so as to prevent it from serving as an incitement to revolutionary counter-violence. Sometimes, however, it may itself resort to using this bipolar scheme when it feels very self-confident; thus, in France, one year after the failure of the revolution of 1848, the Archbishop of Toulouse wrote:

Man's inequality of station, concerning which there has been so much blasphemous talk, is, it is true, the fundamental law of society: without such inequality, the arts, the sciences and agriculture would be doomed to perish and we would all be deprived of the things that are most necessary for life. This law is one of the decrees of the divine wisdom, for God intended the rich to find, in the sufferings of the poor, an opportunity to make the most generous sacrifices, and the poor to find, in the benevolence of the rich, a powerful reason for gratitude and love, so that the unity of human society should be strengthened by the twofold bond of benevolence and need.[8]

When social tensions become too great, what is needed is not so much the prospect of achieving a harmonious relationship as a hope of change. But mere promises of change are not enough. Certain members of the ruling class sometimes become aware, just in time, of the counter-violence that is being organized, and not only do they promise or demand reform so as to appease the discontented, but they also seek to convince people belonging to the same class as themselves of the need for partial reforms. Today the mass media can be used for the high-speed dissemination of such analyses, which are dangerous because they are realistic. They are therefore prepared in a safe place, within an organization such as the Rand Corporation, for instance, and become known to the public only as a result of indiscretions or leaks. It is consequently difficult to study their contents. One has only to think of the reports of the World Bank, the distribution of which is extremely limited, no doubt because they do not give a deliberately falsified picture of reality.

Two centuries ago, any book written in Europe could reach only a small circle of readers, and that circle became even smaller if the writer dealt with such a specialized subject as the corn trade. It was by means of such a book that a member of the French ruling class (in the broad sense), the Geneva banker Necker,[9] alerted the government to the dangers which he felt lay ahead. For, in France, in the 1770s the warning signs of revolutionary counter-violence were becoming more frequent. Necker wrote his book, in fact, with only one reader in view—the king. That he succeeded in convincing the king is clear, since, in the year following Turgot's fall, he was appointed Minister of Finance, in effect Prime Minister. For the purposes of his demonstration, he used the bipolar pattern of antagonism between the 'haves' and the 'have-nots', because, despite its obvious limitations, this was the only illuminating approach to the problem of violence in the French countryside, which had been ravaged since the turn of the century by several famines. The publication of Necker's work was authorized by the king on the very day that the people of Paris looted the bakeries.[10] Necker describes what becomes of the people in times of famine :

When landowners raise the price of food and refuse to raise the price of the labour of industrious men, there arises between those two classes of society a sort of obscure but terrible combat in which it is impossible to count the number of victims, while the Strong oppresses the Weak under cover of the law and the man of property crushes under the weight of his prerogatives the man who lives by the work of his hand. . . . As bread becomes more expensive, the Landowner's empire expands, for once Craftsmen or the Country-dwellers have exhausted their stocks of provisions they are no longer in a position to argue; they have no choice but to work today so as not to die tomorrow, and in this conflict of interests between the Landowner and the Labourer the one stakes his life and that of his family, whereas the other need fear nothing worse than a temporary impediment to his enjoyment of even greater luxury.[11]

The agricultural labourer's diet does not even allow him to build up food reserves in the tissues of his own body. The French chemist Lavoisier, who was the first to measure nutritional energy, wrote in 1777: 'Why is it that by a shocking contrast the rich man enjoys an abundance which is not physically necessary to him and which seems destined for the working man? We should, however, refrain from maligning nature and accusing her of faults which no doubt derive from our social institutions and may be inseparable from them.'[12]

For Necker this violence did in fact derive from institutions, that is to say, from the laws governing property
rights:

No matter how the burden of taxation may be distributed, the
Common People are doomed by the effect of the laws of property
never to obtain more than the bare necessaries of life in exchange
for their work; unless, then, those laws are overthrown and public
order is constantly disturbed by the partitioning of land (a method
which would be unjust as well as impracticable), the authorities
who hold the sovereign and legislative power cannot display their
benevolent intentions towards the Common People except by
assuring them at least of the bare living to which their expectations are reduced, and this depends solely on the wisdom of
the corn laws.[13]

Obviously the reference here is to the wisdom of Necker
himself, who put himself forward as the man best qualified
to regulate the circulation of grain as circumstances might
dictate. It is surprising to see that Necker, writing as a
politician intent on the pursuit of power, nevertheless hinted
at an agrarian reform that would consist in a permanent
process of re-establishing equality in a sphere where it always
tended to diminish, even though he described it as 'unjust',
'impraticable' and 'constantly disturbing public order'. What
he had in mind was obviously an agrarian reform decided in
high places. Adam Smith, at the same period, proclaimed
that 'the freedom of the corn trade is the best security against
famine'.[14] He also reviewed the workers' prospects of organ-
izing themselves: so far as he could see, they were slight or
even non-existent. Since there were but few masters, they
could, according to Smith, come to an agreement to keep
wages down to the lowest level, especially since there were
no laws to stop them from forming associations, whereas
laws existed that prevented the workers from doing so. Like
Necker, he highlighted the contrast between the stocks built
up by landowners and the non-existence of any stocks
belonging to the workers.
   The history of the workers' movement has demonstrated
that Smith was overly optimistic concerning the future
prospects of the classes whose interests he defended. On the
other hand, the history of peasant movements shows what
formidable difficulties are encountered by agricultural
labourers and poor peasants when they want to organize

themselves in order to carry through their own agrarian reform, that is to say, the radical change that alone can banish the spectre of famine for ever.

Famine and international violence

When Christopher Columbus, during his fourth expedition (1502–04), discovered gold on the banks of the Veragua, he named the place Belem, or Bethlehem, and wrote, enthralled, 'Gold, gold, what an excellent product!... Gold is the source of all wealth, gold is the spur to all human activities, and the power of gold is such that it suffices to transport souls to Paradise.'[15] The great voyages made by Europeans during the late fifteenth and early sixteenth centuries marked the first of the decisive stages in the development of world trade and, therefore, stimulated the interest of Europeans in the study of political economy. The spontaneous and somewhat mystical mercantilism of Columbus gave way to more systematic thinking about the problems of international trade, and this was all the more to the point because various states were gradually evolving machinery to cope with such trade. One of the first economists to attempt to establish a theory concerning the distribution of human activities throughout the world, the Frenchman Jean Bodin (1530–96), expressed the opinion that, in international trade, 'there are necessarily nations that gain and others that lose. It is therefore important to control the movement of products, men and money so that France may grow rich'.[16]

Gold and spices did not feed the poor of Europe. There was a sharp increase in their number at the beginning of those 'modern times'[17] and food shortages and famines were all the more severe on that account.[18]

The beginnings of industrialization in England gave rise to new lines of conceptual approach, on which modern economic science still hinges. The discussion around the Poor Law of 1834, the arguments of the Anti-Corn-Law League founded in 1839 by Richard Cobden ('the foremost of duties is to feed the hungry') and the controversy between Ricardo and Malthus over the Corn Laws, are the last examples of a major debate between proponents of different theories concerning agricultural and nutritional problems as they relate to poverty.

The repeal of the Corn Laws and the re-establishment of free trade in 1846 marked the political victory of Ricardo over Malthus and, more generally, of the cities and industrial capitalism over the countryside and the great landed proprietors. The terrible times of food shortage experienced by Europe in 1846–48, and the Irish famine of 1845–49, the last great famine of Western Europe,[19] did not, in spite of the million people who died and the hundreds of thousands who emigrated, lead at the time to any particular development of the theories of conventional economic science. Agricultural and nutritional problems in relation to poverty made a timid reappearance in economic discussions only at the time of the agricultural crisis in the early 1930s, and they came to the fore after the Second World War and have been given particularly close attention in the last few years.

Immediately after the Second World War it became necessary for the industrialized countries to establish new economic relations with the poor countries that were becoming politically independent, at least in name. The literature concerning 'development' that has been produced in the industrialized countries is devoted predominantly to reflections on that necessity. Whether such writings were intended to enlighten decision-makers in the industrialized countries—in which case they were realistic and usually confidential—or to win over the intellectual élite in the poor countries so as to make them the instruments of the policy of the rich countries—in which case they were widely disseminated through university channels—they could not disregard the key problems of agriculture and food for very long.

It is generally recognized that the colonial powers, the industrialized countries of the 'North' or the 'Centre', perpetrated a great deal of violence in their colonies, the poor countries of the 'South' or the 'Periphery', and that famines, at least those that occurred during the colonial period, must be interpreted in this context.

Many contemporary analyses show how the disruptive effects of the colonial powers, interference with land-tenure customs, land rights and farming systems contributed to making the colonized peoples less capable of producing enough food for themselves and, in particular, of building up the stocks needed to tide them over the lean years.

The author of an analysis of Indian famines, the Rev. J. T. Sunderland of Boston, Mass., considering that famine in India is most frequently attributed to climatic factors, begins his study by examining that argument. He maintains, on the one hand, that droughts do not occur in every part of India simultaneously, nor are there any notable climatic changes and, on the other hand, that there exists a good communications network making it possible to transport corn from surplus-producing zones to regions where it is in short supply. He further points out that the irrigation methods that have been used for centuries in India should make it possible to mitigate the effects of local droughts. Casting aside the traditional arguments of 'overpopulation' he observes in addition that 'even under present conditions, (India) produces enough food for all her people'. What then is the true cause of famine in India? 'A poverty so severe that it keeps a majority of all on the very verge of suffering, even in years of plenty, and prevents them from laying up anything to tide them over years of scarcity. . . . India is a land rich in resources beyond most other lands in the world.' For more than two centuries, however, England has drained India's wealth. 'There is no country in the world that could endure such a steady loss of wealth without becoming impoverished. . . . Called by its right name, what is the treatment of India by England? It is the stronger nation sucking the blood of the weaker. It is "Imperialism".' Sunderland published his analysis in the journal *India* in the first month of 1900, and then published it again in the *New England Magazine* in September 1900.[20]

Other analyses of the same kind were published during the same period, either by Indian nationalists such as Romesh Dutt[21] or Dadabhai Naoroji,[22] or by British administrators who shared their convictions, such as William Digby.[23] When Sunderland, rejecting the explanations that were popular in his time—and are also familiar to our ears—laid the responsibility for famine, not on natural or demographic causes, but on 'Imperialism', he was simply developing the opinion expressed in a gory metaphor by Lord Salisbury himself, that is to say, by the representative of that imperialism. Writing after the famines of 1865–67, which, according to the British authorities, killed 2 million persons, and those of 1868–70 (1.6 million dead), and before those of 1876–78 (over 6 million dead), Salisbury, Secretary of State for India, stated in his famous minute of 26 April 1875 that, 'as India must be bled', this had to be done judiciously and, in particular, that great care should be taken in determining the basis for assessment of tax liability: 'The lancet should be directed to the parts where the blood is congested or at least sufficient, not those which are already feeble from the want of it.'[24]

The opening of the Suez Canal in 1870 stimulated British exports of textiles and industrial goods to India, while the volume of Indian cotton exports to the United Kingdom also increased. The Suez Canal also made it possible to export Indian corn to Europe. Whereas we find no references to any participation by Indians in the world corn trade before 1870, Indian exports of cereals during the three years of famine from 1876–77 to 1878–79 amounted to 3.75 million tons. India became the United Kingdom's principal supplier of corn and also exported corn to Belgium, France and Egypt. 'This was first met by the outcry that, for greed, the better classes of the community were exporting the surplus stocks that formerly were stored against times of scarcity and famine.'[25] Between 1883 and 1914, cereals were India's chief export. It was not until 1921 that the country stopped exporting cereals on a regular basis.

The comments on colonial violence that were made by people actually perpetrating it showed that they appreciated the economic dangers of excessive violence before they came to realize its political dangers as national independence movements developed. The weaker these movements were, the more frankly and openly were such comments made. What could be said publicly in India in 1875 could no longer be said publicly at the turn of the century, when the Congress Party was being formed.

During the years following the First World War, defence of the colonial system consisted entirely in highlighting its civilizing mission and enumerating the benefits of progress which colonized peoples owed to their colonizers. The realistic analyses that were needed, however, if the colonial powers were to maintain their dominant position, had to be kept confidential lest they be seen to conflict with the arguments advanced in official statements.

Archives dating from the colonial period confirm that realistic analyses of this kind were in fact made. We can refer, for instance, to the reports of a particularly lucid inspector-general of the French colonies, Bernard Sol. In his report on his mission to Upper Volta in 1932 he recalled that 'from 1926 to 1931 there were three years of famine in Upper Volta':

We may . . . wonder how it has come about that comunities such as those living in the Dedougou rural district, the granaries of which always contained three harvests in reserve and where it simply was not done to eat grain that had not been stored for at least three years, have suddenly become improvident. They had not had any difficulty in surviving the frightful famine of 1914, which was the result of an exceptionally severe drought. Of course their stocks had diminished by the time they were gathering the harvest of 1916–18, but it was not long before they were replenished. The first serious inroads were made into their stocks in 1926, which was a good year for cotton but a bad one for millet. Since that time, these communities, formerly accustomed to opulence as regards food supplies, have lived under extremely precarious conditions. . . . I feel morally bound to point out, however, that the intensification of the policy of giving priority to industrial products has coincided with an increase in the frequency of food shortages. . . . I believe that, under present circumstances, the cultivation of any crop for industrial purposes is harmful to the production of foodstuffs on which the life of the country depends.[26]

In 1921 the President of the Italian Red Cross proposed that the League of Nations should undertake a scientific study of disasters and calamities, including famines. That suggestion led to the founding of a scientific journal entitled *Matériaux pour l'étude des calamités* [Data for the Study of Calamities], published in Geneva from 1924 to 1965. Despite the accumulation of data on droughts, floods, cyclones, earthquakes, famines, etc., the results of that venture were extremely limited, owing to the absence of a theoretical framework for an analysis of the data. Yet a tentative theoretical approach had been outlined as early as 1926 in the journal itself by Corrado Gini, for whom famines represented 'a particular form of economic crisis linked to specific stages in the development of the national economy'.[27] Industrialization seemed to him to be the best way of putting an end to the threat of famine. In other words, he thought that famines were caused by the economic gap between industrialized countries and the others. In the same year,[28] the League of Nations was preparing the World Economic Conference to be convened in May 1927 in pursuance of the Resolution of the Sixth Session of the Assembly (September 1925), the latter having declared that it was 'convinced that economic peace will largely contribute to security among the nations'.

The discussions turned mainly on the question of customs

tariffs between industrialized countries, and the principal result of the Conference was the establishment of an Economic Consultative Committee, to be responsible for keeping under review the implementation of the resolutions and recommendations of the Conference. The Committee did little to change the policy of the League of Nations, which continued to hold the view that security was not a problem of economic relations even though the scope of the debate was limited to those of Member States, and particularly of European countries, but basically a problem of political relations. The best guarantee of security was disarmament.[29]

It was not until the Bruce Reform of 1939–40 that 'the close interdependence between international security and economic and social co-operation' was recognized. The awareness of that interdependence was eventually reflected in the fact that the United Nations Charter established the Economic and Social Council alongside the Security Council, the functions of which were akin to those of the League of Nations.

From 1925 onwards, however, interest began to be shown in feeding the poor, as evidenced by the activities of the Health Organization of the League of Nations (today, the World Health Organization), which arranged for food surveys to be conducted in the industrialized countries, leading to the report written by E. Burnett and W. R. Aykroyd in 1935. In the same year, the Mixed Committee on the Problem of Nutrition—the ancestor of the Food and Agriculture Organization—was set up. In 1936, while the International Labour Office was producing a report called *Workers' Nutrition and Social Policy*,[30] the Mixed Committee was defining basic food needs, particularly in terms of calories, and preparing a report on the problem of nutrition.[31]

The year 1936 also saw the publication of Lord Boyd-Orr's *Food, Health and Income*, which showed that the cost of an adequate diet was beyond the means of close to half of the British population in 1933–34. The following year a conference convened at Bandung by the Health Organization examined problems relating to the health and nutrition of Asian peoples.

Through the experience of their own economic crisis the industrialized countries were at last discovering the age-old link between hunger and poverty. In 1941 the Atlantic Charter referred to the vital importance of securing 'freedom from want for all men in all lands'; in 1942 the McDougall Memorandum stressed that mankind must be liberated from its most pressing affliction, hunger, and, in 1945, at the Conference of Quebec, Boyd-Orr, the first Director-General of the Food and Agriculture Organization, pleaded in favour of a world food policy based on human needs: 'The hungry people of the world wanted bread and they were given statistics. . . . No research was needed to find out that half the people in the world lacked sufficient food for health.'[32] He soon realized that his possibilities of action were limited. In the American journal *Fortune*, of May 1946, an article entitled 'The Food Scandal' contained the following passage: '"Some people are going to have to starve", said the United States Secretary of Agriculture to a Congressional Committee. He added: "We're in the position of a family that owns a litter of puppies: we've got to decide which ones to drown."' *Fortune* commented upon this statement as follows: 'While a half billion people in Europe, Africa and Asia faced hunger and possible death by starvation, Americans continued to eat about 20 per cent more food, measured in calories, than nutritionists recommend as a healthy diet.'

After proposing that a World Food Board be established, with a large budget and extensive powers, Boyd-Orr came up against the opposition of the Truman administration and then of the British Labour Government. The Soviet Union, for its part, had announced that it would not participate in this venture unless the United States and the United Kingdom also did so. When he saw that nothing would come of his proposal, Boyd-Orr resigned from his post as Director-General of the Food and Agriculture Organization. Both Norris E. Dodd and Philip Cardon, who succeeded him at the head of the organization from 1947 to 1956, came from the office of the United States Secretary of Agriculture. However, in recognition of his attempt to overcome the selfishness of the rich countries, Boyd-Orr was awarded the Nobel Peace Prize in 1949.

Immediately after the Second World War, poverty was referred to in official speeches as a kind of disease in itself, without any historical relationship to the development of the more prosperous countries.[33] Accordingly, remedial measures should not be designed to change the nature of the relations between rich countries and poor countries, but should bear directly upon the poor countries. In seeking to ensure their own immunity, the rich countries did not have

to resort to military weapons or economic means (investments and loans), for they could combat the plague endemic
to poor countries by applying a twofold miracle cure in the
shape of science and technology. They offered this cure as
a way of setting the poor on the road to recovery and redemp-
tion with all the more generosity because it did not seem,
at first sight, to be a costly proposition, particularly by
comparison with the Marshall Plan.

However, while science and technology make it possible
to increase cereal yields, for instance, they reduce neither
internal social inequalities nor external dependence. On the
contrary, as has been abundantly demonstrated,[34] techniques
of the 'green revolution' type have increased the disparities
between the rich and the poor, between regions well endowed
with natural resources and less fortunate regions, and have
often had the effect of replacing the latter's direct dependence
for food supplies by a more insidious form of dependence
consisting in the need to acquire fertilizers, pesticides, agricultural machinery and sources of energy, thus providing
multinational corporations with ample opportunity to step
in and reap a profit.

The 'green revolution', by magnifying inequalities and
aggravating the effects of the process of dispossession on the
lives of the poorest, helps to exacerbate structural violence.
Norman Borlaug, the geneticist standard-bearer of the 'green
revolution', was nevertheless awarded the Nobel Peace
Prize, perhaps because the connotations of the words 'agriculture' and 'peace' have been so strongly linked in people's
minds for centuries that they tend to inhibit all critical
thinking concerning the type of agriculture that is represented
by the 'green revolution'.

A geneticist does not operate in an economic and social
vacuum. His selection criteria vary according to the category
of peasants with whom he is concerned and their farming
systems. Furthermore, he may work in a laboratory cut off
from the rural masses but very close to industrial interests.
But he may, on the other hand, try to understand the peasants'
concrete difficulties, enlist their help in seeking to identify
the principal obstacles to development and propose solutions
that are adapted to local conditions, acceptable and readily
assimilated.

For a quarter of a century, the food-aid programmes of
the rich countries did, however, prevent thousands of poor

peasants who were recalcitrant to 'science and technology' from dying. But they also made it possible to prevent thousands of poor peasants from rising in rebellion. We know to what degree bilateral food-aid programmes have become, over the years, an economic, commercial, political and diplomatic weapon calculated to perpetuate and reinforce the bonds of dependence and the social status quo.

The dominant classes and the dominant countries do in fact mean to perpetuate and reinforce their domination. In order to do this, they have to preserve the machinery that is designed to ensure that resources are transferred to them. However, such a transfer system, which enables those who are already well-off to continue to satisfy their acquisitive instincts, sometimes leaves the most needy without adequate stocks, and when that happens they can no longer ensure a regular flow of supplies; what is more, they may even want to change the existing order.

The dominant classes and the dominant countries must then organize a temporary transfer of resources in the opposite direction, and this enables them not only to perpetuate the existing system, but also, in some cases, to reinforce it. A food-aid programme is a good example of such an operation. It is a means of forestalling the development of a political consciousness, which might degenerate into social disorder. It increases the power of the donor countries, which demand all kinds of services in return, and it offers wider opportunities for manœuvring to people in key positions at the national and local levels. This form of aid is not inherently distinguished by all these characteristics. It acquires them only because the context in which it is dispensed is that of international violence and internal inequalities within poor countries. Food-aid schemes could be different. They could contribute to developing the political consciousness of the oppressed and help them to organize themselves for the struggle to abolish conditions of inequality and dependence in order to ensure that development is a self-centred and well-balanced process.

An observer has noted the extent to which the relief centres set up in villages of Bangladesh in 1973–74 reinforced the powers of the élite and turned the workers into beggars. Fighting famine, in such circumstances, means fighting this wilful process of dehumanization. Some village communities decided that no member of the community would set foot in the relief centres and that no aid would be sought from any source outside the village; furthermore, it was decreed that no one should go hungry in the village. What this decision implied was that the foodstuffs available in the village were estimated to be sufficient to feed everyone, but that they needed to be more equitably distributed, and that the richest inhabitants had a duty to donate supplies and/or to provide jobs.

What is true at the local level should also be true at the national level: to refuse the deceptively easy solution offered by a food-aid programme that has to be paid for in a thousand different ways means that a country must rely entirely on its own resources; the people must be roused to action so that, disdaining the mentality of recipients of public assistance, they realize that the scourge of famine must be eliminated by taking immediate steps to resist the acceptance of food-aid programmes on terms determined by the donors, and by pursuing a long-term policy of transforming internal relations of inequality and external relations of dependence in such a way as to build a society that will be more just and more firmly in control of its own development.

It was only at the end of the 1960s that people began to give serious attention to the theme of poverty in the underdeveloped countries as a threat to the prosperity of the rich countries. The most forceful and closely reasoned statement on this subject was undoubtedly made by Robert McNamara in the speech he delivered at Montreal in 1966, when he was United States Secretary of Defence and the Viet Nam War was getting under way:

What is most significant of all is that there is a direct and constant relationship between the incidence of violence and the economic status of the countries afflicted. . . . The gap between the rich nations and the poor nations . . . is widening. By 1970, over one-half of the world's population will live in the independent nations which encircle the southern half of the planet. But this hungering half of the human race will by then command only one-sixth of the world's total of goods and services. . . . Our security is related directly to the security of the newly developing world. . . . Security is development and without development there can be no security.[35]

A less sophisticated expression of the view that established a link between stability and development is to be found in a speech Lyndon Johnson read in the same year (1966): 'There are three billion people in the world and we have only 200 million of them. We are outnumbered fifteen to one. If might did make right, they would sweep over the United States and take what we have. We have what they want.' This declaration, which could complement Necker's sentence which prefaces this article, reflects a particularly muscular conception of the right to be rich among the poor. The latter cannot claim any rights by virtue of the might that they owe to their numbers because it poses a threat to property.

Most of the industrialized countries of the 'First World' subscribed to such analyses. Their rhetoric changed only very slowly as decolonization advanced and as the poor countries set about combining their efforts, particularly from the time of the Cairo Conference in 1961 and the first United Nations Conference on Trade and Development (UNCTAD 1) in 1964 that was held as a result.

The representatives of the First World were almost unanimously opposed to the proposals submitted to that conference by the Third World countries. It must be recorded here, in the interests of historical accuracy, that the representative of the richest country in the First World went so far as to vote against the Third World proposal that follows: 'Economic relations between countries, including trade relations, shall be based on respect for the principles of sovereign equality of states, self-determination of peoples and non-interference in the internal affairs of other countries.'

Whereas the revolutionary approach to international inequalities sets rich, dominant countries belonging to the Centre against poor, dominated countries belonging to the Periphery and thus marks out the field of international violence, people who favour maintaining the status quo emphasize mutual interdependence and the multiplicity of poles of attraction. If a parallel can be drawn between intranational violence and international violence, the very existence of nation-states, reflecting various class alliances and caught up in complex networks of international alliances, certainly blurs the bipolar pattern.

Those who wish to change the existing international order in such a way as to set it moving towards the goal of greater equity and justice, and who are conducting a campaign within their own countries to bring about this change, are aware of the difficulty of combining their efforts at the international level, since each national movement is developing at its own rate and has to contend with specific problems. They make due allowance, in their action, for complexity and multiplicity. If, in their words, they give prominence to the bipolar picture of the situation, they do so because it stimulates their listeners to summon up all their strength for the struggle to achieve a more just international order. People who are in favour of maintaining the status quo know this very well, and consequently emphasize multiplicity so as to make their opponents feel powerless and bewildered in the face of the complexity of the tasks that need to be carried out. The example of UNCTAD 1 does, however, show that the bipolar pattern of antagonism really exists because, even in the matter of voting on proposals, the participating countries fell into two camps, each of which invariably took a unanimous decision as to whether the text presented should be accepted or rejected. The grouping of countries around these two poles of attraction makes it easier to discern the field of operation of the forces of international violence.

It has become increasingly rare in international proceedings for the theme developed by McNamara in his 1966 speech linking the security of rich countries to the development of poor countries to be evoked, because now it is easier to use humanitarian arguments. However, as E. S. Mason, a particularly realistic and lucid economist, wrote in 1955: 'Humanitarianism is not an important national interest; governments simply do not act on the basis of such unadulterated consideration.'[36]

Mason's object, like that pursued by Necker, was to enlighten the dominant classes as to their own interests. The philanthropist's approach, on the other hand, is designed to appeal to the sincere and generous feelings that exist within the rich nations. However, when this approach is given wide coverage by the mass media so as to ensure that substantial foreign-aid credits are voted, it may disconcert certain leaders of the business world and even some economists, who believe that they detect a contradiction between foreign aid and the development of the national economy. It consequently becomes necessary to remind them, albeit discreetly, that 'the principal purpose of foreign aid is to promote the security of our country and, in so far as our security is dependent on others, foreign aid is an essential part of a mutual security policy'.[37]

Aid from the rich countries has made it possible to promote, not the development of the poor countries, but a certain type of industrial and agricultural growth, the unequally distributed benefits of which have enabled the dominant social classes in the poor countries to strengthen their domination. This increase in the wealth, concentrated in the hands of a few, aggravates structural violence in the poor countries. The rich in the poor countries then need to strengthen their military and police forces in order to maintain their domination. The rich countries are thus afforded fresh opportunities to make further profits, as is shown by the substantial growth of arms sales throughout the world.

The potential threat presented by the poor people of the poor countries to the rich people of the world is regarded by the latter as sufficiently serious to justify putting an increasing amount of money into studies concerning the poor. Far fewer studies are devoted to the national centres of power and the nerve centres of the world economy, despite the fact that it is their practices which explain the persistence of poverty, hunger and famine, and even their present or foreseeable tendency to increase. The poor throughout the world, and even the poor countries as a whole, are thus emerging as the new dangerous classes. This is the idea that is suggested—whatever reservations may be made regarding this highly ideological division of our planet into three worlds—by the French expression 'Tiers-Monde', associated with the 'Tiers-État' of prerevolutionary France.[38] The poor of the world today, like the poor of Europe in previous centuries, come alive for us only when we see them through the eyes of the dominant classes; they are merely the subject of writings and speeches, never their authors. They are interviewed, photographed, measured, weighed, analysed, asked to give only a factual account of their work, their daily lives, what they eat, drink and desire. Civil servants define their basic needs in terms of calories, proteins and lengths of cloth.[39] They are advised to have fewer children and to educate them according to our own standards; they are urged to become more enterprising. Tolstoy wrote in 1893, in a booklet on the famine then devastating Russia:

Feed the people! Who then has taken it upon himself to feed the people? It is we, the civil servants, who have taken it upon ourselves to feed the very men who have always fed us and who go

on feeding us every day. . . . It can be said that bread, not to
mention all other forms of wealth, is produced directly by the
people. . . . How is it then that this bread is to be found, not in the
possession of the people, but in our hands, and that, by a peculiar
and artificial process, we have to return it to the people, cal-
culating so much for each person? . . . Must we delude ourselves by saying that the people are poor merely because they
have not yet had time to adjust to our civilization, but that, come
tomorrow, we shall set about imparting all our knowledge to them,
concealing nothing, and that then they will doubtless cease to be
poor . . . Do not all enlightened folk continue to live in the
towns—for what they claim to be a very exalted purpose—and
to eat in the towns the sustenance which is brought there and
for want of which the people are dying? And these are the
circumstances in which we have suddenly started to assure ourselves and everyone else that we are very sorry for the people
and that we want to save them from their wretched plight, a
plight for which we ourselves are responsible and which is indeed
necessary to us. Here is the cause of the futility of the efforts
made by those who, without changing their relationship with the
people, wish to come to their aid by distributing the riches which
have been taken from them.[40]

Notes

1. See B. N. Bhatia, *Famines in India*, p. 324, Delhi, Asia Publishing
   House, 1967.
2. In 1880 a Famine Commission in India laid down the main provisions
   of the famine laws, which, in more or less modified form, are still
   applied in India and Bangladesh.
3. Silvio Gomez de Almeida, *Le risque de famine dans le Nord-Est du
   Brésil*, Paris, INRA-GEREI; Geneva, UNRISD, June 1975, p. 11.
4. K. Suresh Singh, *The Indian Famine, 1967—A Study in Crises and
   Change*, p. 233, New Delhi, PPH, 1975.
5. See the document edited by the author: *Famine-Risk and Famine Prevention in the Modern World—Studies in Food Systems under Conditions
   of Recurrent Scarcity*, Geneva, UNRISD, June 1976, 100 p.
6. 'The miserly owner of stocks of corn refuses, even when offered a fortune,
   to provide his fellow men with the sustenance they lack. The pauper
   breathes his last beside an abundance which is no longer accessible to
   him and on which he neither dares nor is able to lay his hands.' Poster
   of the 'Patriots of 89', in Babeuf, *Le Tribun du peuple*, p. 182, Paris,
   Union Générale d'Éditions (10/18), 1969.
7. Mao Tse-tung, *Analyse des classes de la société chinoise*. Peking, Éditions
   en langues étrangères, 1966.
8. Bruhat-Dautry-Tersen, *La Commune de 1871*, 2nd ed., Paris, Éditions
   Sociales, 1970.
9. J. Necker, *Sur la législation et le commerce des grains*, Paris, 1775;
   and *Œuvres complètes*, Lausanne, 1786. The latter text does not appear
   to have been republished since the eighteenth century. A few quotations
   from it are to be found in K. Marx, *Histoire des doctrines économiques*
   (ed. by L. Kautsky, trans. by J. Molitor), Vol. I, p. 90–5. Paris, Alfred
   Costes, 1950.
10. An episode in the bread riots known as the 'guerre des farines' of
    April–May 1775, which foreshadowed the revolution of July 1789. On

this subject see, for instance, Edgar Faure, *La disgrâce de Turgot*, Paris, Gallimard, 1961.

11. Necker, *Sur la législation et le commerce des grains*, op. cit., Vol. I, p. 87.

12. Lavoisier, *Mémoire sur la respiration et la transpiration des animaux*, read to the Academy of Sciences, Paris, 3 May 1777. See also Brun. 'L'homme, système d'énergie' (Dossier Bis), *Jeune Afrique*, January–June 1975.

13. Necker, *Sur la législation et le commerce des grains*, op. cit., p. 169.

14. Adam Smith, *The Wealth of Nations*, p. 493, New York, The Modern Library, Random House, 1937.

15. Émile G. Leonard, 'La réforme et la naissance de l'Europe moderne', in *Encyclopédie de la Pléiade, Histoire universelle*, Vol. II, p. 12.

16. Pierre Dockes, *L'espoir dans la pensée économique*, p. 80, Paris, Nouvelle Bibliothèque Scientifique, Flammarion, 1969.

17. See for instance B. Geremek, *La Popolazione Marginale tra il Medioevo e l'Era Moderna*, Studi Storici, 1968; and Jean-Pierre Gutton, *La société et les pauvres. Exemple de la généralité de Lyon 1534-1789*, Paris, Les Belles-Lettres, 1971.

18. See for instance François Lebrun, *Les hommes et la mort en Anjou aux XVIIe et XVIIIe siècles*, Paris, Flammarion, 1975. See also texts by Voltaire: 'Dying of poverty and hunger to the sound of the Te Deum'; Boileau, 'Pale-faced want and doleful famine disturb the air with their wailing'; La Bruyère, 'Ordinary citizens, simply because they were rich, had the audacity to swallow at one gulp the food of a hundred families'; and above all the letter from Fénelon to Louis XIV: 'The glory that hardens your heart is dearer to you than justice . . . than the nourishment of your subjects, great numbers of whom are dying every day from diseases caused by famine.'

19. Eastern Europe continued to experience numerous famines, the worst of which occurred in Russia in 1891–92, 1905–06, 1911–15, 1921–22.

20. *New England Magazine* (Boston, Mass.), Vol. XXIII, No. 1, September 1900, cited in W. Dibgy, *Prosperous British India*, pp. 162–70, London, 1901.

21. Romesh Dutt, *Famines and Land Assessment in India*, London, 1900.

22. Dadabhai Naoroji, *Poverty and Un-British Rule in India*, London, Swan Sonnenschein, 1901.

23. Digby, op. cit.

24. Naoroji, op. cit., p.v.

25. Watt, *The Commercial Products of India*, p. 1088, London, 1908. Cf. P. Spitz, *Notes sur l'histoire des transferts de techniques dans le domaine de la production végétale*, p. 6. OECD, 1975 (DSTI/SPR/75–45).

26. Archives Nationales, Section Outremer, Paris, Affaires Politiques, AOF, Haute-Volta, Mission d'Inspection Bernard Sol, 1931–32, in Laurence Wilhelm, *Le rôle et la dynamique de l'état à travers les crises de subsistance : le cas de la Haute-Volta*. (Thesis, Geneva, Institut d'Étude du Développement/Institut Universitaire des Hautes Études Internationales, October 1976. Cf. also Bernard Sol's 1931–32 mission to Niger, in J. Egg, F. Lerin and N. Venin, *Analyse descriptive de la famine 1931 au Niger*, Paris, Geneva, INRA/UNRISD, July 1975. (Presented by P. Spitz.)

27. Gini Corrado, 'Les calamités économiques et sociales', *Data for the Study of Calamities*, pp. 95–111, Geneva, July–September 1926.

28. The year in which Mao Tse-tung's *Analysis of the Classes of Chinese Society* was written and W. H. Mallory's *China, Land of Famine* was published.

29. The World Economic Conference, May 1927, *Final Report*, Geneva, League of Nations, CEI-44(1).

30. *Workers' Nutrition and Social Policy—Studies and Reports (Social and Economic Conditions)*, No. 23, p. 249, Geneva, ILO.

31. 'The Relation of Nutrition to Health, Agriculture and Economic Policy', *Final Report of the Mixed Committee of the League of Nations*, Geneva, 1937, II A–10.

32. Lord Boyd-Orr, *As I Recall*, pp. 162–3, London, McGibbon & Kee, 1966.

33. See, for instance, President Truman's inaugural address of 20 January 1949 and his famous 'Point Four'.

34. Pierre Spitz, 'Les aides alimentaires, techniques et culturelles dans la politique agricole des États-Unis en Inde depuis la défaite du Kuomintang', *Mondes en Développement*, No. 4, 1973; Susan George, *How the Other Half Dies*, Penguin Books, 1976.

35. Robert S. McNamara, *The Essence of Security*, pp. 150–62, New York, N. Y., Harper & Row, 1968.

36. Edward S. Mason, *Promoting Economic Development*, Claremont, Calif., 1955.

37. Edward S. Mason, *Foreign Aid and Foreign Policy*, pp. 33–4, New York, Harper & Row, 1964.

38. The English equivalent does not suggest the same idea, particularly as the expression 'Third World', unlike 'Tiers-Monde', does not imply limiting the number of parts to three.

39. An attempt to find an alternative to this approach is made in the research work undertaken by the United Nations Research Institute for Social Development (UNRISD, Geneva) on the dual theme of 'livelihood' and 'participation', and, in particular, the research project entitled 'Food Systems and Society'.

40. Leo Tolstoy, *La Famine*, Paris, Éditions Perrinot, 1893.

'Institutional' violence, 'democratic' violence and repression

Pierre Mertens

Research Worker at the
Institute of Sociology
of the Free University
of Brussels

The two opposing forces of violence

The violence that is referred to these days as 'violence' (as though there were only one kind), the violence that makes the headlines, is almost invariably that of the rebel, the 'desperado'—call him what we will. And the context of this violence, which might tend to explain, if not justify it, is generally not mentioned. The news media, in this respect, are simply reflecting the ideological stance adopted by the ruling power. The violence we hear about, that we are told so much about, is often no more than the reprisals taken by dissidents in response to prior violence, which, although less obvious, is as profound as it is insidious, because it is embodied in an institution. It might be described, in other words, as the home-made violence of 'amateur' retaliation against the 'professional' violence practised by a regime which, by its abuses of power, has shown itself to be oppressive.

We might reasonably be asked, as Dom Helder Camara has done, to consider 'that injustice, wherever it occurs, is a form of violence' and that 'it can and must be proclaimed that is constitutes everywhere the leading form of violence'.[1] It is this initial and primordial violence that leads to the formation of a 'spiral of violence' in which every act of violence leads to further violence, like the murderous rages of the Atreids.

As Marcuse has clearly pointed out, when faced with violence on the part of a domineering ruling order that has grown tyrannical in one or another respect, 'there seems no alternative to meeting the violence head on'.[2] The argument is as old as history. We see it in *Antigone*[3] and in the Bible, in which, as we know, there is violence and violence;

there is the 'good' violence 'that does violence to the violent man'.[4]

How, in fact, can the oppressed cast off his violent role? Has he not been coached in it by the oppressor? Engels suggests that the role was created not by the revolutionary himself but by the state. Hence, 'it is when they affirm class violence that the oppressed actually create a society in which they lay claim to the moral values officially reserved for the non-violent'.[5] Here one can see the first intimation of the need for dictatorship by the proletariat. Similarly, Georges Sorel, in a more ambiguous doctrine, contrasts the healthy violence of the oppressed with the might and ferocity of the ruling class and advocates recourse to general strikes'.[6] Much later Frantz Fanon asserts that what is valid for the proletarian is also valid for the colonized subject.

The revolutionary does not make this profession of faith from a questionable love of violence; he believes in taking up arms to hasten the advent of a world based on a just peace, a peace that will truly recognize the legitimate claims of the people. He therefore believes that violence adopted in order to attain that world will entail the sacrifice of a firebreak in a temporary period of purgatory. Thinkers who are uneasy about this view have often condescendingly termed it a naive 'postulate'. But is their criticism justified? As Sartre has responded, 'I know that violence is necessary and has always been necessary for a transition from one form of society to another; but I do not know what kind of order will perhaps follow it.'[7] Dissidents, however, have no illusions concerning the 'status' to which they are likely to be relegated by the power they oppose; when it encounters the institutional violence of the ruling order, the violence 'of resistance' is necessarily destined to remain illegal.

As might be expected, the supporters of 'good' violence come up against a number of detractors, some of whom even hope to remain 'apolitical' and to take shelter behind purely humanistic professions of faith. Certain pacifists, for example, would like to think that non-violence has a better chance of disarming the opponent's violence, however powerful, than the desperate violence of the minority, which is bound to provoke new violence—the violence of repression. Anyone who reads the works of Gabriel Marcel and Jean-Marie Müller[8] will find non-violence extolled as the surest, most radical and quickest way of changing the world. By contrast, a number of social scientists hold that the struggle for peace entails a rigorous examination of the nature of war[9] and that, without such knowledge, doctrinal non-violence becomes mere sermonizing. This view aside, there are other sound reasons for questioning this kind of pacificism. All too often, those who condemn violence *per se* tend to regard the injustices and inequalities with which the status quo abounds as inevitable, unchangeable 'decrees of fate' to which we must necessarily become resigned.[10]

Let us also bear in mind that, as Maurice Merleau-Ponty long ago pointed out: 'To teach non-violence is to[11] consolidate the violence that is already established, i.e. a system of production that makes poverty and war inevitable.'[12] And, defending 'progressive, necessary' violence—none other than the 'good' violence we have already come across—he went on to attack the 'retrograde' violence inherent in liberal societies but deliberately hidden behind a purely formal system of ethics.[13]

Anyone who invokes non-violence—either in praise or condemnation—is likely to lapse into oversimplification and crude generalizations. There are as many forms of non-violence as there are of violence, and most advocates of non-violence agree on only one point: a refusal to resort to arms except in cases of extreme necessity. Consequently the term 'non-violence' is ambiguous and deceptive. Dom Helder Camara preferred to do without it: 'I do not much like the term "non-violence". I infinitely prefer Roger Schutz's expression "the violence of men of peace", or indeed any definition that is clearly distinct from "pacifism". How can we expect the young to renounce armed violence if we do not offer them in its place something strong, effective and capable of obtaining concrete results?'[14]

Let us consider the 'successful' advocates of non-violence, those who achieved the objective they had set themselves and had sufficient charisma for the purpose. There are very few, two of the most famous being Gandhi and César Chavez. Mahatma Gandhi's stages of evolution, from his first fast and the strike of 1918 up to his death, provide a perfect example. Initially he believed that the only unjust action was one 'that harmed none of the opposing parties'.[15] This subsequently led him to assert: 'For the sake of non-violence, we practice violence on a large scale. Fearful of spilling blood, we torment people day after day till their blood runs dry.'[16] He reproached himself with this and became afraid that passive resistance and civil disobedience, like the 'satya-graha' that formed their ideological basis, might represent another source of wrongful suffering for the opponent, and he actually called off a railway strike 'so as not to torment the government'.[17] A strange scruple indeed.

He finally perceived, however, that many advocates of passive resistance had adopted that stance only through weakness and an inability to answer force with force. In the end he discovered that there is violence in non-violence and that, ideally, it should strive to be 'the non-violence of the strong'.[18]

The path of his evolution is clear. And it should be noted that in the eyes of his opponents—who were not mistaken—Gandhi very quickly appeared dangerous and therefore violent. 'Victimologists' would not hesitate to regard civil disobedience—particularly on a large scale as in the case of the 1930–31 protest march against the salt excise laws, or the boycott of British textiles—as an extreme form of provocation. Proof that the major prophets of Gandhian non-violence were seen by their opponents as thinly disguised terrorists is manifest in the fate meted out to them: to Gandhi, to Martin Luther King, to Lambrakis and, going back to the two earliest pacifists, to Socrates[19] and Jesus. They paid for their principles. Although they had not put themselves outside the law, they had operated on its fringes—and that sufficed to strip them of its protection.

Indeed, Gandhi's strategy—apart from the ideology that inspired and set it in motion—succeeded in mobilizing the people precisely because of an inherent 'violence' that precluded any compromise.[20]

The case of César Chavez is no less revealing. In order to wrest from the authorities better conditions for the Mexican migrant agricultural workers in California this militant trade unionist preached neither social peace nor class co-operation. He even challenged the idealism and morality that prompted some to deny the existence of any conflict. He urged transformation of the existing structures, advocating social revolution in its full sense. And it was by force that he prevented the rent strike from being broken, by setting up strike pickets and boycotting 'bad laws'. Once again, the adversary was not mistaken in seeing the 'Chicanos', with Chavez as their leader, as 'Viet-Cong' waging a kind of 'guerrilla' warfare.[21]

Pacifists, however, are not the only ones to denounce the necessary recourse to violence. There is the objection raised by sociologists who fear glorification of violence for its own sake and decry the attraction it exerts on certain thinkers of the left today. Hannah Arendt, for example, attempts to demythify the violence advocated by the American 'new left', which draws its inspiration from the message of such people as Sorel, Pareto, Fanon and Sartre. She fears that 'purifying' violence, sanctioned as an end in itself, does not constitute a valid answer in the social debate. She therefore feels justified in relegating both the unorthodox left and the forces of repression to the same level, condemning them equally on the grounds that the violence of each feeds on that of the other. She does, however, admit that 'in certain circumstances, violence is the only way to balance the scales'.[22] But what exactly are those circumstances?

In much the same way, Friedrich Hacker does not hesitate to condemn all forms of violence and all those who resort to it or advocate it. He has no qualms, for example, in writing: 'Sartre, Fanon, Eldridge Cleaver, Che Guevara, Ho Chi Minh and Mao Tse-tung all celebrate and ritualize their own violence, representing it as an instrument of deliverance and freedom and a source of unity and abnegation. On the authority of their shameless ideologies they sanctify violence with the name of counter-violence and extol the triumph of inhumanity in the destruction of man'.[23] Moreover, later in this argument, we find the author lumping together Ho Chi Minh, Castro, Nixon, Hitler, Mussolini and Stalin.[24]

Such is the curious pot-pourri to which Hacker's argument leads. It is an example, in fact, of the kind of amalgamation, sometimes unintentional, that may well result from putting oneself, as does Hacker, so far 'above' politics and ideologies that one loses sight of things. As Jean-Marie Domenach has observed: 'We are very quick to condemn violence from whatever source; we denounce wars, insurrections and reigns of terror with a blithe lack of discrimination; but when we do this we strike merely at the most visible aspect of violence and retreat into a fragile moralism.'[25]

Indeed, is it 'reasonable' to remain neutral towards the Guatemalan and the Dhofar peasants and the power that is wiping them out, towards the South African rebels who are the victims of the apartheid practices of the Pretoria government? Can we maintain a 'serious' attitude only at this price? Anyone who is thus determined not to take sides, even if prompted by humanitarian principles, exposes himself either deliberately or unconsciously to the risk of rushing to the aid of that structural violence he has finally refused to recognize as such; he thereby becomes both its accomplice and its hostage. It is also the best way of attaining to the detachment of a false pacifism,[26] which guarantees a permanently stainless conscience. Kurt Vonnegut, speaking one day of the lack of feeling shown by the 'silent majority' in the United States towards the bombing of Viet Nam, used the term 'hysterical indifference'.[27]

In the final analysis, Hacker's argument is based on the assumption that revolutionary violence itself creates the elements of a situation in which it offers and presents itself as the only possible way out and the sole conceivable response to institutionalized violence. Such an attitude leads to a sweeping and final abandonment of efforts to identify the causes of violence rather than to worry about its effects.

For some, counter-violence possesses the major drawback of prolonging structural violence without providing the means of fighting it effectively, since counter-violence results in triggering repression that is capable at any time of crushing it.[28] By virtue of a kind of Pascal-like gambling on the eventual establishment of a free and just society, even left-wing thinkers such as Roger Garaudy appear to have reached the conclusion that it is impossible for a society free of violence to emerge from the purifying fire of revolutionary violence. In any case, this vision of an all-renewing revolution is held to be nothing more than wishful thinking on the part of Nietzschean-oriented intellectuals[29] who are cut off from the masses and are really not particularly concerned about the 'public good'.

Others believe that the institutional forms of violence are those to be curtailed and attacked; they view resistance to them as a right and even a duty, resistance being 'the motive force needed for the genuine development of liberty'.[30] Human rights, those supreme values of peace and respect for life, have often had to be seized by revolutionary violence (in 1688 in Great Britain, in 1776 in the United States, in 1789 and beyond in France), sometimes in its bloodiest form. Does this mean we have to agree with Marcuse when he tells us that 'Revolutionary terror is different from white terror, because revolutionary terror—by its very terror—entails its own transcendence towards a free society'?[31]

There is only one problem: all too often, no sooner does the revolution dawn than it is betrayed or perverted

Institutional violence in democracies

We shall now turn our attention mainly to violence in democracies. Totalitarian violence, after all, is axiomatic, and we shall merely refer to it here and there for the purpose of comparison. The violence found in democracies, although omnipresent, is not of the same obvious kind. It nevertheless has occasion to show itself, both in domestic affairs—against citizens or foreign immigrants—and in foreign relations. Let us examine the forms it takes in the political, economic and cultural spheres.[32]

Political violence

A totalitarian state makes use of violence as a system of government; a democracy resorts to it only selectively or intermittently in what are referred to as 'periods of crisis', at which times even those international conventions that insist on respect for human rights contain provisions for suspending the application of most of those rights.[33] Since the gravity of the situation is theoretically assessed by the government, the door is left open to possible abuse. The term 'crisis' implies a threat to the regime. In order to stay in power, rulers who have reached a point at which their followers have disowned them or become a minority may overturn the true democracy of the country and replace it by a merely formal democracy. And the army may well be helping them behind the scenes. Every democratic constitution contains provisions to enable the government to assume special powers. Here again, there is a constant danger of abuse of power.

Even the sacrosanct dogma of the separation of powers is sometimes alarmingly breached, either occasionally or continuously. In many democracies the panoply of the judiciary includes special courts whose 'mission' is to permeate the wall between the judicial and the executive franchise. The establishment of a whole range of 'specialized' forces of repression,[34] which exist on the very fringe of the law in its strict sense, is hardly reassuring.[35] The penitentiary system too, in its disregard for modern thought and attitudes and in its failure to conform to the goals it sets itself, frequently constitutes a bastion of conservatism.[36] Psychiatric institutions hardly differ from prisons.[37]

States also have ways of censoring the information media or of using them to communicate their own propaganda. We shall look at this aspect in greater detail when we examine intellectual and cultural violence.

The increased bureaucratization of the services that are 'placed at the disposal' of those being administered leads to the 'data processing' of citizens; the computer is installing itself among us without our knowledge; this inevitably means the invasion of privacy.

There are whole categories of citizens who are condemned to marginality either because they do not quite fit into the 'normal' pattern of the social majority[38] or simply because of certain taboos.

Edward Sagarin notes that even today 'the homosexual is still highly stigmatized and treated cruelly by society'.[39] It has frequently been suggested that the murder of Pier Paolo Pasolini on 2 November 1975 was a political crime, in the strict sense of the word. In our opinion,[40] although the murder was clearly political, it was political not only in the strict sense of the word, which minimizes the crime, but in the larger sense as well—the puritanism, the prejudices, the conventions, the irrevocable condemnation of 'deviance' by a particular society at a given point in its limited evolution. It goes without saying that the same conditions can apply to 'sexual minorities', political dissidents,[41] the 'handicapped' of every kind, those who are 'stigmatized' because of their race and all the 'non-conformist' occupations, etc.

Goffman notes that, if we abandon the role allotted to us by society, we run great risks—either of losing face or of losing our freedom.[42] He might have added that we may also lose our lives.

There are judicial means of protesting against the possible abuses and threats we have mentioned. In all democracies there are the constitutional freedoms that are their very foundation and without which they would cease to exist. International instruments—which generally take precedence over domestic legislation—confirm or reinforce these safeguards. Unfortunately, though, because they are often too abstract to take into account the concrete human being situated in a specific social reality,[43] their protection is, at least to some extent, theoretical.[44]

At the international or transnational level, a certain kind of rhetoric that magically invokes the tenets of democracy can create a smokescreen. In the name of the intrinsic virtues of parliamentary government, even as serious an organization as the Council of Europe unhesitatingly retained Turkey within its ranks, despite the fact that, at the time, Turkey was as repressive domestically towards progressive elements as it had been aggressive externally in its attempts to annex Cyprus.[45]

Economic violence

One does not have to be a Marxist to recognize the fact that the capitalist system as such is based on violence done to the proletariat. What the Marxists have done, not surprisingly, is to take this fact as their cornerstone and as a total justification of the criticism they level at 'property, which is based on the violence of the ruling class'. Hence their conception of wage-earning labour, which during the last century was no better than forced labour and whose qualities of bondage and alienation, in the opinion of many, can never be entirely destroyed by means of successive improvements and humanitarian reforms alone.[46] It is essentially this quality that they see as constituting class violence—'the routine, dehumanized, institutional violence that is inherent in the structures of the capitalist state'.[47]

It may be said, therefore, that we are still burdened today with the legacy of this type of enslavement, so much so that many Marxists are themselves forced to admit that, under socialist as well as capitalist regimes, the production sector is based on coercion.

In the distribution sector, the capture and control of markets, the implacable application of the laws of competition and the appearance of new forms of high-pressure salesmanship, which, for the poorly paid, become snares and delusion, are accompanied by new forms of credit and concentrations of capital for the purposes of exploitation, dumping, various kinds of stock-market speculation, etc.[48] We see today the strides made by a whole new genre of 'white-collar delinquency', a delinquency of profit, an economic delinquency 'that has nothing in common with the kind of delinquency punished by the penal code'.[49]

It will be said that all these dangers or defects are hardly disguised. But very few people are prepared to consider them in terms of institutional violence, because what is happening here is that a particular form of society is aiding and abetting a particular class, and vice versa.

Oddly enough, it is often only when the 'sins' of capitalism reach an international scale that their violent nature is unmasked beyond all doubt—as when the development of the multinational corporations was denounced by the Russell Tribunal at its 1975 session in Brussels, concerning 'American crimes in Latin America'. Similarly, certain economic enfranchisement measures (acts of nationalization, for example, or the denunciation of unfair agreements previously concluded with large foreign companies, such as the International Petroleum Company in Peru, may be seen as a means of 'emancipating' nations formerly subject to the colonial yoke. The full force of the phenomenon can be seen in the 'economic war' waged among capitalist countries and between capitalist and socialist countries, especially when it concerns arms exports.[50] All too often, a Third World country's pseudo-development is presumed to take place amidst incalculable squandering of the country's natural resources, through overexploitation of the toiling masses and—as a frequently inevitable corollary—repression linked to this 'economic policy' with widespread unemployment and aggravation of the existing underdevelopment.[51] Here we are once again entering the realm of totalitarianism but, this time, it is a totalitarianism that, riding roughshod over an entire population, enjoys a special relationship with the 'free world'. Finally, there exist national minorities who see their social subjection as a kind of colonization from within. Stokely Carmichael and Charles V. Hamilton cite the case of economic relations between the black community and the rest of American society, which reflect the former's status as a colonized community.[52]

In sum, the economic violence done to human communities 'literally shortens the lives of social groups or defenceless peoples'.[53]

There is a final remark to be made about this economic violence within capitalist society. A trend in sociology has been to try to define, in particular, the social significance of the right to die not just at any time or anywhere[54] and to reveal the inequality that still exists in this respect: 'How can there be equality in death when there is so little in life?'[55] We feel that, in the context of a study of violence in general, this point was worth reiterating.[56]

Lastly we may note that, while the right to strike forms the standard legal remedy for institutional economic violence—and we know how fierce a struggle was needed to obtain recognition of this right—a growing number of workers today consider it neither adequate nor always capable of obtaining a satisfactory response to every claim arising within its field of action. The new remedies employed as a result are of questionable legality: 'wildcat' strikes, unauthorized production, the occupation of factory premises, forcible detention of managers, etc.

Intellectual violence

In a monumental thesis entitled *Totalitarian Languages*,[57] Jean-Pierre Faye suggests that history is created 'by being recounted' and cannot be created otherwise. It is necessary, therefore, to assess the effect of this 'narrative' on 'the account given by history of itself'. The establishment produces its own language to such an extent that it assumes a monopoly of official terminology. This helps us to understand how whole populations can blindly follow a demented or hysterical dictator and the handful of strongmen who put him into power and keep him there. This unfathomable enigma and the absurdity it represents can be comprehended only in terms of the extension of a form of language and of its uses and abuses. 'With Dr Goebbels', says Faye, 'history turned into a horror story from which humanity was to escape only after a considerable time.'[58] Totalitarianism, at least, can be regarded as irrational and pathological in many respects, but the abuse of the power of words can be proved in democracies too.

Any culture is intimately associated with a given society, which gives birth to it, nurtures it, teaches and thereby propagates it and, up to a point, imposes it. In asserting its own existence, it thereby denies the existence of other cultures or, at the very least, supplants them and behaves 'as if' they did not exist.

Those imperialistic conquests that presented themselves as vehicles of progress inspired by a 'civilizing mission' turned into what Robert Jaulin[59] has called 'ethnocides', i.e. assaults on the lives of certain communities in terms of what they were, the destruction (less military than psychological at times) of civilizations whose cultural identity was quite simply denied. It was an ethnocentric policy, a 'white peace' imposed by force, allegedly inspired by the best intentions and always operating by means of 'self-extension' at the expense of the other party with pretensions to wholeness. The massacres resulting from this blindness continue.

Let us look now at the consequences of the imposition of culture 'at home'. We refer in our societies to 'general culture'. But is it as general as we pretend?[60] Claude Javeau, the Belgian sociologist, clearly demonstrates in this connection the way in which bourgeois culture drives out popular culture.[61] In its place there springs up that bastard form shamefully described as 'mass culture', or what Richard Hoggart terms 'candy-floss' culture,[62] the commercial culture carried out by the sensationalist press and other mass media and promoted so lavishly that it is offered not so much as a choice as communicated by a sort of 'bludgeoning' process.

By way of a brief digression, let us consider the fact that, in Belgium, sport comes under the Ministry of Culture. This is not as illogical as it appears. On the contrary, it represents an endorsement—albeit probably a fortuitous and unintended one—of the role played by sport, together with the ideology and mythology that surround competitive sporting events, in 'mass culture'. Sport, in fact, obeys the laws of profitability, bureaucratic and hierarchical organization, publicity and propaganda that we have seen to be applicable in other fields.[63] It has its part to play in the capitalist system of industrial production and it is also perfectly suited to the propaganda requirements of many socialist states.

In particular, the exercise in sublimation known as the Olympic Games has always provided fodder for scribbling of the most inane kind. These games, for all their supposedly 'apolitical' nature, have never failed to stir up chauvinism, aggressiveness (even though concealed and unavowed) and the commercialization of values.[64] We should remember the bloody police repression that marked the 1968 games in Mexico.

States have the power to exercise varying degrees of control over the mass information media. They own (or hold a majority interest in) 'national' radio and television broadcasting channels. They can 'concentrate' the weight of the press or give selective assistance channelled towards certain newspapers. They can issue propaganda, either directly or indirectly (by the judicious selection of news and the relative importance given to different items). Direct censorship persists even in those parts of the press reputed to be the most free. The role played by advertising has a tremendous influence on the fate of newspapers and 'colours' them while reinforcing constantly the values of a society based on consumption.

As information is one of the keys to power, it is by no means easy to gain access to the 'media'. And freedom of the press does not mean much unless it is accompanied by a 'right to be informed'.[65] There must be freedom to print both news and comment if 'information starvation' is to be avoided. Both misinformation and failure to inform do violence to the reader.

Turning to another form of cultural violence, we must underline the social discrimination that persists in education, its lack of genuine democratization and the inequality of opportunity that is still the rule rather than the exception in so many 'exemplary' democracies.

We must also say a few words about the relationship between the man of science and authority, together with the responsibilities it entails. The scientist sometimes inadvertently becomes the faithful servant of an ideology over which he has no control.[66] Authority depends on science to provide it with rationales. 'Political power, which is undeniably violent, has to give itself the appearance of being founded on the natural order so that it can rely upon a consensus rather than on physical force. In order to do this it, constantly makes use of prevailing patterns of belief so as to shape them to its own advantage.'[67] The greatest danger at present stems from the assertion that a technocracy deemed to be governed by a form of objective rationality can afford to do without 'ideological chimeras'. It is alleged to be 'possible henceforth for politically neutral professional élites to organize society scientifically in the general interest'.[68]

What democratic remedy is there for cultural violence? There is intellectual protest with all its recent innovations: open universities, alternative schools and 'free television', not to mention scientific research and literature and artistic creativity, which for the time being at least are still bastions of liberty in our 'advanced liberal' régimes. Even if the non-conformist intellectual is more often than not fated to play the court jester and to be read by the bourgeois class he professes to detest, there may—at any time and in any society—emerge a man or woman who will cry out, when the need comes, 'J'accuse', and who will represent, as it has been said Zola represented, 'an instant in the conscience of mankind'.

Repression
of counter-institutional violence

The legal function

Many jurists in all good faith draw a distinction between the law and the state it serves, seeing the law as apolitical and as enjoiyng a kind of autonomy that places it firmly above the political arena. This blatantly disregards the fact that the law has an ideological content. It comes to the aid of the existing structures when necessary, supports the established authorities and champions of the status quo. But all this is done with the invocation of sacrosanct words and concepts. The law of nations, in particular, is studded with such ideas as 'the right of peoples to self-determination', 'the duty to refrain from interfering in the internal affairs of states', and 'the prohibition of aggression', to say nothing of the 'human rights' and 'fundamental freedom' that would appear to constitute safeguards against injustice, inequality and arbitrary treatment. However, it is all too obvious that, in spite of *jus cogens* and all the paraphernalia of international justice, it is possible for the worst iniquities to be perpetrated with impunity in the name of an ideology—provided that the ideology is dominant. The myth of a 'law of disarmament', to take but one example, is sufficient to illustrate the point.[69]

It is also well known that the equality of defendants before the law is a polite fiction.[70] People are tried not as individuals but as representatives of a class; certain trials are treated as 'non-political' even where the charge involved is by no means free of political motivation.[71] The esoteric character of legal terminology and the pomp of legal procedure tend to intimidate the defendant and form part of a mechanism more likely to crush the poor than the rich. It is theoretically possible, of course, for justice to be one thing and law another, the latter having no responsibility for the ambiance in which it is applied. In every society, however, the legal code always undeniably constitutes a statement of the 'rules of the game'.[72]

Because of the trappings of the law, however, because of the cloak of morality that protects it, and even because of its own formalism as well, it can turn on those who framed it for their own use—by clients who manage to insist on the letter of the law and force it at last to express that truth latent in its verbal varnish. Fact and fiction thus can sometimes coincide; authority can be caught in the trap of its own legalism. Over and against those jurists who toady to authority, it is still possible to conceive of a non-hierarchic form of justice in which sanctimonious phrases would at long last give way 'to justice based on freedom and equality'.[73]

Repression of 'terrorism'

Nazi crimes during the Second World War, it will be recalled, were so unspeakably horrible and so unprecedentedly barbaric that in 1945 new legal concepts had to be invented to deal with them: concepts such as 'crimes against humanity', formally recognized by Article 6 of the Nuremberg Tribunal Charter, and formally recognized on 9 December 1948 by the Convention on the Prevention and Punishment of the Crime of Genocide. These innovations by no means pleased all jurists, some of whom deplored the threat they posed to the principle of non-retroactivity in penal law. References to 'the law of the victor' were heard.

But the law also has a short memory. Twenty years later, when the crimes in question were nearly due to become prescribed, it was almost decided not to uphold the principle of imprescriptibility for punishment and prosecution with respect to those crimes. The assumptions on which the statute of limitations is normally based in penal law were invoked, despite the fact that not one could be applied to the circumstances in question. Those same states that today believe in punishing terrorism by individuals were very tempted at that time to show great indulgence towards crime sponsored and organized by a state that had itself become guilty of murder.

The whole history of 'terrorism', as a concept in law, rests upon a fiction sanctioned initially by the Convention for the

Prevention and the Repression of Terrorism. From then on it was accepted that terrorism would not be recognized as a political crime. 'Depoliticizing' the concept denied the 'terrorists' the privilege allowed those who commit acts recognized as political—that a political offender cannot be extradited. In every text dealing with the subject, whether in general or specific terms, attempts at definition are always replaced by a depoliticization. Far more important, in virtually every case there is no mention of state terror. 'Terrorism' is always perpetrated by the other party, the opponent, the dissident, the rebel. And yet every state possesses ammunition in its legal arsenal for successful prosecution, especially on charges of contravening the 1949 Conventions on Humanitarian Law.

What then is the rhyme or reason for this incrimination? Is it to some extent intended to create a kind of 'aggravating circumstance'? This is no mere debate between differing schools of thought, however. The argument is not without importance. The 1937 Convention never obtained the necessary ratifications to come into force.

Nevertheless, on 27 January 1977, the Council of Europe adopted a European Convention on the Suppression of Terrorism, which suffers from the same invalidating defects as those already mentioned. This convention is concerned not only with avoiding the kind of 'blackmailing terrorism' (hijacking, kidnapping, etc.) that most people would condemn but even with the most traditional violent political acts. As Jean Salmon says, it is a wonder they left out 'hold-ups at the point of a dagger or Mauser rifle'.[74] It would not matter if extradition had not become the rule in all these cases, in defiance of every principle that traditionally forbids extradition for political offences.[75] But, of course, in the eyes of the convention the 'political offence' has now virtually ceased to exist. Heribert Golsong, Director of Legal Affairs at the Council of Europe,[76] contends that there never was a generally accepted definition of 'political offences'. And so the argument for suppressing 'terrorism' (equally undefined, for obvious reasons) rests on this juridical lacuna. The one minute exception to the application of the text is hardly sufficient to set our minds at rest. The proviso in question stipulates that the intentions of the state requesting extradition are to be taken into consideration—as though such states were in the habit of divulging their intentions.

With the ratification of this document the political offence has been abolished and with it the right to asylum. This 'disappearance' of the political crime is of particular interest in that the concept was promoted in the first place by regimes that considered it necessary to give recognition to 'the autonomy of politics' as against economic power; it was thus a 'liberal' idea making it possible 'to wipe out the power wielded in practice by economic forces'.[77] In other words, it was not something invented by revolutionaries. As often happens in law, however, a concept may be given a meaning unsuspected by its author and turned against him. It is precisely to prevent that eventuality that the principle in question has now been reduced to nothing by the very people who created it.

Perhaps we shall be told that the new convention, as the fruit of the 'good tree' of Europe, can hardly be very evil: are not the member states of the Council of Europe democratic by definition?

When the European Convention for the Protection of Human Rights was signed in 1950, some people did not see the purpose of including, *inter alia*, a provision relating to torture. Here again, was not torture unthinkable in a member state of the Strasbourg body? And then came the Cyprus affair, the war in Algeria, the dictatorial regime of the Greek colonels. It had not been a mistake, after all, to provide 'for every eventuality'.

As for 'European terrorism', we have seen it in the Baader-Meinhof affair (in the Federal Republic of Germany), with bans on professional activity and 'suicides' in prison; we have seen it in the 'strategy of tension' (in Italy); we have seen it in torture in Ulster (in the United Kingdom); we have seen it in the Abu-Daoud affair, that faithful echo of the Ben Barka affair (in France). We have seen it in the erstwhile fascism of Greece and in the present highly troubled state of Turkey. These countries will in the future be able to get virtually anyone extradited—to all intents and purposes simply by asking. Are we really justified in being reassured so easily?

Nor have we looked yet at certain internal legal measures and legislative adjustments that have enabled repression to be intensified. Let us merely note that, on the whole, they reflect the ambiguities found in international law.

Torture under democracies

Just as, when we speak of 'terrorism', we think only of the terrorism practiced by dissidents, we link 'torture' with 'totalitarian' states.

In its *Report on Torture* Amnesty International demonstrated that torture was practiced in more than sixty countries. Under a dictatorship the practice is hardly surprising, since it is part of the system. Some places are veritable strongholds of torture. But what about it when it happens in an advanced, liberal regime?

Following the investigation by Amnesty International and the official inquiries set up in Great Britain, the European Commission of Human Rights was able to establish that after the launching of 'Operation Demetrius' in Ulster on 9 August 1971, hundreds of people were arrested, sent to detention centres and subjected to 'various forms of interrogation'. These consisted essentially of five methods described as 'sensory deprivation'. This is known more familiarly as 'clean' torture, since it is supposed to leave no traces. Its after-effects are in fact such that some of the former detainees are still suffering today from incurable traumas. Special coaching had been provided by experts in the methods in question for the purpose of the operation. Given the degree of preparation and the scale of the operation, it is difficult to give credence to the suggestion lamely put forward by the accused government that these incidents were mere 'errors of judgement' of the kind that can always occur in war. A secondary defence, mentioned also in some of the conclusions reached in the reports drawn up by the official British inquiries, was the fact that the people subject to 'ill-treatment' were believed to be terrorists or at least IRA sympathizers. In other words, each case would be merely the exception that proves the rule: it is only suspected terrorists who are tortured. This is, in fact, a widely held view.

When it comes to the most heinous offences against law, jurists always give the impression of being somewhat bewildered and at a loss. It is exactly as though they found it immensely difficult to define any enormity—which is understandable enough. To provide a highly detailed definition of genocide, crimes against humanity, or torture, filled with subtle distinctions, would be considered inhuman. But to abandon all distinctions is to risk lumping together into the same general category a haphazard assortment of acts that differ widely in their degree of barbarity. What is certain, in any event, is that by virtue of the actual text of the new convention itself (Article 15) torture is one of the very few acts in the application of law that is never tolerable in any circumstances. It would be utterly monstruous if this were not so.

The accused government made the curious point that this was 'clearly not the kind of situation the drafters of the convention had in mind, being concerned in the post-war period to prevent the resurgence of Nazi-type situations. There was no question here of that kind of situation or regime, nor was it a case of a military dictatorship persecuting its opponents'. In a sense, this was the best thing that could be said; in another, it was the worst possible thing to say if the British Government was really trying to exonerate itself. Similarly, the vehemence with which it protested that the case had nothing in common with the notorious precedent of tortures in Greece was something of a two-edged weapon. And what can we make of the defendant's reference to the damages paid to the victims, surely in itself tantamount to recognition of its own responsibility?

We are not suggesting that any reasonable person would attempt to equate the British Government with regimes specializing in torture. But is this not the point: that the lesson to be learned from the affair is that a state so different in every way from those at which our present criticism is directed nevertheless resorted to such practices? We may note, more-over, that repressive measures are to an increasing extent forming an integral part of the general societal functions exercised by the ruling order.[78]

At what point, then, does torture become 'institutional'? So institutional, in fact, that we find the doctor, whose presence all too often amounts to complicity, collaborating with the interrogator?

'Torture by the state', writes Vidal-Naquet, 'is in fact nothing more nor less than the most direct and the most immediate form of domination of one man by another, in other words, the very essence of politics.'[79]

234 *Pierre Mertens*

Conclusion

Of all the evils that give rise to violence and sometimes form
a basis for it, there is one more deadly than all the rest that
any study of the subject has a duty to stress, for the work will
otherwise remain a mere formality. We are referring to what
Egil Fossum has described as 'violence by omission', i.e. 'tacit
violence, that product of the social structure that takes the
form of famine, disease and humiliation and is reflected in the
statistics on life-expectancy, infant mortality, calorie intake,
frequency of epidemics, etc.'. As Robin Clarke points out,
in the final analysis there is as much violence in the way in
which each nation treats its underprivileged classes—or, in the
case of the southern hemisphere, underdeveloped peoples—as
in an attack on a bank messenger or café owner by a gang
of thugs.[80]

This understatement nevertheless has the merit of revealing
a glimpse of a world in which violence is ubiquitous and
occurs simultaneously at every level in the form of injustices
and inequalities that damage and threaten the whole social
edifice. Let us reflect on this before announcing that there
is no such thing as legitimate violence or just war. And let us
ask ourselves first of all whether, in a world of flagrant social
injustice, there is not more violence in maintaining the status
quo than in upsetting it. 'In order to understand my actions',
Leilah Khaled advises us, 'you will have to analyse their
underlying causes.'[81]

Is it really too much to ask? And does her request bear
the stamp of hysteria or of humility?

1. Dom Helder Camara, *Spirale de violence*, p. 16, Paris, Desclée de
   Brouwer, 1970.
2. H. Marcuse, *La fin de l'utopie* [Das Ende der Utopie], p. 8, Paris,
   Éditions du Seuil et Delachaux et Niestlé.
3. Cf. Simone Fraisse, *Le mythe d'Antigone*, Paris, Armand Colin, 1974.
4. Xavier Léon-Dufour, 'La violence selon la Bible', *Esprit* (Paris),
   February 1970, p. 327.
5. See F. Engels, *Théorie de la violence*, p. 37, Paris. Ed. 10/18, 1972
   (preface by Gilbert Mury). See also pp. 201, 224 and 261.
6. See *Réflexions sur la violence*, new edition, Paris, Marcel Rivière, 1972.
7. Interview, 17 June 1973, in Francis Jeanson, *Sartre dans sa vie*, p. 296,
   Paris, Éditions du Seuil, 1974.
8. Jean-Marie Müller, *L'évangile de la non-violence*, Paris, Plon, 1971.
9. See Gaston Bouthoul, *Lettre ouverte aux pacifistes*, Paris, Albin Michel,
   1973.
10. Jacques Ellul is no exception to the rule. See *De la Révolution aux
    révoltes*, Paris, Calmann-Lévy, 1972 ('Liberté de l'esprit' collection).

11. As Pope Paul VI urged the diplomats accredited to the Holy See. See *Le Monde*, 18 January 1977.

12. Quoted by d'Astier de la Vigerie, in *La Violence* (Semaine des intellectuels catholiques), 1967, p. 26, Paris, Desclée de Brouwer.

13. See Maurice Merleau-Ponty, *Humanisme et terreur*, p. IX, Paris, 1947. It will be remembered that Merleau-Ponty became involved in a heated argument with Albert Camus on this subject, the echoes of which can be found in 'Ni victimes ni bourreaux', in Albert Camus, *Essais*, pp. 280 et seq., 332 et seq., Paris, Gallimard. See also Maurice Weyembergh, 'Merleau-Ponty et Camus', in *Annales de l'Institut de Philosophie* (Free University of Brussels), 1971, pp. 53–99.

14. Dom Helder Camara, *Les confessions d'un évêque : conversations avec José de Broucker*, p. 164, Paris, Éditions du Seuil, 1977.

15. Erik H. Erikson, *La vérité de Gandhi*, p. 324, Paris, Flammarion, 1974. The author is a Western psychoanalyst who had access to sources that had long remained unpublished.

16. Ibid., p. 355.

17. Ibid., p. 327.

18. See Roger Garaudy, *Pour un dialogue des civilisations*, p. 185, Paris, Denoël, 1977.

19. In this connection, see the ideas expressed by Maurice Clavel, in *Nous l'avons tous tué*, Paris, Éditions du Seuil, 1977.

20. On this subject, see Garaudy, op. cit., p. 181.

21. See Peter Matthiess, *Sal si puede: César Chavez and the New American Revolution*, pp. 158–9, New York, Random House, 1970. For a comprehensive view of the social progress triggered off by Chavez, see Jean-Marie Müller and Jean Kalman, *César Chavez — Un combat non violent*, Paris, Fayard, Le Cerf, 1977.

22. Hannah Arendt, *Du mensonge à la violence*, p. 173, Paris, Calmann-Lévy, 1972.

23. Friedrich Hacker, *Agression et violence dans le monde moderne*, p. 103, Paris, Calmann-Lévy, 1972.

24. Ibid., p. 129.

25. *La violence*, Semaine des intellectuels catholiques, op. cit., p. 31.

26. Even a 'non-violent' such as J. M. Müller expresses reservations about any kind of attempt to apply the same censure indiscriminately in this way to both oppressors and oppressed (see *L'évangile de la non-violence*, op. cit.).

27. Quoted in Noam Chomsky, *Guerre en Asie*, Paris, Hachette, 1971.

28. See Ellul, op. cit., p. 297.

29. Ellul, op. cit., p. 213. Hence the accusation levelled at them of formulating, albeit unwillingly and unwittingly, a programme oriented towards fascism. See R. Aron, *Histoire et dialectique de la violence*, pp. 242–3, Paris, Gallimard, 1973.

30. Marcuse, op. cit., p. 49.

31. Ibid., p. 69.

32. In order to study this subject, reference may usefully be made to the report prepared by S. C. Versele and A. Van Haecht on 'Institutional Violence' for the Twenty-third International Criminology Course at Maracaibo, in August 1974. We have based ourselves here on the approach to the subject adopted in their report, which represented the conclusions of a working group of Belgian experts from the Institute of Sociology of the University of Brussels. See *Revue de l'Institut de Sociologie*.

33. See the European Convention on Human Rights, Article 15.

34. Particularly in respect to the checks made on foreigners as such, with the underlying racialism that this almost inevitably implies.

35. For studies on France, see Denis Langlois, *Les dossiers noirs de la police française*, 1973; Casamayor, *La police*, Paris, Gallimard, 1973; R. Backmann and C. Angeli, *Les polices de la nouvelle société*, Paris, Maspéro, 1971; Bertrand des Saussaies, *La machine policière*, Paris, Éditions du Seuil, 1972; G. Denis, *Citoyen policier*, Paris, Albin Michel, 1976; etc.

36. See Michel Foucault, *Surveiller et punir*, Paris, Gallimard, 1975; also

P. Deyon, *Le temps des prisons*, Lille, Université de Lille III, 1975; D. Briggs, *Fermer les prisons*, Éditions du Seuil, 1977; B. Remy, *Journal de prison*, Paris, Hachette, 1977; etc.

37. See Thomas Szasz, *Fabriquer la folie*, Paris, Payot, 1976; *La loi, la liberté et la psychiatrie*, Paris, Payot, 1977; and the works of R. Laing, D. Cooper and F. Basaglia; also Roger Gentis, *Les murs de l'asile*, Paris, Maspéro, 1973.

38. And 'wherever there are norms, there is deviance', as we are reminded by Albert Cohen in *La déviance*, p. 13, Paris, Éditions Duculot, 1971. This notion includes all those who, for one reason or another, are 'stigmatized' in the sense used by Erving Goffman, *Stigmate — les usages sociaux des handicaps*, Paris, Éditions de Minuit, 1975.

39. Steven de Batselier and H. Laurence Ross (eds.), *Les minorités homosexuelles*, p. 265, Paris, Éditions Duculot, 1973.

40. See our study 'Pasolini dissident et martyr', *Pro Justitia* (Brussels), No. 11/12, 1976, pp. 85–114.

41. It is worth remembering that in totalitarian countries opposition may in itself be regarded as 'mental illness'.

42. See Erving Goffmann, *Les rites d'interaction*, Paris, Éditions de Minuit, 1974.

43. It is notorious that women as such, for example, have found these instruments of little use for the purpose of claiming equality of treatment with men.

44. In this connection, see our study 'Égalité et droits de l'homme : de l'homme abstrait à l'homme *"situé"*, in *Travaux du Centre de philosophie du droit de l'Université libre de Bruxelles*, Vol. IV, 1975, pp. 266–302.

45. We should also guard against the ethnocentric reflex shown by so many Western democrats who always tend to prefer, in a Third World country, a purely formal parliamentary democracy (where the leaders of the opposition are in prison or under house arrest, elections are rigged, etc.) to a single-party people's democracy, even if the right to differ genuinely exists within it. On these matters, see our study: 'La violence qui ne dit pas son nom', *La pensée et les hommes*, No. 1, June 1976, pp. 1–5.

46. Marx indeed held that such measures could never eliminate the rivalry that this mode of production engenders among the wage-earners themselves.

47. See Engels, commentary by G. Mury, op. cit., p. 42.

48. 'An elegant opportunity for "respectable people" to be dishonest', write Christian de Brie and Pierre Charpentier, who add: 'As far as taxes are concerned, evasion is engendered by the legislation itself: first and foremost among frauds are those organized or tolerated by the law.' In 'La criminalité aujourd'hui', *La Nef*, pp. 31–2.

49. Michel Labeyrie, 'La montée de la violence', pp. 9–12.

50. Which 'alone make it possible to balance the national accounts, since national production capacity always tends to be underutilized'. See J. Grapin and J. B. Pinatel, p. 206.

51. Paul Vieille and Abd-Hassan Bani-sadr (eds.), *Pétrole et violence. Terreur blanche et résistance en Iran*, pp. 11, 63, Paris, Anthropos, 1974. See also François Partant, *La guérilla économique — les conditions du développement*, especially pp. 149 et seq., Paris, Éditions du Seuil, 1976.

52. Ibid., p. 29.

53. Claude Julien, op. cit., p. 11. See also his *L'empire américain*, 1968, and especially Pierre Jalée, *Pillage du Tiers Monde*, Paris, Maspéro, 1976.

54. See Serge Karsenty, *La culpabilité des survivants*, in 'La mort à vivre', *Esprit* (Paris), 1976, No. 3, p. 476.

55. Luce Giard, *Esprit*, op. cit., p. 412.

56. On this subject see, for example, Jean Ziegler, *Les vivants et la mort*, Paris, Éditions du Seuil, 1975; J. M. Domenach, 'L'énergie du deuil', *Esprit*, op. cit., p. 421; M. Féraud and O. Querouil, *Les territoires de la mort*, Paris, Le Centurion, 1976; Odette Thibault, *La maîtrise de la mort*, Paris, J. P. Delarge, 1975; P. Ariés, *Essais sur l'histoire de la mort en Occident du Moyen âge à nos jours*, Paris, Éditions du Seuil, 1975.

57. Ed. Hermann, 'Savoir' series, 1972. See also *Théorie du récit*, by the same author, issued simultaneously by the same publisher.

58. Interviewed by J. M. Palmier in *Le Monde*, 13 October 1972.

59. See Robert Jaulin, *La paix blanche. Introduction à l'ethnocide*, Paris, Éditions du Seuil, 1970; *Le livre blanc de l'ethnocide en Amérique* (texts collected by R. Jaulin), Paris, Fayard, 1972; *La décivilisation. Politique et pratique de l'ethnocide* (edited by R. Jaulin), Paris, Ed. Complexe, 1974. See also Lucien Bodard, *Le massacre des Indiens*, Paris, Gallimard, 1970; J. Meunier and A. M. Savarin, *Le chant du Silbaco*, privately printed, 1970; and Ettore Biocca, *Yanoama*, Paris, Éditions Plon, 1968.

60. See Versele and Van Haecht, op. cit.

61. See Claude Javeau, *Haro sur la culture*, Paris, Éd. de l'Université de Bruxelles, 1975.

62. R. Hoggart, *The Uses of Literacy*, London, Penguin, 1957.

63. In this connection see Jean-Marie Bröhm's remarkable *Sociologie politique du sport*. Paris, J. P. Delarge, 1976.

64. See Paul E. Ohl, *La guerre olympique*, Paris, Robert Laffont, 1977.

65. Bernard Voyenne, *Le droit à l'information*, p. 8, Paris, Aubier-Montaigne, 1970.

66. Referring to the still unexplained disappearance of the atomic physicist Majorana, Leonardo Sciascia wonders whether some scientists may not have had similar scruples in advance and refused to co-operate in the work of death (see Sciascia, *La disparition de Majorana*, Paris, Lettres nouvelles, 1977). Regarding Oppenheimer's case, see particularly Margret Boveni, *De la trahison au XXe siècle*, Paris, Gallimard, 1970.

67. *Discours biologique et ordre social*, a collective work containing a conclusion by Pierre Archard, p. 280, Paris, Éditions du Seuil, 1977. In the same connection, see also the final report of the Workshop on Interrelations between Biology, Social Sciences and Society, Unesco, 18–22 March 1974 (doc. SHC.74/CONF.801/13), particularly the papers presented by Godelier and Morin. In addition, see *L'idéologie de/dans la science*, Paris, Éditions du Seuil, 1977. On the question of science's connection with military policy, see Georges Menahem, *La science et le militaire*, Paris, Éditions du Seuil, 1976.

68. See Pierre Birnhaum, *La fin du politique*, Paris, Éditions du Seuil, 1975; also Jürgen Habermas, *La technique et la science comme 'idéologie'*, Paris, Gallimard, 1973.

69. See Robin Clarke, *We All Fall Down*, London, Penguin, 1969.

70. See Nicolas Herpin, *L'application de la loi*, Paris, Éditions du Seuil, 1977.

71. See the Goldmann affair as described by the accused himself. Pierre Goldmann, *Souvenirs obscurs d'un Juif polonais né en France*, Paris, Éditions du Seuil, 1975.

72. See André-Jean Arnaud, *Essai d'analyse structurale du Code civil français. La règle du jeu dans la paix bourgeoise*, Paris, Librairie générale de Droit et de Jurisprudence, 1972. See also, by the same author, 'La paix bourgeoise', *Quaderni fiorentini per la storia del pensiero giuridico moderno*, 1973, No. 2. Finally, see Michel Miaille, *Une introduction critique au Droit*, Paris, Maspéro, 1977; Bernard Edelmann, *Le Droit saisi par la photographie*, Paris, Maspéro, 1973; the special issue of the journal *Contradictions* on 'Le droit en question' (April 1977) and E. Novoa Monreal, *El derecho como obstáculo a cambio social*, Mexico City, 1975.

73. To reiterate the hope expressed by Ernst Bloch in *Droit naturel et dignité humaine*, Payot, 1976.

74. 'La Convention européenne pour la répression du terrorisme : un vrai pas en arrière', in *Journal des Tribunaux* (Brussels) as a reply to a study by Bart De Schutter on the same subject entitled: 'La Convention européenne pour la répression du terrorisme : un (faux) pas en avant ?' *Journal des Tribunaux*, 26 March 1977.

75. See Stefan Glaser, 'Le terrorisme international et ses divers aspects', *Revue internationale de droit comparé*, 1973, pp. 837–8. The author refers to a principle that 'as everyone knows, is firmly rooted in inter-

national law'. See also Georges Levasseur, 'L'entraide internationale en matière pénale, 'extradition', in *Juris-classeur de droit international*, 'Droit pénal international', Leaflet 405-B.

76. See *Ici l'Europe*, 1977, No. 1, p. 5.
77. Christian Panier, 'La déliquescence de la notion de délit politique', in 'Le droit en question', *Contradictions*, No. 11, April 1977, p. 17.
78. See André-Clément Decouflé, in a forecast entitled 'L'industrie de la répression dans les systèmes capitalistes avancés', Antwerp, 1973.
79. *La torture dans la République*, p. 175, Paris, Éd. de Minuit, 1972.
80. Robin Clarke, op. cit.
81. Leilah Khaled, *Mon peuple vivra*, p. 145, Paris, Gallimard.

Women and social violence

Head of the Sociology
Department, Dartmouth
College, Hanover, N.H.,
United States

Elise Boulding

Introduction:
the structure of social violence

The image of man the warrior, the conquering hero, has evolved together with the image of the conquering god as humanity has moved from the simpler modes of relationship of hunting and gathering peoples and early horticultural societies[1] to the increasingly complex patterns of social dominance we know today. Zeus the all-powerful, ruling over a pantheon of heroic rapists, has been the inspiring model for the male sex[2]. The model for the woman out of the same mythology has been submission to rape.

An end to that type of submission is necessary for the fuller development of the humanity of both men and women. Do we therefore conclude that giving women equal opportunity with men to do all the things that men now do would make the world more peaceful and just? One extreme view is that, by replacing male dominance with female dominance and by making all rulers and legislators women would bring world peace.

The battle of the sexes, present as a theme from earliest historical records, is that each sex feels victimized and oppressed by the other. This sense of victimization is an ever-fresh source of further structural arrangements and behavioural contortions that disfigure the body social and impede the self-actualization of individual women and men. The same ugly act of violent rape that shatters the woman victim physically and psychically can be seen as the frantic effort of an infantile male, beset by intolerable, gnawing incompleteness,[3] to assert wholeness and humanity. The effort to 'look inside' both victim and victimizer leads us to view the issue of social violence differently. We are not yet even at the threshold of understanding the processes by which children, essentially bisexual in the prepubertal stage, might achieve mature non-pathological adult role integration of their bisexual and their distinctive one-sex characteristics. However, if violence-inducing sex-role pathologies are widespread in settled societies as we have known them for the past 12,000 years, beginning with primitive communities, then this must be taken into account in efforts to reduce levels of societal violence.

The ideal of the androgynous human being, partaking of both the assertive characteristics ordinarily associated with the male and of the nurturant characteristics associated with the female has been present in the historical records at least since the time of the universal religions, as witness the personalities of Buddha and Jesus. In a fumbling and round-about way, it is this role model that is being rediscovered by contemporary movements of transsexual and lesbian liberation. Each group is seeking wholeness in its own sex. The more peaceful and just society sought by both reformist and radical political movements will certainly require androgynous personalities to make it work. The politics of dominance, however radical politically, will always give us more of what we already have—asymmetrical and mutually hurtful exercises of power in all its forms.

The same socialization strategies that prepare boys to be soldiers and policemen also co-opt women as mothers, wives and sisters into that preparation process. The concept of structural violence, that which frames behavioural violence, refers to the organized institutional and structural patterning of the family and the economic, cultural and political systems that determine that some individuals shall be victimized through a withholding of society's benefits, and be rendered more vulnerable to suffering and death than others. That structural patterning also determines the socialization practices that induce individuals to inflict or to endure according to their roles. This latter aspect of structural violence is conceptually related to the fact that structural violence establishes the culturally accepted threshold for physical violence in a society.

Women experience both structural and behavioural violence more sharply than men because social definitions of their biological equipment assign them to a special secondary descriptor (female) as a limitation on their social status at every level in a given social hierarchy. The effects of this are to ensure that the unequal distribution of resources, which is hierarchically determined in all but the simplest societies, becomes 'extra unequal' for women. When food, tools and supplies are short, women do without before men do. Pregnant and lactating women and adolescent girls are culturally assigned less food than their bodies need in many societies.[4] They face recurring risks of death in childbirth. At the same time, in all but the most industrialized and wealthy societies, women carry a heavier work load than men, responsible for the triple production roles of breeder, feeder and producer for the family unit, where men have only a single production role.[5] In addition, they must be ready at any time to render sexual service to men, often involuntarily. Concomitantly, they are excluded from decision-making roles, both domestically and in public affairs. Socialized into the same culture of violence as men, though with different role specifications, women themselves use violence when and where they can to protect and enhance their status.

In the remainder of this essay, I will present an analysis of women as victims, and women as aggressors, under specified conditions of structural and behavioural violence, concluding with an examination of women's initiatives for overcoming the victim-victimizer trap.

Women as victims

How the institutional structures of society victimize women

While there are many differences in social structure between First, Second and Third World societies, there are some common features of patriarchal family structure that inflict deprivation on women in all these societies. One aspect is the patriarchal household itself, in which the male head of the household has the power of life and death over the women and children of his family. The patriarch will protect his women from other men, but there is little or no protection from the patriarch. Court intervention to protect abused women (or children) has always been very limited, the practice of such intervention being even more limited than the concept. Therefore the vulnerability of women to the vicissitudes of the male temperament within the household is one aspect of the structural violence inherent in the institution of the patriarchal family. Mushanga[6] has dramatically documented this for some African societies, and also provides a useful survey of contemporary research on women as domestic victims in all societies. Another face of this structural violence shows itself in the situation of the one-third or more women of child-bearing age in every society who are unpartnered (never married, widowed, deserted or divorced).[7] Many of these women maintain single-parent households unaided, and are totally vulnerable to rape and economic exploitation; they have neither patriarch nor court to protect them.

By the inverted logic of the rules of patriarchy, prostitution and rape and the auxiliary institution of pornography are seen as safeguards to the institution of the family. By providing men with sexual satisfaction outside the family, they protect wives from 'unreasonable demands'. The underlying perception of women on the part of men that makes pornography, rape and prostitution possible is that of objects varyingly available for erotic stimulation. Generally it is the one-third of women outside the patriarchal family who are considered 'available'; the penalties in most cultures for being discovered using another man's property for erotic stimulation are high.

Increasingly, rape is being presented as a central theme in the oppression of women.[8] The definition of woman-as-object on which the institution of rape is based is the enabling dynamic that supports prostitution and pornography on the one hand, and the woman as non-person in political and economic roles on the other. Oddly, the diminution of the woman-as-property theme currently being achieved, as law courts evolve a definition of women as individuals with rights of their own, is having practically no effect on the underlying social perception of woman-as-object. Instead, the same pseudo-libertarian ethic that leads to support of the pornographic industry has led to a rhetoric of sexual liberation that has convinced many women that the traditional woman's modest behaviour is prudish, old-fashioned and self-destructive. Through this liberation rhetoric a 'large new reservoir of available females was created to expand the tight supply of sexual goods available for traditional exploitation, disarming women of even the little protection they had so painfully acquired'.[9]

More broadly speaking, the patriarchal imprint keeps women from sharing in economic, cultural and political roles according to their abilities, because of stereotypic notions about what is appropriate for women. This form of structural violence is closely linked with the rape-prostitution-pornography syndrome of treating women as objects, systematically preventing their full participation in the society to which they render so many forms of forced service.

The two-thirds of women inside male-headed households are not necessarily more structurally protected than unpartnered women. In historically recurring times of economic depression and social stress the individual household (whether male- or female-headed) bears the ultimate burden of that stress through having fewer resources with which to feed and care for family members. There is considerable evidence[10] that the less resources a family has available to meet needs, the more violence will take place within the family.[11] Periods of unemployment are thus likely to be periods of increased woman-beating.

Another worldwide depression such as that of the 1930s will certainly increase woman-beating around the world, and not only in the lower classes. Levinger's United States study of divorce applicants found that nearly one out of four middle-class wives cited physical abuse as the reason.[12] While the actual beating experienced by women is behavioural violence, the patterns of socio-economic and political organization that make women easy victims of their husbands are examples of structural violence.

Women as victims of behavioural violence

Because women are 'easy' victims, they experience a great deal of direct behavioural violence in every society. One of the major breakthroughs of the contemporary women's movement is found in its success in getting rape defined as a criminal, punishable offence against the woman raped, rather than against her husband or her family. Brownmiller's[13] definition of the criminal act of rape ('If a women chooses not to have intercourse with a specific man and the man chooses to proceed against her will') represents a substantially new definition of woman as person in relation to the sexual act. Though it will be slow to be accepted, it will have far-reaching consequences. The documentation on the extent to which women have suffered rape historically and in the present is only beginning.[14] Since 'no more than half of all reported rapes are the work of strangers',[15] a great deal of rape happens in family and familiar community settings. Rape of young children by fathers, male relatives and family friends is being increasingly reported to the authorities in American cities. Every investigation of rape undertaken so far is uncovering far more rape experience than expected among women who range from toddlers to old women. When comparable investigative and reporting procedures are established in all countries, it may turn out that rape is an almost universal experience for females.

While increasing attention is being given to rape as a criminal act, and new bills updating and rationalizing sections of the criminal law codes dealing with rape and other sexual offences are now pending in several countries, including Canada, the United Kingdom and the United States, there appears to be a general increase in the level of sexual assault in major cities around the world in this century, along with a general increase in urban crime rates, after a decline in urban violence towards the end of the last century.[16]

Wife-beating appears to be only a little less prevalent than rape as a phenomenon experienced by women. Every society has proverbs on wife-beating similar to the Russian: 'A wife may love a husband who never beats her, but she does not respect him.' It is not clear whether men ever had absolutely unlimited rights to beat their wives, but there are many folk and quasi-legal traditions as to the size of the whip that may be used,[17] and how much physical damage it is reasonable to inflict.

A certain amount of prostitution is practiced under conditions of near or absolute slavery for the woman. The international white-slave traffic still persists today after three-quarters of a century of effort to eradicate it. There were International Agreements for the Suppression of the White Slave Trade in 1904, 1910, 1921 and 1933. The United Nations General Assembly adopted a Convention for the Suppression of Traffic in Persons and Exploitation of the Prostitution of Others in 1949, followed by a resolution in 1959. A United Nations background paper prepared for International Women's Year points out that the international traffic in women for prostitution continues on a much larger scale than is reported to or controllable by INTERPOL, and frequently involves very young girls and women lured abroad by false job promises. Women migrant workers are particularly vulnerable to exploitation.[18]

In times of war and civil rebellion women endure capture and torture, regardless of whether they have themselves been active in the fighting, simply because they are the wives, mothers or daughters of activists. Amnesty International reports regularly on the imprisonment and torture of dissidents in countries around the world. It appears that women often get particularly brutal treatment. An Uruguayan army officer sent an open letter to Amnesty International denouncing torture in his own country:

practically all prisoners, irrespective of age or sex, are beaten and tortured. . . . The women are a separate category: the officers, non-commissioned officers and the troops greet the arrival of young women detainees with delight. I personally witnessed the worst aberrations committed with women, in front of other prisoners, by many interrogators. Many of the women prisoners are only held for the purpose of discovering the whereabouts of their husband, father or son, that is, they themselves have been accused of nothing.[19]

Gruesome details have appeared on the torture of Vietnamese women during the war in Indo-China. A sobering account of torture borne during the French-Algerian war by Algerian women reared in seclusion can be read in Tillion.[20]

The torture of women always includes some variant of rape. That rape is such a prominent theme in the physical abuse of women brings us back to the basic fact of the structurally ensured position of women as erotic object-cum-victim in contemporary societies, modernized or not. The resulting pathologies display themselves at every level of human interaction from the neighbourhood to the international community.

Women as aggressors

No matter how victimized, human beings are subjects as well as objects, and help to maintain the very structures that victimize them. Thus women in their roles as wives and mothers give vital reinforcement to military structures by socializing battle-ready sons and docile daughters. Since boys spend much of their prepubertal life with their mothers, it is impossible to minimize the role of mothers in creating the aggressive, fight-happy, rape-ready male. By forcing male children to repress tears and expressions of emotion and of pain, mothers directly contribute to the emotional infantilism

of the adult male, who has grown up without adequate techniques for working through his feelings.[21] Techniques for
'hardening' boy children exist in every society. Newspaper
accounts in the autumn of 1976 of Lebanese mothers taking
their children to the Bridge of Death in Beirut to watch
soldiers dropping bodies and burning them give a little glimpse
of an age-old practice. A Beirut pediatrician tells of parents
bringing their hospitalized children, wounded by sniper bullets
and shrapnel, wooden Kalashnikov rifles and toy pistols as
toys during their recuperation. The anti-war-toy movement
started by mothers in Europe and North American in
the 1960s[22] has almost disappeared.

The pressures put on women by their own position as
objects have historically been translated by women into practices of treating children as objects. De Mause's *History of
Childhood*[23] documents the widespread cruelty of mothers
(and fathers) to children from ancient times. Infanticide is a
crime usually committed by women. Women may turn on
their husbands as well as on their children, when a husband's
behaviour becomes intolerable. There are cases of husband-
beating reported from time to time that seem to be an inversion
of the usual wife-beating story.[24]

On the whole, however, women endure their lot without
resorting to physical violence. (Other forms of violence,
especially tongue-lashing, are well known as women's 'special'
techniques. So are forms of 'non-violent' manipulation,
trickery and deceit.) There are far fewer women criminals in
every society than men, and many countries have so few
women prisoners that they have no special prison facilities for
women, thus leaving them vulnerable to many unscheduled
punishments by male fellow prisoners. Just as rising crime
rates are considered an index of 'development' for Third
World countries,[25] so crime rates may be considered an index
of liberation for women.[26]

The same observation on women's propensities for violence crime could be made about women's performance as
fighters: they are not normally given the opportunity, but
when they are, they perform well. There have been a number
of successful, empire-expanding warrior queens in history.[27]
Every army has had its quota of women who dressed as men
and fought like men. Most freedom fighters in recent and
current wars of liberation in the Third World have included
women in their ranks. Tania,[28] the guerrilla who died with

Che Guevara in Bolivia, was a notable example. Le Thi Rieng, who led the women's commando group that occupied the United States Embassy during the Tet offensive, killed two hundred United States personnel and left the National Liberation Front flag flying over the building, is a military heroine in every sense of the word. As a role model, Le Thi Rieng conveys many conflicting messages. So does Madam (General) Dinh, Deputy Commander of the PLAF, after her leadership in the 1960 En Tre uprising.[29] Forty per cent of the PLAF fighters were women. In the United States, women are receiving gruelling combat training at the Air Force Academy in Colorado, and like many men they have mixed feelings about this training.[30] Currently thirty-six countries and territories report to the United Nations on women in military service, with participation levels from a high of 6 per cent (New Zealand) to a low of less than 1 per cent (Malaysia). Israel, Guinea and Mali conscript women. Women also serve in the civilian police forces of a number of countries.

In spite of increasing levels of physical training and prowess, women are still far more the victims than the victimizers when it comes to violence. Brownmiller is convinced 'that the battle to achieve parity with men in the critical area of law enforcement will be the ultimate testing ground on which full equality for women will be won or lost'.[31] Since skill, not size and strength, are now the prime factors in law enforcement, and very probably in military action also, we might look ahead with Brownmiller to the time when women will make up 50 per cent of all armies, national guards, state and local police, and the judiciary.

An end to victimization and violence?

Increasing economic opportunities, improved medical technologies for birth control and abortion, and increased legal protection for women leave them less dependent on a patriarchal system and more in control of their procreative, socio-economic and civic behaviour. Their own initiatives in redefining their social roles and the institutional constraints on those roles are breaking down centuries-old traditions about appropriate behaviour for both sexes.

The International Tribunal on Crimes Against Women, for example, was conceived at Fem, an international feminist

camp in Denmark, in 1974 as a feminist response to International Women's Year. It was timed to close on 8 March,
International Woman's Day. Simone de Beauvoir greeted
the 2,000 women from thirty-two countries who were present.[32]
Conducted along highly participatory lines, the Tribunal was
organized around testimony about crimes against women.
Workshops planned action in relation to different categories
of crimes, and produced resolutions defining goals and
strategies.

The pace of the Tribunal initiatives is certainly faster than
the pace of United Nations initiatives in regard to women,
born of the International Women's Year. As the entire United
Nations programme is geared to long-run structural changes,
it does little to ease the pressure of immediate inequalities and
suffering. More training and job opportunities, better health
and welfare facilities and the promotion of rights to a range
of public goods including credit are all important aspects of
United Nations programmes for women. The closest the
United Nations comes to dealing with women as immediate
victims of direct violence, however, is in a statement of
proposed future projects ('if funds become available') from
the Crime Prevention and Criminal Justice Section of the
Centre for Social Development and Humanitarian Affairs in
the United Nations Secretariat. The proposed projects are:
(a) reducing female criminality, (b) equal participation of men
and women in the administration of criminal justice, and
(c) combating prostitution and the illicit traffic of women.[33]

Conclusion

In the short run, we will probably see an increase in the violent
behaviour of women as they test out their new opportunities.
Simon's figures on crime rates tell us that this is already
happening. I would interpret these figures as a transition
phenomenon. Where the transition will lead is up to us. It
could lead towards a new era of justice and peace. Continuing
expansion of the coparticipation of women and men in every
field will be necessary for this to happen, and it can only
happen if we are prepared to engage in a type of self-conscious
valuing and choosing such as human beings have embarked on
only in the great axial periods of human history. We did it
at the time of the birth of the universal religions, when women

and men both experienced a great loosening of traditional ties and the emergence of new social roles. We did it again in the nineteenth century, when movements of social reform and spiritual regeneration swept all continents. The medieval women's movement, a key part of that reform and regeneration, was but one of many heralds of a new style of human relationships. The androgynous role model is still available as a reference, however implausible it may seem for the development of new forms of human relations in which human males and females will be less frustrated, more self-actualizing and gentler than they are now, closer to the true essence of our humanity.

Notes

1. The mingling of the more mystically-oriented mother-godless religions of the Mediterranean with the heroic father-god religions brought to Greece by the Achaean warriors storied by Homer creates some interesting anomalies in Greek mythology. The conquering warrior automatically has the right to rape, but rape becomes euphemistically redefined in many of the Greek myths, for example in the story of Leda and the Swan, or Europa and the Bull. Cf. Colin Turnbull, *The Forest People*, New York, Simon and Schuster, 1968; Richard B. Lee and Irven DeVore (eds.), *Man the Hunter*, Chicago, Aldine, 1968.
2. James Robertson, *Money, Power and Sex*, London, Marion Boyars, 1976.
3. The nature of the conceptual problem is reflected in such studies as Bruno Bettelheim's *Symbolic Wounds* and Mary Jane Sherfey's *Nature and Evolution of Female Sexuality*, reflecting respectively male and female perspectives on human sexuality. Bettelheim, *Symbolic Wounds: Puberty Rites and the Envious Male*, Glencoe, Ill., The Free Press, 1954; Sherfey, *The Nature and Evolution of Female Sexuality*, New York, Random House, 1972.
4. Alan Berg, *The Nutrition Factor*, Washington, D.C., The Brookings Institution, 1973.
5. Ester Boserup, *Woman's Role in Economic Development*, New York, St Martin's Press, 1970.
6. Tibamanya Mwene Mushanga, 'The Victimization and Victimology of Wife in Some of the East and Central African Communities', paper prepared for the Second International Symposium on Victimology, Boston, Mass., September 1976.
7. Elise Boulding, *Women in the Twentieth Century World: International Women's Year Studies on Women as a Resource*, Beverly Hills, Calif., Sage Publications, 1976; and her *The Underside of History: A View of Women Through Time*, Boulder, Colo., Westview Press, 1977. Boulding (1976), op. cit.
8. Susan Brownmiller, *Against Our Will: Men, Women and Rape*, New York, Simon and Schuster, 1975.
9. Shumalith Firestone, *Dialectic of Sex: The Case for Feminist Revolution*, New York, Morrow Company, 1970.
10. See Suzanne K. Steinmetz and Murrary A. Straus (eds.), *Violence in the Family*, New York, Dodd, Mead & Company, 1974; and especially Morton Bard, 'The Study and Modification of Intra-Familial Violence', ibid., p. 127–39.
11. J. Dollard et al., *Frustration and Aggression*, New Haven, Yale University Press, 1939.
12. Steinmetz and Straus, op. cit., p. 7.

13. Brownmiller, op. cit.
14. Statistics on rape in the societies that report them are almost meaningless because the taboos against reporting are so strong, and the experience of those who do report are so punishing. See the United States studies by Diana E. J. Russell, *The Politics of Rape: The Victim's Perspective*, New York, Stein and Day, 1975; Andra Medea and Kathleen Thompson, *Against Rape*, New York, Farrar, Straus and Giroux, 1974; and John M. MacDonald, *Rape: Offenders and Their Victims*, Springfield, Ill., Charles C. Thomas, 1971.
15. Brownmiller, op. cit., p. 400.
16. Ted Robert Gurr, *Rogues, Rebels and Reformers: A Political History of Urban Crime and Conflict*, Beverly Hills, Calif., Sage Publications, 1976.
17. Robert Calvert, 'Criminal and Civil Liability in Husband-Wife Assaults', in Steinmetz and Straus, op. cit., pp. 88–91.
18. United Nations, 'Current Trends and Changes in the Status and Roles of Women and Major Obstacles to be Overcome in the Achievement of Equal Rights, Opportunities and Responsibilities', a conference paper for IWY, New York, United Nations (E/CONF.66/3/Add.&), 1975; United Nations, 'Exploitation of Labour through Illicit and Clandestine Trafficking: Note by the Secretary General', New York, United Nations (E/CN.6/5821), 1973.
19. 'Uruguayan Army Officer Denounces Torture', *Amnesty Action*, Amnesty International, 2119 Broadway, Room 309, New York 10023, Vol. 3, No. 2, April 1976.
20. Germaine Tillion, 'Prehistoric Origins of the Condition of Women in "Civilized" Societies', *International Social Science Journal*, Vol. XXIX, No. 4, 1979.
21. For an enlightening discussion of marianismo, the complementary institution to machismo in Latin society, see Cornelia Flora, 'The Passive Female and Social Change: a Cross-Cultural Comparison of Women's Magazine Fiction', in Ann Pescatello (ed.), *Female and Male in Latin America: Essays*, pp. 59–85, Pittsburgh, Penn., University of Pittsburgh Press, 1973.
22. Among the leading international women's organizations promoting such a movement were the Women's International League for Peace and Freedom and Women Strike for Peace.
23. Lloyd de Mause, 'The Evolution of Childhood', in Lloyd de Mause (ed.), *The History of Childhood*, pp. 1–74, New York, Psychohistory Press, 1974.
24. Valerie Solanis, 'Excerpts from the SCUM (Society for Cutting Up Men) Manifesto', in Robin Morgan (ed.), *Sisterhood is Powerful: An Anthology of Writings from the Women's Liberation Movement*, pp. 514–18, New York, Vintage Books, 1970.
25. Marshall Clinard and Daniel Abbott, *Crime in Developing Countries*, New York, Wiley and Sons, 1973.
26. Rita James Simon, *Women and Crime*, Lexington, Mass., Lexington Books, 1975.
27. Cf. Boulding, 1977, op. cit.
28. Marta Rojas and Marta Rodriguez Calderón (eds.), *Tania: the Unforgettable Guerrilla*, New York, Random House, 1971.
29. Cf. Boulding, 1976, op. cit., Chap. 7; see also Viet Nam Women's Union 39, *Women of Vietnam* (Hang Chuoi-Hanoi, Socialist Republic of Viet Nam), No. 1, 1976; Fall also writes in detail of the tradition of heroism of women in Indo-China, Bernard B. Fall, *Street without Joy*, p. 131–43, Harrisburg, Penn., The Stockpole Company, 1961.
30. Grace Lichtenstein, 'Kill, Hate, Mutilate!', *New York Times Magazine*, 5 September 1976, pp. 10, 37–42.
31. Brownmiller, op. cit., p. 388.
32. They came from Austria, Belgium, Brazil, Canada, Chile, Denmark, the United Kingdom, France, the Federal Republic of Germany, Greece, the Netherlands, India, Iran, Iceland, Ireland, Israel, Italy, Japan, the Republic of Korea, Luxembourg, Mexico, Norway, Portugal, Puerto Rico, Saudi Arabia, Scotland, South Africa (including a black

woman), Spain, Sweden, Switzerland, the Syrian Arab Republic and the United States. The American and Australian delegations included 'aboriginal' women's testimony.

33. United Nations, 'Summary of Research Activities Related to Women Being Undertaken by the United Nations System of Organizations', Background Paper No. 3, Expert Group Meeting on the Establishment of an International Institute on Research and Training for the Advancement of Women, New York, United Nations, 17–23 February 1976.

Appendix

Interdisciplinary Expert Meeting on the Study of the Causes of Violence

Paris, 12–15 November 1975

Extracts from the Final Report

Questions of theory and method

10. A theoretical discussion was initiated by a certain number of participants. The adequacy of quantitative methods for the study of political violence was challenged. In addition, a number of participants called in question the methods imported from countries in the 'centre' as they were applied to countries of the 'periphery'. The main questions in the field of theory and methods related to systems of causality, transdisciplinarity, the historical setting of violence and its definition.

Systems of causality

11. In one participant's view, there were in this regard four main streams of thought which must be denounced as lacking any theoretical basis, particularly when one moves into the international arena: (1) the tendency to equate the outbreak of violent conflict with a miscalculation, misperception or error in strategy, as if it were really possible to define the difference between 'the objective state of affairs' and what is foreseen or perceived; (2) the tendency to equate political conflict with personal conflict, a tendency found at every turn in those abstract typologies which, in fact, serve only to obscure the concrete relationships between levels of violence; (3) the tendency to establish a one-way equivalence between inegalitarian structure and conflict. Instead of seeking the mechanical cause of violence in the existence of an inegalitarian structure, one should look for the dialectical cause of inegalitarian structure in conflict; (4) the tendency to equate knowledge with metrology.

12. Another general observation which particularly

engaged the attention of the meeting concerned the need, when investigating the causes of violence, to reject the unidimensional approach inherited from certain behavioural sciences, the ingrained habit of defining the variables and then identifying the key or independent variable and the dependent variables in the belief that it was possible to change the whole system by changing the key variable. In fact, at the macro-sociological level, this was a highly dubious way of proceeding, since the phenomena were subject to multiple causes and it was in no way possible to modify a system by acting on one single variable or even, often, on several of them. For example, if one started with the idea that the arms race between East and West was essentially based on the intellectual and political climate of the Cold War, this variable could be modified and after a five-year wait, one found that nothing had changed. What was needed was a concept of configurational causality. Generally speaking, an epistemological discussion of the concepts of cause and determination would seem to be necessary.

Transdisciplinarity

13. All participants agreed that it was no longer possible to make any progress unless a multidisciplinary and even trans-disciplinary approach were adopted which would define the interdependence of the subfields involved in the study of violence, and would establish correlations between them. It might, for example, be necessary to consider what conditions were more likely to lead respectively to the appearance of individual violence and collective violence, that of society as a whole or of international society. In order to make progress in this direction, one participant recommended using the simulation method so as to break down the compartmentalized and hierarchical structure governing psychology, sociology and the study of international relations; where possible, specialists with qualifications in several fields should be used for such studies.

The historical setting of violence

14. Another general observation of theoretical significance was made from several points of view. This concerned the need for any investigation or research into the causes of a

given form of violence to take the historical dimension fully and specifically into account: either particular methods of investigation had to be worked out according to the historical and cultural characteristics of the population being studied or else, in the view of other participants. This is because one was led to study the violence as the outcome of a succession of previous forms of violence, histori- cally determined and—to a greater or lesser degree—insti- tutionalized or organized in structures, or finally, because one referred explicitly to the nature of the social system in which the phenomenon of violence was being studied, in terms of which mode of production was currently dominant and what features distinguished socio-economic and national structures as well as historical blocs in non-European societies.

15. The statements expressing the points of view of the 'peripheral' countries provided an opportunity for putting forward several levels of theoretical and political concern. One participant, on the basis of a 'historico-critical' approach, asserted that the fundamental characteristic distinguishing the East from the West was in fact its conception of the rational use of political violence. The immense time-span covered by 'hydraulic' social and cultural systems led in the end to a symbiotic view of social organization and to the need to limit the level of violence inside the system in order to avoid its disintegration and destruction. The dialectic of the Yin and the Yang, of the top and the bottom, must continue, without at any time jeopardizing social cohesion. The political history of the West and its philosophical history from Aristotle onwards started from quite different principles and included a practice of political violence taken to extremes. In the East, on the other hand, where violence was minimal, and was at the same time a fundamental factor in the preservation of society, its ethical impact was also much less strong.

16. It was not thought desirable to go very deeply into this discussion, seeing the variety of starting points, but it is fair to say that two ideas nevertheless emerged from it on which the meeting was able to express a consensus.

Definition of violence

17. Firstly, it was not desirable to start with a narrow, legal definition of violence or with a biological or medical (clinical or therapeutic) approach to the problem, such as involves a

form of causality situated at the level of the individual. On the contrary, it was agreed that research into the causes of violence should be based on a broad socio-cultural concept of the phenomenon. Against the common background or framework thus established the various participants were able to project their information, their personal observations, their field surveys or research.

18. Secondly, it was no longer possible to study violence as an exclusively negative phenomenon seen in terms of aggressive behaviour. It also had to be seen as a method of pursuing positive interests by other means, or as the response made in reaction to a less visible negative violence present in the whole of the social structure.

Guidelines for the understanding of violence

19. The statements made in this general discussion concerned either major disciplinary themes or themes of vital interest in the modern world.

Disciplinary themes

20. The group made up of criminologists itself defined the limitations of that discipline within the framework of a rigorously legal point of view. In the opinion of one participant, that dividing line should be retained; from a criminological point of view, it was essential to make a clear distinction between criminality and other phenomena of violence—in other words, violent forms of political revolt could not be equated with delinquency. To make that distinction was not inconsistent with the way in which criminologists had shown that study of the causes of individual criminal violence must be linked with definition of the delinquent personality in social and economic terms. Some experts even said that in certain cases the law itself could be regarded as a determinant of violence and that one had to ask in general to what extent the law facilitated, hindered or simply followed the changes which determined social behaviour; it was essential to pursue a just criminological policy, such that the activities of the agencies combating crime (legislation, courts, police, prisons) did not themselves engender violence. One participant asked

for the study of prison revolts to be the subject of specific research, since the prison world could be regarded as a reflection of society at large where violent relationships were concerned. The important work of the Fifth United Nations Congress on Prevention of Crime and Treatment of Offenders was referred to as relevant to recent research in the field of penal law and criminology.

21. The group of psycho-sociologists discussed ideas and problems concerning the biological attributes and psychological traits of the individual personality and group-induced behaviour changes. According to a number of participants, some progress has been made in their discipline in regard to this subject, but there had been scarcely any fresh discoveries for about fifteen years, and this was not the fruitful line to pursue in order to study the phenomenon of violence on a large scale. It was nevertheless agreed that it was neither possible nor desirable to make a clear-cut distinction between the study of interpersonal relationships and the study of social and cultural conditions. It was noted that more violence existed in societies undergoing rapid social and economic changes and that the people taking part, for example, in racial disturbances in certain developed countries were also those who, during their lifetimes, had experienced the most rapid changes either upwards or, possibly, downwards, whereas the permanently underprivileged sections of the population tended rather to be apathetic. According to one participant, the literature on the subject suggested that it was not economic growth as such which engendered violence but social and cultural change. The most fruitful field for research today was the relationship between the interpersonal level and the social and cultural level.

Themes of vital interest for the modern world

22. It was considered vital to elucidate not only the economic causes of wars and institutional and structural forms of violence but also their final causes, particularly on the economic plane (the profits accruing from violence). In the view of some participants there is, in fact, a direct and positive correlation between the development of violence and the development of capitalism, between the use of violence and the expansion of capitalist production relations, between underdevelopment and imperialism. Other participants saw

clearer evidence of a correlation between the increase of violence in the Third World and the reduction of military violence in the industrialized countries following the reduction of international tension. Finally, some participants thought that this reduction of military violence in countries at the 'centre' was being accompanied by an increase in criminal violence and violence between sectors, groups or communities (men-women; whites-blacks; teachers-pupils).

23. A number of experts expressed their concern with regard to the particular characteristics of the violence to which women were subject, and stressed the importance attaching to an examination of the role of women in relation to the structure of domination. One expert underlined the fact that male domination should be considered as a social, political and economic system of oppression and exploitation which embodied and supported the bases of structural violence as well as of direct violence, and stressed the need to study the implications of the fact that, notwithstanding their disarmed position in society, women are paradoxically obliged to support masculine combatant groups and masculine systems of structural violence.

24. Other participants stressed the specific character attaching to repressive violence or institutionalized structural violence in southern Africa and Latin America, where it was used to resist change. Reference was also made to the question whether it was legitimate to use violence as a means of eliminating alienation and acquiring self-determination and freedom for oppressed or colonized nations. These questions should preferably be dealt with at regional meetings bringing together specialists and other representatives from several countries in the region. One participant, who was also Secretary-General of the African Association of Political Science, said that he was particularly in favour of this method, adding that out of the twelve research projects currently being undertaken under that association's auspices, four were directly concerned with the theme of violence in the sense towards which the Meeting seemed to be moving. Another participant referred specifically to the inadequacy of certain Western investigating techniques for the analysis of large, heterogeneous, pluralist societies, where recourse must be had to new methods for the purpose of appraising the phenomenon of violence.

25. With regard to terrorism, it was noted that it had never

been accurately defined as a notion. It could only be defined if it were recognized that there was also a 'state terrorism' which frequently preceded the other kind. One would not define an act which was 'terrorist by its nature' except by linking institutional terrorism with the terrorism of the desperado, which was frequently nothing more than an amateur response in opposition to professional violence. From this point of view, it would be necessary to study even what must be termed 'democratic violence'—i.e. the violence expressed and exercised through the institutions of the liberal democratic countries themselves—and not to restrict the scope of the concept of structural violence exclusively to authoritarian or totalitarian régimes.

26. A large number of participants felt that research should be done as a matter of priority on the problem of the relationship between armed violence and the production and export of armaments by a small number of countries producing sophisticated weapons, as the material fact of the general phenomenon of militarization. In this respect, the idea should be challenged that the maintenance of a lasting peace is based on a balance of armaments in the 'centre' and on balanced transfers of armaments to the 'periphery', without any real disarmament. In any case, 'conventional' weaponry now included sophisticated antipersonnel devices and was developing police-control technology. In the view of some experts, the problem of the increasing technological refinement of instruments of violence was not merely a question of weapons, but must now be extended to include police records and investigation methods and psychological or psychiatric techniques and forms of treatment. Generally speaking, a certain kind of structural violence was induced by the level of technology, because of the authoritarian types of discipline required in certain sectors (nuclear energy) and the contribution these could make to the militarization of social relationships.

27. Mention was made of the growing use of torture as one of the most flagrant violations of human rights and a particularly alarming form of direct and institutional violence. Although the United Nations had this matter on its agenda and although it had been studied by the Fifth United Nations Congress on the Prevention of Crime and the Treatment of Offenders, it was a phenomenon which should be the subject of very extensive research so that an understanding of its

causes could contribute to the search for measures to prevent it in all regions.

28. One of the experts suggested that attention be directed to the analysis of the roles of non-élite groups in the causes of violence and the prospects for social change, arguing that, while the role of élite groups (imperialist powers, national political and economic ruling classes, etc.) has tended to preoccupy attention in the past, it may be that the role of the masses (the poor, the exploited, women, racially and ethnically subjugated groups, the politically and economically oppressed) is ultimately more decisive to the maintenance or overthrow of conditions leading to violence.

Remarks made by observers

29. Several observers made an important contribution to the debate on the theme of the Meeting and to identifying the priority problems relating to violence in their fields of competence. Two representatives from teachers' organizations drew the attention of the participants to the rapid increase of violence in schools and of attacks on school premises. They proposed that this problem should be thoroughly investigated so as not only to reduce the amount of such violence but also to find ways of teaching pupils non-violent solutions to their interpersonal problems. Other observers stressed the harmful effects of the representation of violence by the mass media and the way in which they manipulated violence, exposing the public at large to the 'blackmail of violence'. One observer, after stressing the importance for an understanding of violence of the work done on it by his Institute, made particular mention of a study which, since January 1968, had been keeping a count of the occurrence of political violence in the world. He suggested that, with the support of Unesco, this research should be extended back to 1945 in order to cover the phenomenon of violence in the nuclear age. The link between violations of human rights as a form of violence and the kinds of society which engender violence was mentioned by another observer. The relationship between violence and the centralization of political and economic structures was also mentioned as a subject deserving study. One comment urged a higher participation of women in similar meetings. Finally, it was observers who drew attention to the importance of what might be called 'victimology' in the

study of violence (in other words a more precise knowledge of the victims and not simply of the perpetrators of violence), to the role of population growth as a factor contributing to violence, to non-violent action to bring about social change and to certain other aspects of violence already mentioned by the experts.

Recommendations for future research relating to violence and its underlying causes

30. After the general discussion, the meeting examined suggestions for further research which, in the view of the participants, deserved consideration in the formulation of projects of study and research within the framework of Unesco's programmes, in accordance with the main orientations established for the Medium-Term Plan. Among the objectives to be used in formulating this plan the following were considered to be particularly relevant to issues involving violence:

Promotion of research aimed at assuring human rights (Objective 1.1).

Promotion of the appreciation and respect for cultural identity of individuals, groups, nations and regions (Objective 1.2).

Improvement of the status of women (Objective 1.3).

Promotion of peace research (Objective 2.1).

Promotion of the study of international law and study of international organizations (Objective 2.2).

Development of education for peace and international understanding (Objective 2.3).

Promotion of the formulation of global multidisciplinary interpretation of development (Subobjective 3.1.A).

Studies of socio-cultural conditions, systems of values, motivations and procedures for participation by the population likely to foster endogenous diversified development (Subobjective 3.1.B).

Contribution to the development of infrastructures and programmes in the social sciences with a view to increasing the different societies' ability to find ways of solving social and human problems (Subobjective 3.1.C).

Greater collaboration by young people as well as by certain groups of society, e.g. disadvantaged groups, in educational scientific and cultural activity (Objective 6.4).

Contribution to the working out of concerted approaches to
the problems of social disharmony (Objective 6.5).

31. It was not possible, at the present stage of the formulation
of Unesco's Medium-Term Plan, to make specific recommendations concerning each of these objectives and subobjectives.
The recommendations for further research and study constitute, therefore, an overview of themes which would contribute
to a better understanding of violence in the contemporary
world if they could be undertaken within the framework of
Unesco's programmes using not only an interdisciplinary or
multidisciplinary approach but also transdisciplinary methods
and soliciting the collaboration of social scientists from
different regions and cultural systems of the world.

32. Some participants suggested that an important contribution to the understanding of the causes of violence would
be made by a large-scale and systematic survey of existing
literature on the subject. One suggestion concerned a survey
of behaviouralist and structural-functionalist writings on the
subject which would be arranged by themes. A second suggestion was for a critical examination of work dealing with
the relation between rapid socio-cultural change and the
occurrence of violence. A third was for a survey of the different theoretical approaches prevailing in socialist countries,
Western countries and countries in the Third World. A fourth
suggestion was for a statistical comparison of types of political
violence since 1945. A fifth was for a general treatise offering
an overview of the political economy of violence. Rather than
recommending one or several such major undertakings, it was
decided to enumerate themes for projects or as more specific
studies to be undertaken within the framework of a larger
programme.

33. Several suggestions were made as to groupings of the
suggested study and research themes. One suggestion, for
example, concerned subsuming all the themes under 'structures of domination' and 'structures of liberation'. Some
participants felt that such a division would overemphasize
structures to the expense of other relevant violence-inducing
phenomena. Whatever subdivisions were to be used, however,
it was generally agreed that social and economic structures
should occupy an important place in the study of the causes
of violence. It was clear to all participants that any grouping
of subjects would have advantages and disadvantages and
would necessarily involve overlapping between and within

the main headings. The presentation finally agreed upon was, therefore, considered as adequate for the purposes of the meeting. The order in which the headings and the specific subjects were presented corresponded roughly, though not entirely, to the main priorities which the participants had in mind. It was recognized that the relations between the sexes involved highly important dimensions of violence which cut across many of the themes suggested.

34. The listing of suggested themes leaves open the question of the most appropriate method to use in conducting study and research relating to each one of them. Some require field work, others constitute in themselves approaches to the study of causes of violence, while others require library research applying historical, sociological and other methods. Moreover, there has been no attempt to go from the general to the particular or to maintain a common level of generality.

35. Finally, the participants were not all ready to accept all the suggested themes either as appropriate to Unesco's fields of competence or as scientifically well formulated. However, the participants agreed that they do reflect, on the whole, the main aspects of violence relevant to vital contemporary social and economic issues and are, for that reason, deserving of further research.

36. The participants agreed that the papers presented at the meeting could be used as a basis for a publication dealing with methods, theories and research trends on the causes of violence. It would be worthwhile, however, to condense radically in some places, particularly as regards behaviouralist contributions to the study of violence, and to allow the authors to modify their manuscripts in the light of the discussion and supplement the bibliographical references where appropriate. Additional papers should be included covering some important perspectives not dealt with in the existing papers, in particular as regards violence and relations between the sexes, the philosophical and ethical dimensions of violence, the methodological problems of the study of violent crime, etc.

Suggested themes for further research and study

Violence, the structures of domination,
processes of social change and development

(a) The role of women in structures of domination and in achieving social change.
(b) The effects of rapid social change in terms of increase or decrease in violence.
(c) Aspects of violence that impede social and economic development.
(d) Violence and processes of socialization and desocial-ization.
(e) Non-violent means of social change as a way of achieving peace and solving human rights problems.
(f) Relations between structures of violence and victims of violence.
(g) Institutionalized violence, subversion and political repression.
(h) Manifestations of violence at school.
(i) The role of youth in structures of domination and in achieving social change.
(j) Processes of perpetuation of violence.

Violence and emerging world patterns

(a) International systems and the prospects of demilitarization and disarmament.
(b) Aspects of violence that negate the process of peace at regional, hemispheric and international levels.
(c) The scientific and technological revolutions and their consequences for mass violence.
(d) Militarization of social relations and its effects on violence in different types of societies.
(e) Structures of violence and the establishment of a new international economic order.
(f) Relations between the major powers and violence in the Third World, particularly the arms race and arms transfers to the Third World.
(g) Situational contexts of violence (geopolitical regions, types of society, family patterns and levels of development).
(h) The economic problems of the capitalist world and their effects on violence in the Third World.

Violence and processes of national liberation

(a) National self-determination and the right to use force as recognized by the United Nations.
(b) The role of multinational corporations in situations of national liberations.
(c) Colonialism, neo-colonialism and imperialism as causes of violence.
(d) Unequal exchange and export of finance capital and their effects on national liberation.
(d) Participation of women in national liberation struggles as recognized in the resolutions of the International Women's Year Conference in Mexico City.
(e) Internal divisions and strife within revolutionary groups as an additional ingredient of violence.

Violence, population and deprived social groups

(a) Violence and relations between the sexes.
(b) Poverty, social inequality and violence.
(c) Violence and population expansion.
(d) The role of institutional violence in alienation processes and cultural deprivation.
(e) Racism, apartheid and violence.
(f) Ethnic group relations and violence.
(g) Other forms of intergroup violence, including religious, linguistic, regional, class, etc.

Conceptions and perceptions of violence in contemporary cultures and civilizations

(a) Violence seen as a historical process composed of successive stages.
(b) Cross-cultural study of structural violence and human rights, including the rights of women.
(c) The role of transdisciplinary research in harmonizing the results of research on violence in different parts of the world.
(d) Philosophical and ethical justifications of violence.
(e) Comparative criminal policies and approaches to violence.
(f) Role of social scientists in supporting and opposing the process of violence.
(g) A world-wide survey to determine how to measure intent to commit violence in different societies.

(h) Perception of violence by the public and its manipulation by the media.
(i) Violence and conceptions of the quality of life.
(j) Comparative analysis of criminological conceptions of the causes of violence.
(k) Comparative statistics of criminal violence.

Participants (as of 1975)

ABDEL MALEK, Anouar. Maître de recherches, Centre National de la Recherche Scientifique (CNRS), Paris.

CARROLL, Berenice A. Executive Editor of *Peace and Change: A Journal of Peace Research*, United States.

FALS BORDA, Orlando de. Professor, Bogotá.

GALTUNG, Johan. Professor of Peace and Conflicts, University of Oslo.

JOXE, Alain. École des Hautes Études en Sciences Sociales, Paris.

KHAN, Rasheeduddin. Professor of Political Science and member, Indian Council of Social Science Research, New Delhi.

KLINEBERG, Otto. Director, International Centre for Intergroup Relations, Paris.

MERTENS, Pierre. Secretary, Centre du Droit International de l'Institut de Sociologie de l'Université Libre de Bruxelles.

NEWCOMBE, Alan. Co-editor, 'Peace Research Abstracts', Canadian Peace Research Institute.

NYATHI, Vunguza M. Co-ordinating Secretary, Southern Africa Research Association, Lusaka, Zambia.

OLISA, Michael S. O. Director, Peace Research Institute of Nigeria, Nsukka, Nigeria.

POKLEWSKI-KOZIELL, Krzysztof. Deputy Editor, *Panstwo i Prawo*, Warsaw.

SENGHAAS, Dieter. Peace Research Institute, Frankfurt.

SHAMUYARIRA, N. M. Secretary-General, African Association of Political Science, Dar es Salaam.

SHUPILOV, V. P. All-Union Institute for the Study of the Causes of Crime and the Elaboration of Preventive Measures.

TAYLOR, A. J. W. Professor of Clinical Psychology, Wellington, New Zealand.

Non-governmental organizations

Amnesty International.
Co-ordinating Committee for International Voluntary Service.
Federation for the Respect of Man and Humanity.
Friends World Committee for Consultation.
International Centre of Films for Children and Young People.
International Commission of Jurists.
International Federation of Senior Police Officers.
International Federation of University Women.
International Fellowship of Reconciliation.
International Film and Television Council.
International League for the Rights of Man.
International Peace Research Association.
War Resisters' International.
Women's International League for Peace and Freedom.
World Confederation of Organizations of the Teaching Profession.
World Federation of Democratic Youth.
World Peace Council.
World Union of Organizations for the Safeguard of Youth.

Delegations

Permanent Delegation of Argentina to Unesco.
Permanent Delegation of Chile to Unesco.

Other institutions

Centro de Investigaciones y Dociencia Económicas, Mexico City, Mexico.
French Institute for Polemology, Paris.
International Federation of Human Rights, Paris.
International Society for Research on Aggression, Birmingham, United Kingdom.
Review *Études*, Paris.
Rijksuniversiteit te Leiden, the Netherlands.
Society for Peace and Conflict Research, Groningen, the Netherlands.

As a concept it unifies disparate phenomena
such as wars, torture, football hooliganism
& rape p85   Violence is negative. p85
excluding anything one does not reject,
including anything we reject.   reprehensible
p27 "Reprehensible", of its effects & not in itself

Sorel — spirit of democracy has
generated the modern concept of
violence & has given it a perjorative
overtone — Didedort . . . . . .
p28/29
Little, in fact, that is new in the
phenomena p1

Galtung — typology — ideological position